The *New* BIG BOOK of LOGOS

David E. Carter editor

book design
Suzanna M.W.

layout & production
Graham Allen
Christa Carter

The New Big Book of Logos

First published in 2000 by HBI,
an imprint of HarperCollins Publishers
10 East 53rd Street
New York, NY 10022-5299

ISBN: 0688-17890-1

Distributed in the U.S. and Canada by
Watson-Guptill Publications
1515 Broadway
New York, NY 10036
Tel: (800) 451-1741
         (732) 363-4511 in NJ, AK, HI
Fax: (732) 363-0338

Distributed throughout the rest of the world by
HarperCollins International
10 East 53rd Street
New York, NY 10022-5299
Fax: (212) 207-7654

First published in Germany by Nippan
Nippon Shuppan Hanbai
Deutschland GmbH
Krefelder Strasse 85
D-40549 Dusseldorf
Tel: (0211) 5048089
Fax: (0211) 5049326
nippan@t-online.de

ISBN: 3-931884-71-6

Printed in Hong Kong by Everbest Printing Company
through Four Colour Imports, Louisville, Kentucky.

Once upon a time, there was a big book.

A **Big Book of Logos**. It became a major seller. Well, not by John Grisham or Stephen King standards, but in the world of graphics, it was huge. It actually cracked the circle of the top 3% of ALL books sold on Amazon.com.

Graphic designers really, really liked this book. And when a book is that successful, **you know what happens**: a sequel.

So, the publishers huffed, and they puffed, and they convinced David Carter to do another Big Book of Logos. (He wanted to call the book "Green Eggs and Ham", but that title was already taken.) **THIS is THAT book**.

And, oh yes, they reminded him that this sequel had to be just as good as—or better than—the original. Someone said something about "an offer you can't turn down."

We listened carefully, and selected about 2,500 outstanding logos that had been designed in the last three years. And, once again, **The NEW Big Book of Logos** will go into the design world and say "We've done it again."

This book, combined with its predecessor, contains well over 5,000 great logo designs. This may be one of the best sources of logo design ideas ever assembled. (Or maybe not. That's for you to judge. But we think you'll find this great collection to be inspirational.)

To paraphrase W.P. Kinsella, "Publish it and they will buy."

David E. Carter

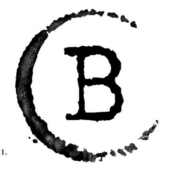

1.

PRETTY GOOD PRIVACY™

2.

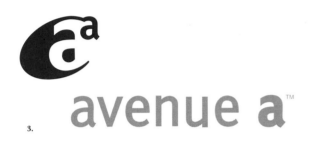

avenue a™

3.

ALTA

4.

ATRéVA™

5.

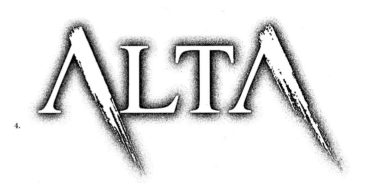

Charter™
COMMUNICATIONS®

A WIRED WORLD COMPANY

6.

blue nile

7.

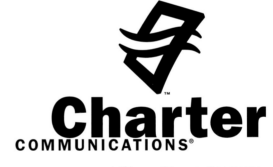

grape finds℠

8.

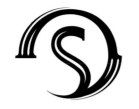

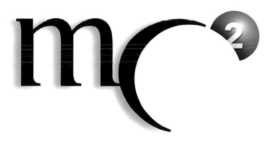

9.

STEWART CAPITAL MANAGEMENT

10.

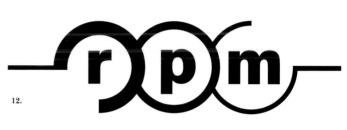

innoVentry™

11.

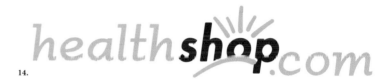

rpm

12.

mc²

13.

healthshop.com

14.

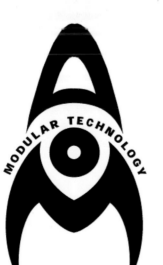

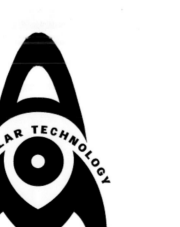

MODULAR TECHNOLOGY

15.

(all)
Design Firm Hornall Anderson Design Works

1. Client   Best Cellars
   Designers   Jack Anderson, Lisa Cerveny,
   Jana Wilson Esser, David Bates,
   & Nicole Bloss

2. Client   (PGP) Pretty Good Privacy
   Designers   Jack Anderson, Debra
   McCloskey, Michael Brugman,
   Heidi Favour, Jana Wilson Esser,
   & Katha Dalton

3. Client   Avenue A
   Designers   Jack Anderson, Debra
   McCloskey, Tobi Brown,
   Henry Yiu, James Tee,
   & Gretchen Cook

4. Client   Alta Beverage Company
   Designers   Jack Anderson, Larry Anderson,
   & Julie Keenan

5. Client   Wells Fargo "Atreva"
   Designers   Jack Anderson, Kathy Saito,
   Alan Copeland, Cliff Chung,
   & Chris Sallquist

6. Client   Charter Communications
   Designers   Jack Anderson, Lisa Cerveny,
   Jana Wilson Esser, Mike Calkins,
   David Bates, Julia LaPine,
   & Sonja Max

7. Client   Blue Nile
   Designers   Jack Anderson, Bruce Stigler,
   Gretchen Cook, Henry Yiu,
   & Sonja Max

8. Client   grapeThus
   Designers   Jack Anderson, Lisa Cerveny,
   Gretchen Cook, Jana Wilson
   Esser, & Mary Chin Hutchison

9. Client   SaviShopper.com
   Designers   Jack Anderson, Ryan Wilkerson,
   Naomi Davidson
   & Margaret Long

10. Client   Stewart Capital Management
    Designers   Jack Anderson, Debra
    McCloskey, David Bates,
    & Lisa Cerveny

11. Client   Wells Fargo "innoVentry"
    Designers   Jack Anderson, Kathy Saito,
    Sonja Max, & Alan Copeland

12. Client   (RPM) Wells Fargo
    Designers   Jack Anderson, Kathy Saito,
    Sonja Max, & Alan Copeland

13. Client   MC²
    Designers   Jack Anderson & Margaret Long

14. Client   Healthshop.com
    Designers   Jack Anderson, Mary Hermes,
    Mike Calkins, David Bates,
    & Holly Finlayson

15. Client   K2 Corporation
    Designers   Jack Anderson, Andrew Smith,
    Taro Sakita, & Mary Chin
    Hutchison

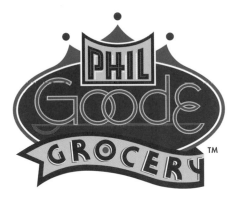

1.

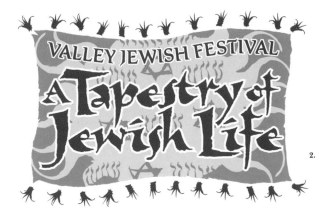

2.

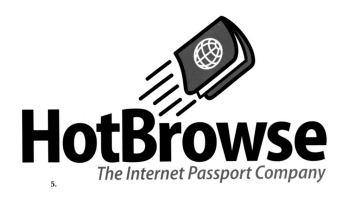

3.

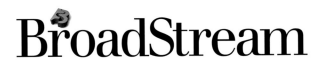

4.

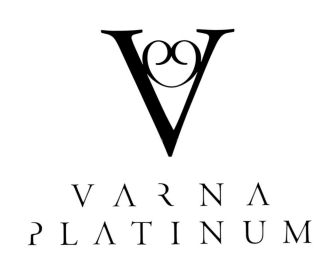

5.

BroadStream

6.

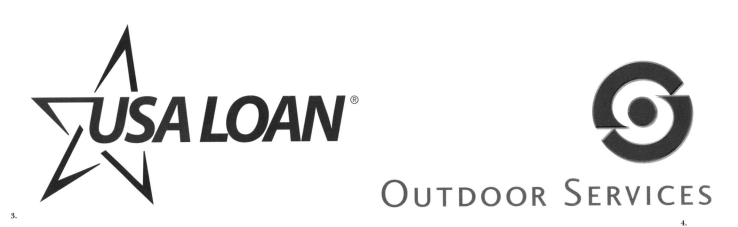

7.

MORPHEUS
MUSIC

8.

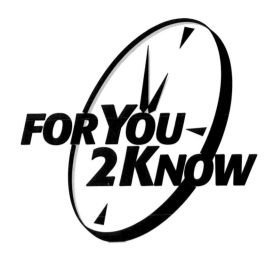

9.

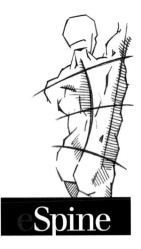

eSpine

10.

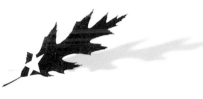

TRADITION BANK

11.

Eclipse™

12.

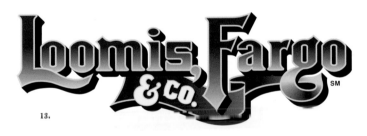

13.

!PCU

HOUSTON POSTAL CREDIT UNION

14.

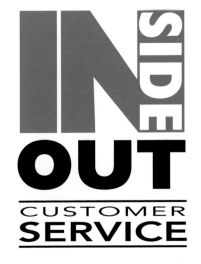

INSIDE OUT

CUSTOMER SERVICE

15.

1
Design Firm Sayles Graphic Design
2 - 10
Design Firm Glyphix Studio
11 - 15
Design Firm The Focus Group

1. Client   Phil Goode Grocery
   Designer   John Sayles

2. Client   The Jewish Federation/
              Valley Alliance
   Designer   Paul Ruettgers

3. Client   USA Loan
   Designer   Brad Wilder

4. Client   Outdoor Services
   Designer   Brad Wilder

5. Client   HotBrowse
   Designer   Brad Wilder

6. Client   Broadstream
   Designer   Brad Wilder

7. Client   Varna Platinum
   Designer   Brad Wilder

8. Client   Morpheus Music
   Designer   Brad Wilder

9. Client   City of Los Angeles
   Designer   Brad Wilder

10. Client   eSpine
    Designers Eric Sena & Brad Wilder

11. Client   Tradition Bank
    Designer Kirk Davis

12. Client   TeleCheck
    Designers Dan Feder & Kelly Johnson

13. Client   Loomis, Fargo & Co.
    Designer Kirk Davis

14. Client   Houston Postal Credit Union
    Designer Kelly Johnson

15. Client   Solvay Polymers
    Designer Kelly Johnson

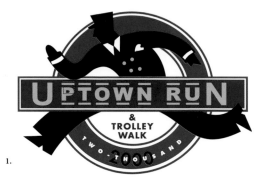

1.

2.

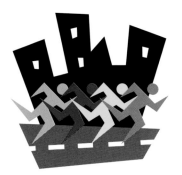

DEEP ELLUM DASH

3.

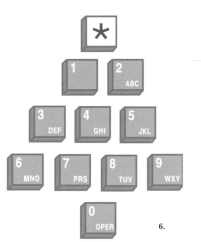

4.

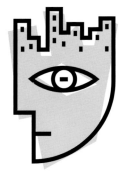

DEEP ELLUM

5.

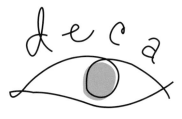

6.

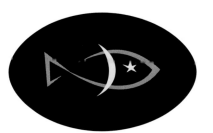

7.

1 - 7
Design Firm   Squires & Company

1. Client   Uptown Run, Annual 5K,
                  10K Run
    Designer   Christie Grotheim

2. Client   DECA Art Gallery
                  Featuring Local Artists
    Designer   Christie Grotheim

3. Client   Deep Ellum Dash '97
                  10K Fun Run
    Designer   Paul Black

4. Client   Aqua Star, Pools and Spa
    Designer   Paul Black

5. Client   Deep Ellum Association
                  An Historic Industrial
                  Area of Dallas
    Designer   Paul Black

6. Client   Communigroup
    Designers   Amy Chang & Brandon Murphy

7. Client   Sushi Nights, Restaurant and Bar
    Designer   Christie Grotheim

(opposite)
Design Firm   Dixon & Parcels Associates, Inc.

    Client   Eggland's Best, Inc.

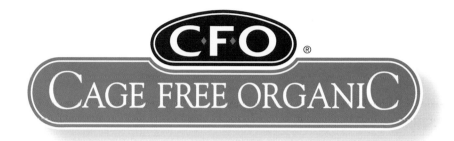

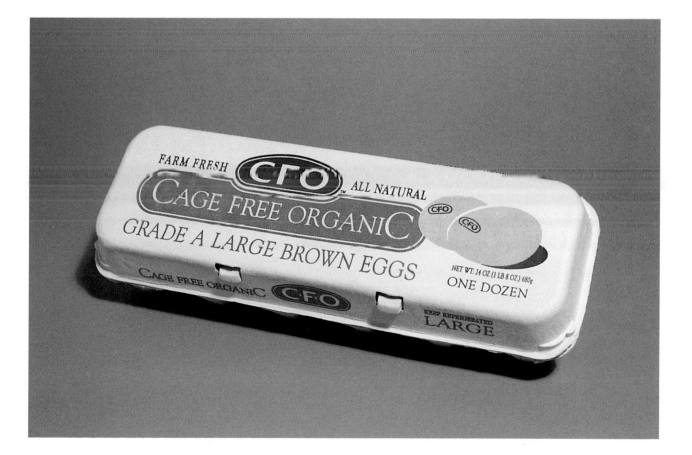

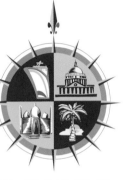

CYBER LIBRARIANS.COM

1.

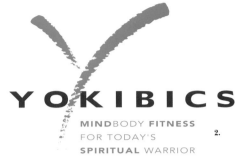

YOKIBICS

MINDBODY FITNESS
FOR TODAY'S
SPIRITUAL WARRIOR

2.

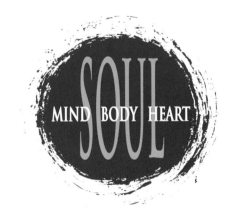

POWER
TRAVEL

3.

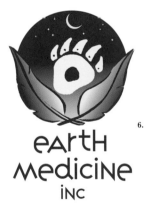

KITCHENS
by
DESIGN

4.

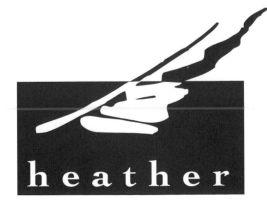

SOUL
MIND BODY HEART

5.

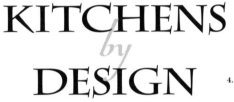

eArtH
Medicine
iNc

6.

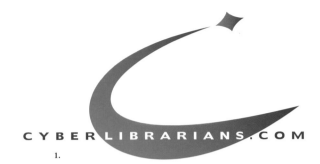

heather

7.

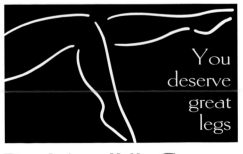

You
deserve
great
legs

Dr. Julius W. Garvey

8.

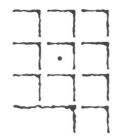

mark d. bennett, cpa

9.

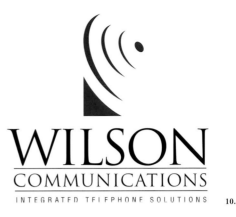

10.

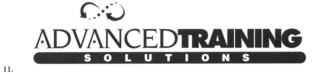

11.

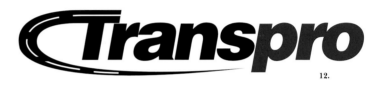

12.

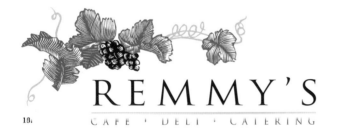

13.

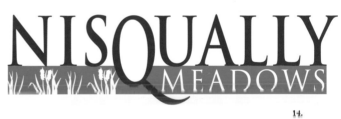

14.

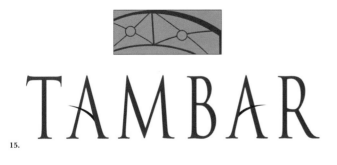

15.

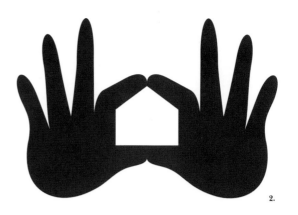

1.

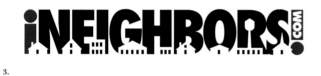

3.

Wesley 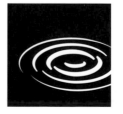 Village

4.

5.

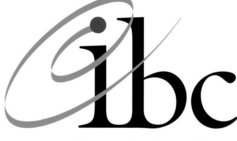

Interactive Brand Center

6.

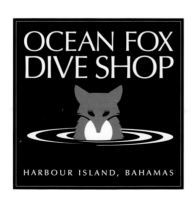

7.

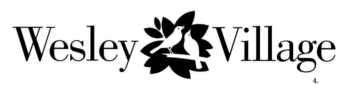
8.

eventra

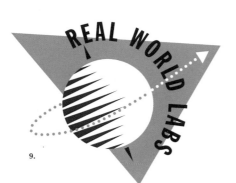

9.

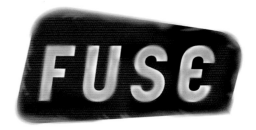

10.

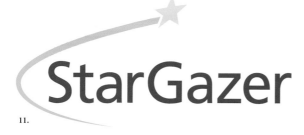

11.

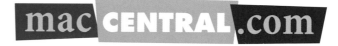

12.

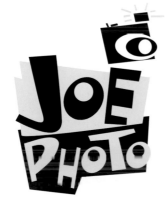

13.

NETWORK

SOCIETY™ 14.

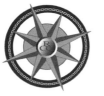

THE RIDGE
COMMUNITY CHURCH

15.

1 - 8
Design Firm Tom Fowler, Inc.
9, 12, 14
Design Firm Edmonds Design
10, 11, 13
Design Firm Fuse, Inc.
15
Design Firm Graphic Technologies

1. Client   Ross Products Division/
           Abbott Laboratories
   Designer   Thomas G. Fowler

2. Client   St. Luke's LifeWorks
   Designer   Karl S. Maruyama

3. Client   Reynolds and Rose
   Designer   Karl S. Maruyama

4. Client   United Methodist Homes
   Designers   Thomas G. Fowler
           & Karl S. Maruyama

5. Client   Haute Decor.com
   Designers   Thomas G. Fowler
           & Elizabeth P. Ball

6. Client   IBC
   Designer   Elizabeth P. Ball

7. Client   Ocean Fox Dive Shop
   Designer   Thomas G. Fowler

8. Client   Eventra
   Designer   Karl S. Maruyama

9. Client   Network Computing Magazine
   Designer   Nancy Edmonds

10. Client   Fuse, Inc.
    Designer   Russell Pierce

11. Client   PairGain—StarGazer
    Designer   Russell Pierce

12. Client   Mac Publishing/MacWorld
    Designer   Nancy Edmonds

13. Client   Joe Photo
    Designer   Russell Pierce

14. Client   Network Computing Magazine
    Designer   Nancy Edmonds

15. Client   The Ridge Community Church
    Designer   Gary Thompson

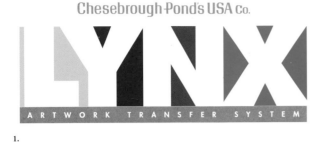

1.

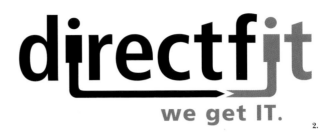

2.

centricity

3.

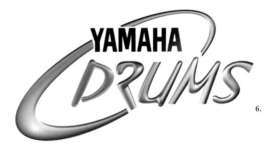

4.

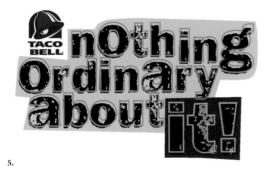

5.

6.

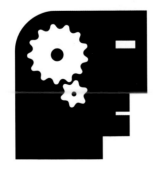

7.

1
Design Firm **Tom Fowler, Inc.**
2 - 6
Design Firm **Fuse, Inc.**
7
Design Firm **Squires & Company**

1. Client   Chesebrough-Ponds USA Co
   Designer Elizabeth P. Ball

2. Client   DirectFit
   Designers Matthew Stainner
             & Mike Esperanza

3. Client   Centricity
   Designer Russell Pierce

4. Client   PairGain
   Designer Mike Esperanza

5. Client   Taco Bell—Nothing Ordinary
             About It
   Designer Russell Pierce

6. Client   Yamaha Corporation of America
   Designer Kristi Kamei

7. Client   I Think, Inc.
   Designers Clark Bystrom & Paul Black

(opposite)
Design Firm **Miriello Grafico Inc.**

   Client   Eastpack
   Designer Ron Miriello

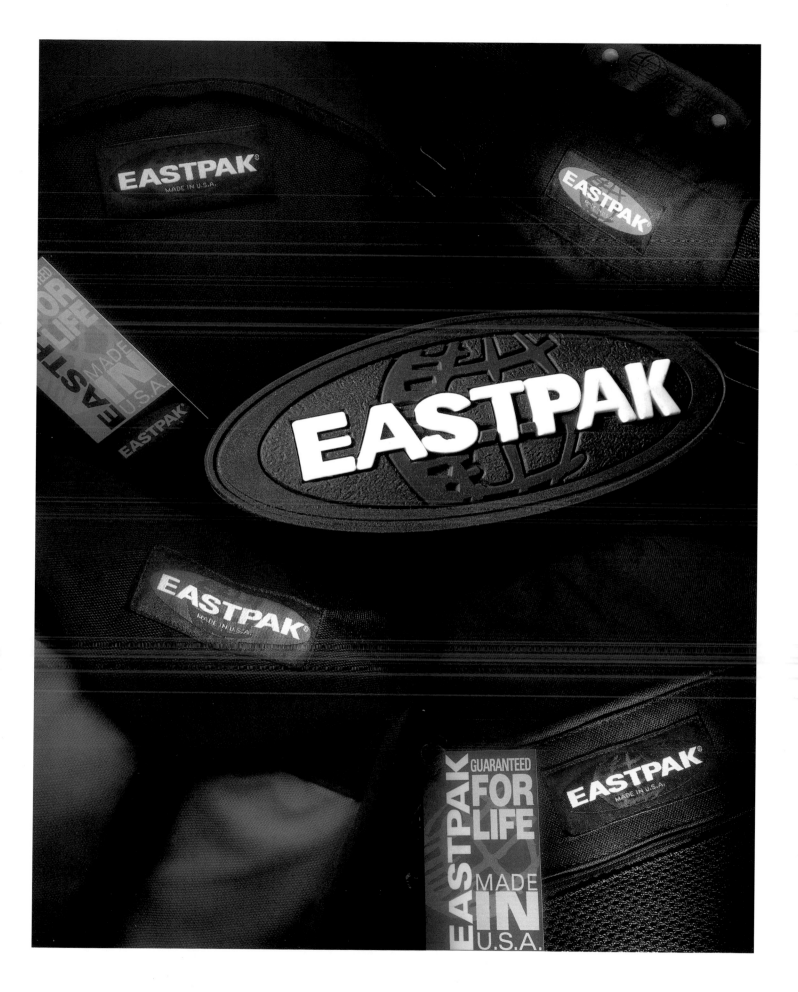

15

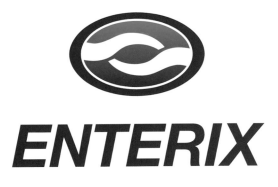
K I D C O N C E P T S

1.

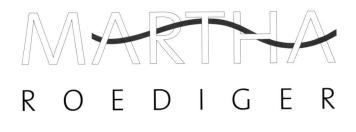
MARTHA
R O E D I G E R

2.

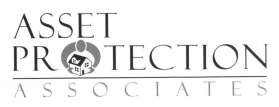
tom mcpherson
P H O T O G R A P H Y

3.

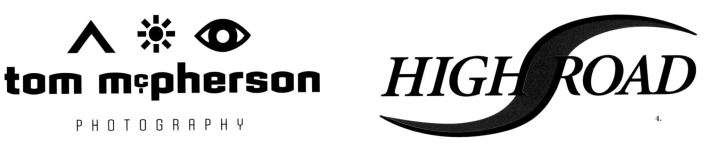
HIGH ROAD

4.

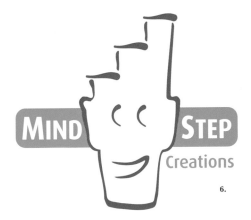
ENTERIX

5.

MIND STEP
Creations

6.

ASSET
PROTECTION
A S S O C I A T E S
PROTECTING WHAT YOU HAVE EARNED
FOR THE REST OF YOUR LIFE

7.

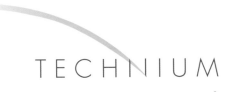
TECHNIUM

8.

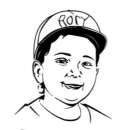

The *Rory* David Deutsch
F O U N D A T I O N
Brighter Tomorrows for Children
With Brain Tumors

9.

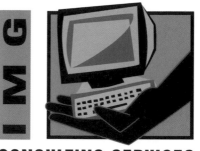

CONSULTING SERVICES

10.

GEORGE ORLOFF, M.D.

11.

ResourceLink

12.

MACGUFFIN
management

13.

DEEP ELLUM
Arts Festival

14.

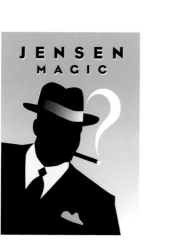

15.

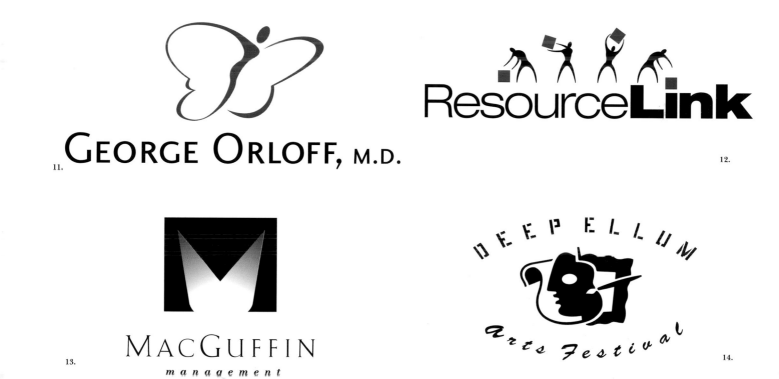

1 - 6		
Design Firm	**Thibault Paolini Design Associates**	
7 - 10		
Design Firm	**Design Moves, Ltd.**	
11 - 12		
Design Firm	**Glyphix Studio**	
13 - 15		
Design Firm	**Squires & Company**	

1. Client	Kid Concepts	
Designers	Renée Fournier & Sue Schenning	
2. Client	Martha Roediger	
Designer	Renée Fournier	
3. Client	Tom McPherson Photography	
Designer	Renée Fournier	
4. Client	Talus	
Designer	Sue Schenning	
5. Client	Enterix	
Designers	Judy Paolini & Sue Schenning	
6. Client	Mind Step Creations	
Designer	Sue Schenning	
7. Client	Asset Protection Associates	
Designers	Laurie Freed, Bill Sprowl, & Jennifer Rayburn	

8. Client	Technium, Inc.	
Designers	Laurie Freed, Bill Sprowl, & Jennifer Rayburn	
9. Client	Rory David Deutsch Foundation	
Designers	Laurie Medeiros Freed, Eric Halloran, Jennifer Rayburn, & Bill Sprowl	
10. Client	Information Management Group	
Designers	Laurie Freed, Jennifer Rayburn, Bill Sprowl, & Amy Forbes	
11. Client	George Orloff, M.D.	
Designer	Eric Sena	
12. Client	ResourceLink	
Designer	Eric Sena	
13. Client	MacGuffin	
Designer	Christie Grotheim	
14. Client	Deep Ellum Arts Festival	
Designers	Thomas Vasquez & Paul Black	
15. Client	Jenson	
Designer	Paul Black	

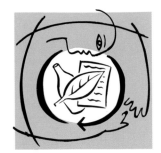

Palo Alto
Recycling
Program

1.

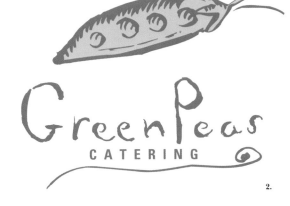

2.

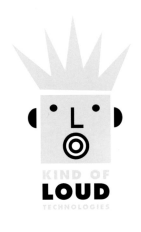

KIND OF
LOUD
TECHNOLOGIES

3.

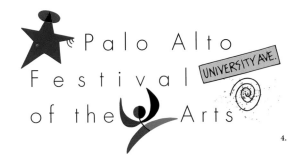

Palo Alto
Festival
of the Arts

UNIVERSITY AVE.

4.

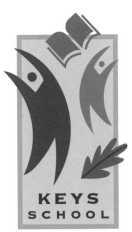

KEYS
SCHOOL

5.

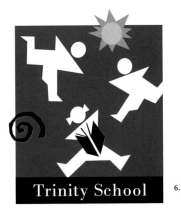

Trinity School

6.

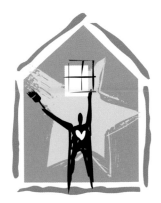

7.

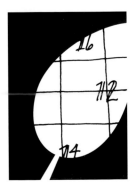

8.

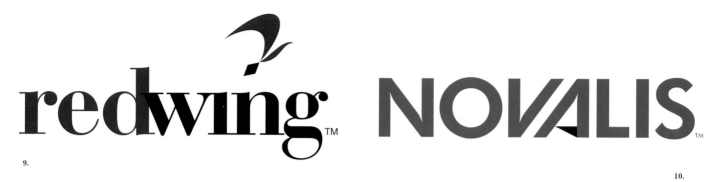

9.

10.

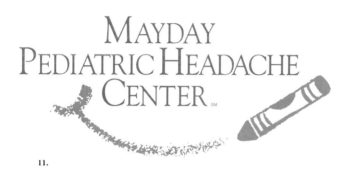

11.

Cosmetic Surgery Center of Lancaster ℠
at Lancaster General Hospital Health Campus

12.

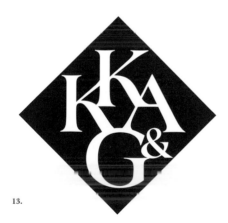

13.

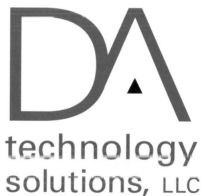

14.

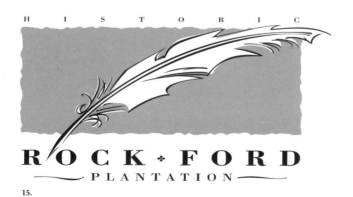

15.

1 - 8
Design Firm **Artefact Design**
9 - 15
Design Firm **Albert/Bogner**
 Design Communications

1. Client City of Palo Alto
  Recycling Program
 Designers Artefact Design

2. Client Green Peas Catering
 Designers Artefact Design

3. Client Kind of Loud Technologies
 Designers Artefact Design

4. Client Palo Alto Festival of the Arts
 Designers Artefact Design

5. Client Keys School
 Designer Kim Schwede

6. Client Trinity School
 Designer Artefact Design

7. Client Christmas in April—
  Mid Peninsula
 Designer Artefact Design

8. Client Tom Richman & Associates
 Designer Artefact Design

9. Client Red Wing
 Designers Kelly Albert,
  & Marie Elaina Miller

10. Client Novalis
 Designer Marie Elaina Miller

11. Client Maday Pediatric
  Headache Center
 Designer Kelly Albert

12. Client Cosmetic Surgery Center
  of Lancaster
 Designer Kelly Albert

13. Client Kegel, Kelin, Almy, Grimm
 Designer Marie Elaina Miller

14. Client DA Technology Solutions
 Designer Marie Elaina Miller

15. Client Historic Rockford Plantation
 Designers Kelly Albert,
  & Marie Elaina Miller

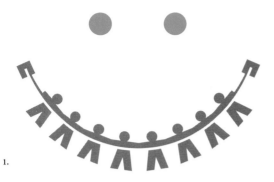

1.

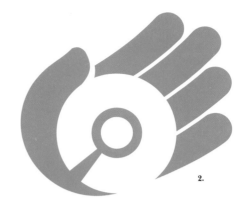

2.

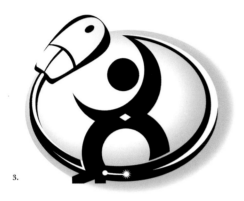

3.

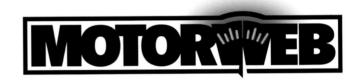

MOTORWEB

4.

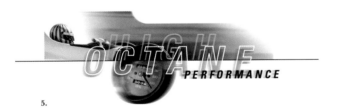

5.

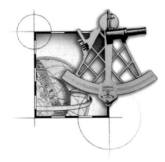

6.

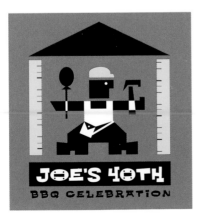

JOE'S 40TH
BBQ CELEBRATION

7.

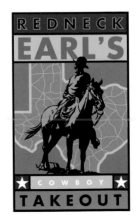

REDNECK
EARL'S
COWBOY
TAKEOUT

8.

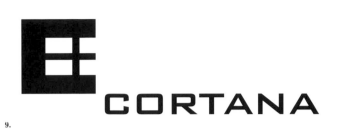 **CORTANA**

9.

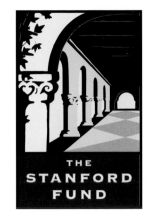

THE STANFORD FUND

10.

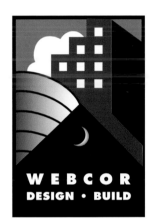

WEBCOR DESIGN · BUILD

11.

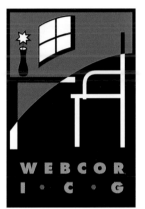

WEBCOR I · C · G

12.

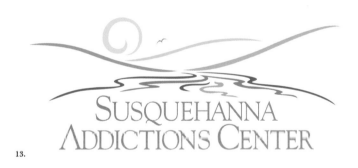

SUSQUEHANNA ADDICTIONS CENTER

13.

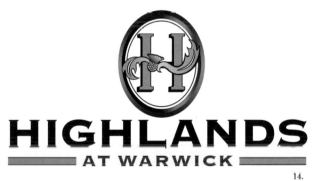

HIGHLANDS AT WARWICK

14.

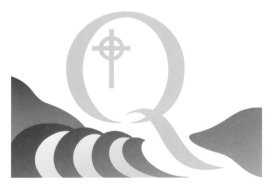

15.

1, 3, 4		
Design Firm	**Ross West Design**	
2, 5, 6		
Design Firm	**GA Design**	
7 - 12		
Design Firm	**Artefact Design**	
13 - 15		
Design Firm	**Albert/Bogner Design Communications**	

1. Client	Dr. Andrew J. Kapust DDS	
Designer	Ross West	
2. Client	Microsoft	
Designer	Ross West	
3. Client	Ross West Design	
Designer	Ross West	
4. Client	Microsoft	
Designer	Ross West	
5. Client	Washington Mutual	
Designer	Ross West	
6. Client	Microsoft	
Designer	Ross West	
7. Client	Joe's 40th Birthday	
Designer	Kim Schwede	

8. Client	Redneck Earl's Cowboy Takeout
Designer	Artefact Design
9. Client	Cortana Corporation
Designers	Artefact Design, Kim Schwede
10. Client	The Stanford Fund
Designer	Artefact Design
11. Client	Webcor Builders, Inc.
Designer	Artefact Design
12. Client	Webcor Builders, Inc.
Designer	Artefact Design
13. Client	Susquehanna Addictions Center
Designers	Kelly Albert & Marie Elaina Miller
14. Client	Highlands at Warwick
Designer	Kelly Albert
15. Client	Quarryville Retirement Community
Designers	Kelly Albert & Marie Elaina Miller

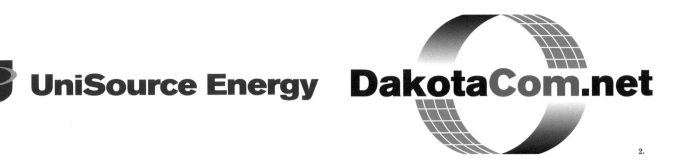

UniSource Energy

1.

DakotaCom.net

2.

certified organic

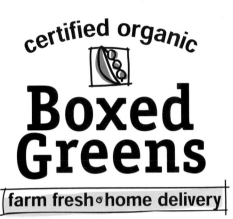

Boxed Greens

farm fresh • home delivery

3.

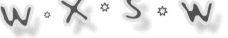

W ✱ X ✱ S ✱ W

West by Southwest Entertainment

4.

SUN CITY
VISTOSO
COMMUNITY
FOUNDATION

5.

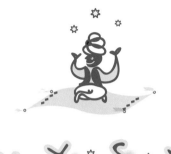

Best **Mortgage** Finders, Inc.

The best source for your home loan.

6.

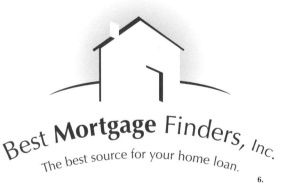

welcome back

about us

our portfolio

7.

aire

8.

22

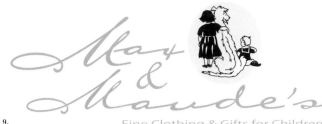

9.

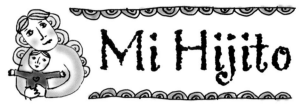

Favorite Childhood Originals for Infants & Toddlers

10.

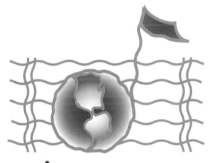

11.

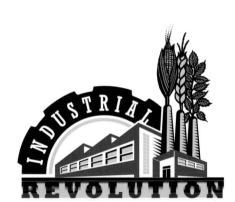

12.

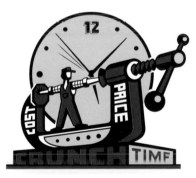

13.

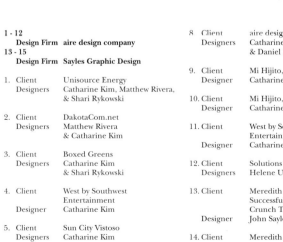

14.

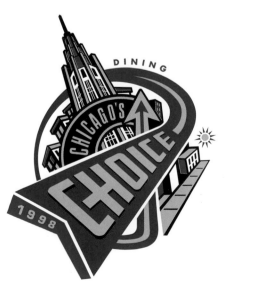

15.

1 - 12
Design Firm aire design company
13 - 15
Design Firm Sayles Graphic Design

1. Client   Unisource Energy
    Designers   Catharine Kim, Matthew Rivera,
                  & Shari Rykowski

2. Client   DakotaCom.net
    Designers   Matthew Rivera
                  & Catharine Kim

3. Client   Boxed Greens
    Designers   Catharine Kim
                  & Shari Rykowski

4. Client   West by Southwest
                  Entertainment
    Designer   Catharine Kim

5. Client   Sun City Vistoso
    Designers   Catharine Kim
                  & Matthew Rivera

6. Client   Best Mortgage Finders, Inc.
    Designer   Shari Rykowski

7. Client   aire design company
    Designer   Catharine Kim

8. Client   aire design company
    Designers   Catharine Kim
                  & Daniel Morrison

9. Client   Mi Hijito, L.L.C.
    Designer   Catharine Kim

10. Client   Mi Hijito, L.L.C.
    Designer   Catharine Kim

11. Client   West by Southwest
                  Entertainment
    Designer   Catharine Kim

12. Client   Solutions
    Designers   Helene Upson & Catharine Kim

13. Client   Meredith Corporation
                  Successful Farming:
                  Crunch Time
    Designer   John Sayles

14. Client   Meredith Corporation
                  Successful Farming:
                  Industrial Revolution
    Designer   John Sayles

15. Client   Chicago Tribune
                  "Chicago's Choice"
    Designer   John Sayles

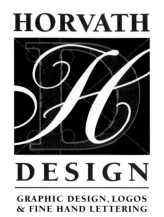

HORVATH
DESIGN

GRAPHIC DESIGN, LOGOS
& FINE HAND LETTERING

1.

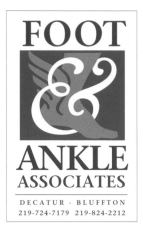

FOOT
&
ANKLE
ASSOCIATES

DECATUR · BLUFFTON
219-724-7179 219-824-2212

2.

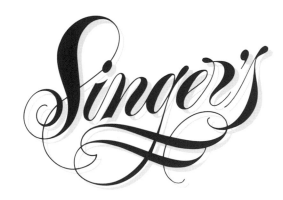

Baggerie

K A N S A S   C I T Y

3.

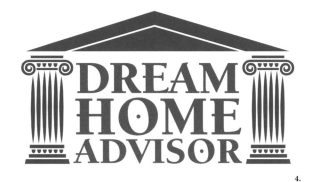

DREAM
HOME
ADVISOR

4.

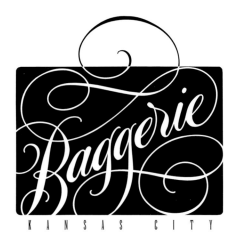

Singer's

5.

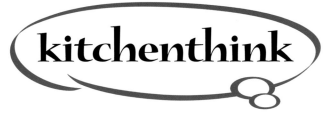

kitchenthink

C R E A T I V E   C O N S U L T I N G

6.

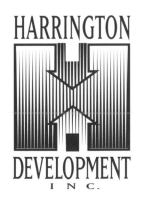

HARRINGTON
DEVELOPMENT
I N C .

7.

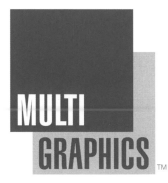

MULTI
GRAPHICS ™

8.

24

OMAN

9.

ENNISKNUPP

10.

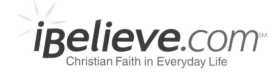

11.

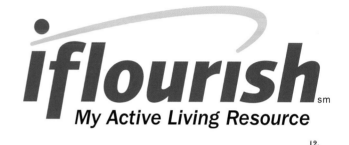

12.

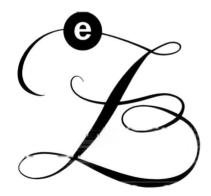

13.

14.

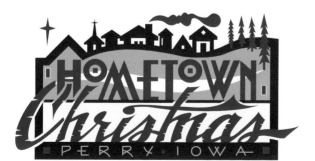

15.

1 - 7
Design Firm Horvath Design
8 - 14
Design Firm Liska + Associates, Inc.
15
Design Firm Sayles Graphic Design

1.	Client	Horvath Design
	Designer	Kevin Horvath
2.	Client	Foot & Ankle Clinic
	Designer	Kevin Horvath
3.	Client	Baggerie
	Designer	Kevin Horvath
4.	Client	Dream Home Advisor
	Designer	Kevin Horvath
5.	Client	Singers Restaurant
	Designer	Kevin Horvath
6.	Client	Kitchen Think
	Designer	Kevin Horvath
7.	Client	Harrington Development
	Designer	Kevin Horvath

8.	Client	Multigraphics
	Designer	Andrea Wener
9.	Client	Oman Photography
	Designer	Steve Liska
10.	Client	EnnisKnupp & Associates
	Designer	Liska + Associates, Inc.
11.	Client	iBelieve.com
	Designer	Liska + Associates, Inc.
12.	Client	iFlourish.com
	Designer	Liska + Associates, Inc.
13.	Client	Elizabeth Zeschin Photography
	Designer	Bonnie Giard
14.	Client	Reptile Artists Agents
	Designer	Holle Andersen
15.	Client	Patee Enterprises "Hometown Christmas"
	Designer	John Sayles

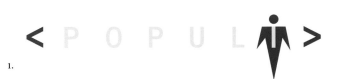

1.

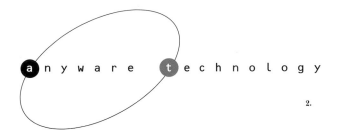

2.

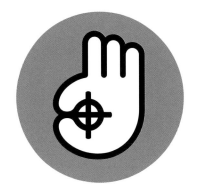

3.

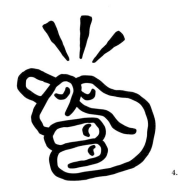

4.

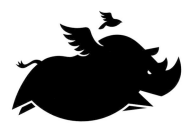

5.

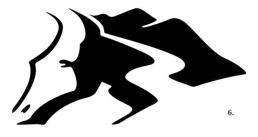

6.

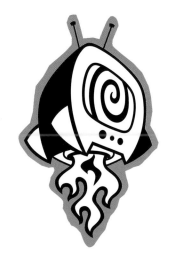

7.

1 - 9
Design Firm **Squires & Company**

1. Client   Populi
   Designers   Brandon Murphy & Amy Chang

2. Client   Anyware Technology
   Designer   Brandon Murphy

3. Client   Pro Color Imaging
   Designers   Kristine Murphy
               & Brandon Murphy

4. Client   Loomis Productions
   Designer   Kristine Murphy

5. Client   Black Rhino Graphics
   Designers   Kristine Murphy
               & Brandon Murphy

6. Client   Hill Country Equestrian Lodge
   Designers   Bryan Hynecek
               & Brandon Murphy

7. Client   Moving Pictures Editorial
   Designers   Kristine Murphy
               & Brandon Murphy

(opposite)
Design Firm **Squires & Company**

8. Client   Deep Ellum Dash '98,
                Annual Fun Run
   Designer   Christie Grotheim

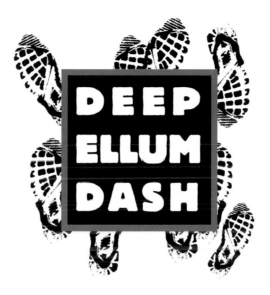

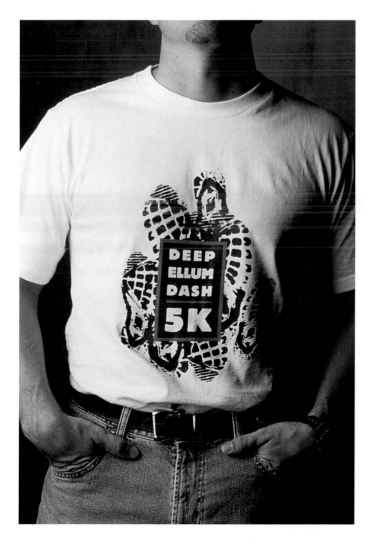

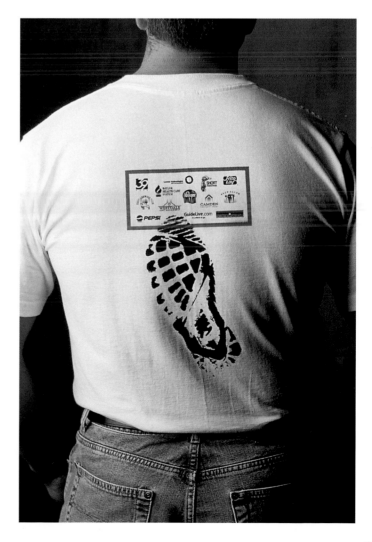

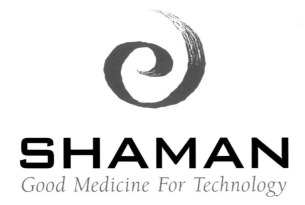

SHAMAN
Good Medicine For Technology

1.

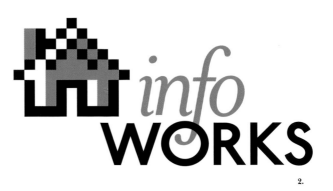

info
WORKS

2.

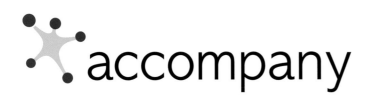
accompany

3.

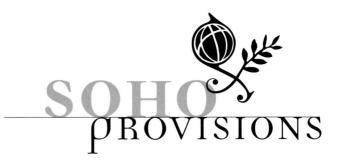

4.

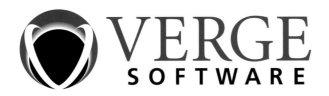
VERGE
SOFTWARE

5.

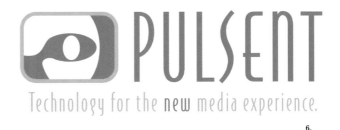
Technology for the new media experience.

6.

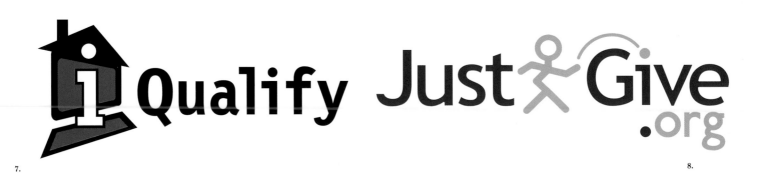
Qualify

7.

Just Give
.org

8.

28

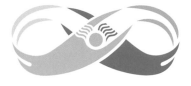

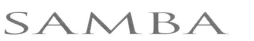

SAMBA

9.

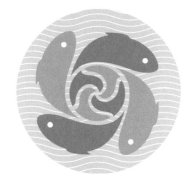

10.

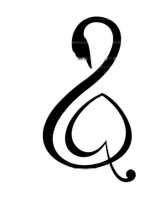

11.

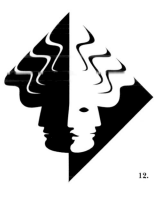

12.

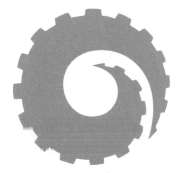

13.

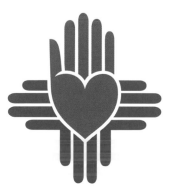

14.

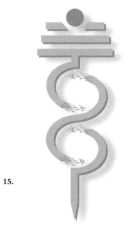

15.

1 - 8
Design Firm Diesel Design
9 - 15
Design Firm Macnab Design
Visual Communication

1. Client   Shaman
    Designer   Amy Bainbridge

2. Client   Info Works
    Designer   Aaron Morton

3. Client   Accompany
    Designer   Aaron Morton

4. Client   Soho Provisions
    Designer   Pam Purser

5. Client   Verge Software
    Designer   Luis Dominguez

6. Client   Pulsent
    Designer   Luis Dominguez

7. Client   iQualify
    Designer   Heather Bodlak

8. Client   Just Give.org
    Designers   Amy Bainbridge
                 & Luis Dominguez

9. Client   Samba
    Designer   Maggie Macnab

10. Client   Truchas Hydrologic Associates
    Designer   Maggie Macnab

11. Client   Swan Songs
    Designer   Maggie Macnab

12. Client   MUSE Technologies Inc.
    Designer   Maggie Macnab

13. Client   CSI Technologies Inc.
    Designer   Maggie Macnab

14. Client   Heart Hospital of New Mexico
    Designer   Maggie Macnab

15. Client   Oriental Medicine Consultants
    Designer   Maggie Macnab

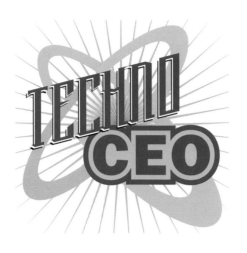

1.

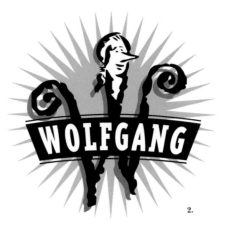

2.

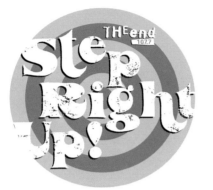

3.

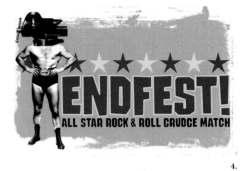

4.

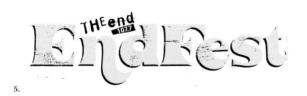

5.

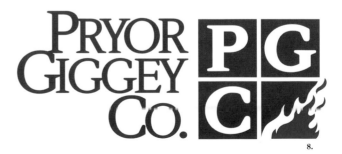

6.

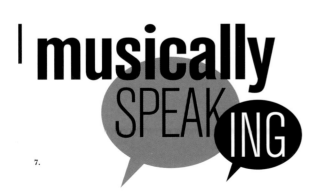

7.

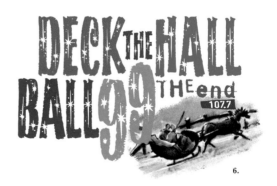

8.

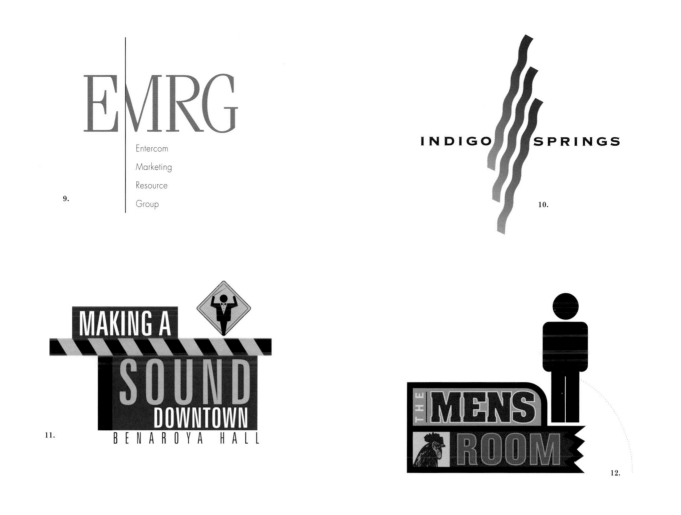

EMRG

Entercom

Marketing

Resource

Group

9.

INDIGO SPRINGS

10.

MAKING A SOUND DOWNTOWN
BENAROYA HALL

11.

THE MENS ROOM

12.

Stravinskys the Nightingale

SEATTLE SYMPHONY

13.

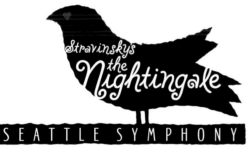

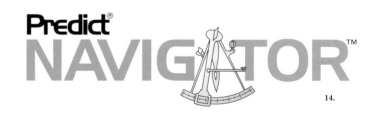

Predict® NAVIGATOR™

14.

n.

Michael Luis & Associates

15.

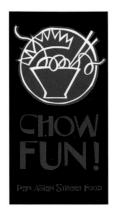

1.

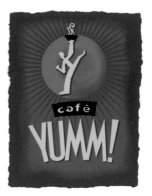

2.

Chambers
Cable

3.

Chambers
PRODUCTIONS

4.

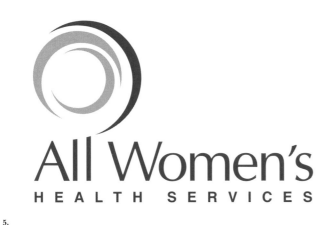

All Women's
HEALTH SERVICES

5.

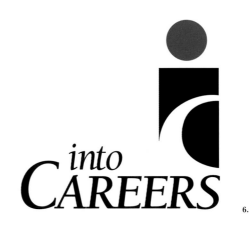

6.

PARK 5

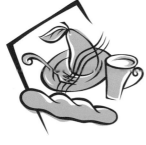

BISTRO

7.

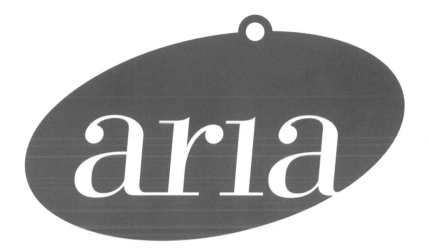

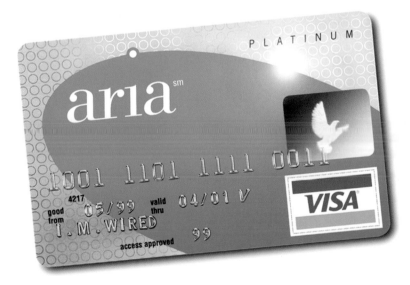

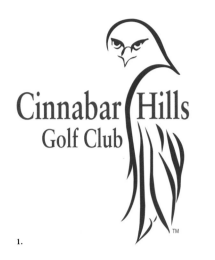

1.

HAMPTON
FINANCIAL
PARTNERS

2.

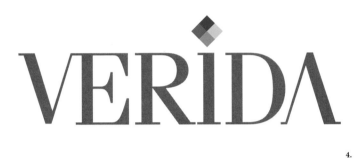

INFINET
INCORPORATED

3.

VERİDA

4.

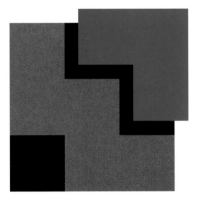

5.

Point Connect

6.

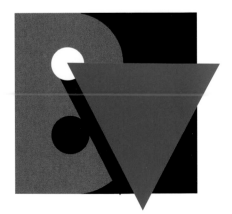

7.

1

Design Firm Bauer Holland Design

3

Design Firm Cathey Associates, Inc.

2, 4 - 7

Design Firm Triad, Inc.

1. Client   Cinnabar Hills Golf Club
   Designers   Julie Holland & Suzanne Bauer

2. Client   Hampton Financial Partners
   Designer   Michael Dambrowski

3. Client   InfiNet, Inc.
   Designer   Gordon Cathey

4. Client   Verida Internet Corp.
   Designer   Diana Kollanyi

5. Client   PointConnect Inc.
   Designer   Michael Dambrowski

6. Client   PointConnect Inc.
   Designer   Diana Kollanyi

7. Client   PointConnect Inc.
   Designer   Michael Dambrowski

(opposite)
Design Firm Donovan and Green

   Client   Faroy
   Designers   Janet Johnson & Ryan Paul

FAROY

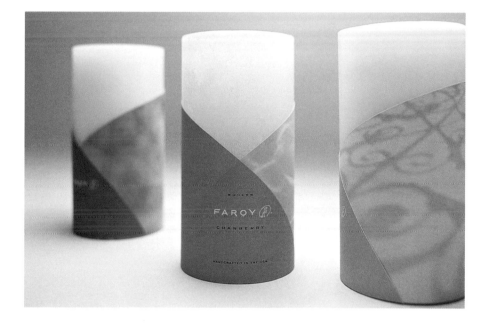

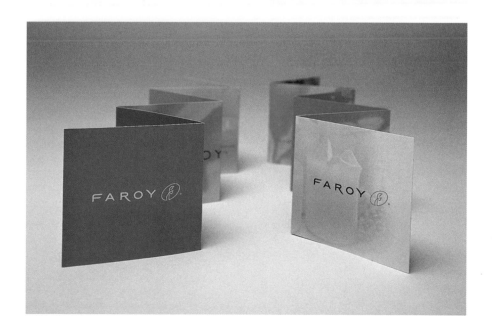

M@llNet™

1.

Unifications
Custom Rug Design

2.

PROTAB

3.

OneSource
Communications, Inc.

4.

state of mind

5.

VO5

6.

LEAP

7.

BioNexus Foundation
Connecting
Global Life Science

8.

ATCC

9.

electric stock

10.

Jet Silver

11.

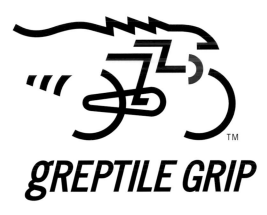

GREPTILE GRIP

12.

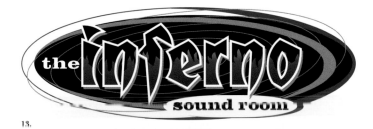

the inferno sound room

13.

The FIREHOUSE

14.

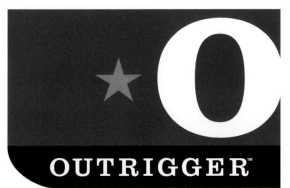

★ O OUTRIGGER

15.

1

Design Firm Donovan and Green

2 - 4

Design Firm Cathey Associates, Inc.

5 - 7

Design Firm Desgrippes Gobé

8 - 10

Design Firm Stephen Loges Graphic Design

11 - 15

Design Firm Phoenix Creative

1. Client   MallNet
   Designer   Janet Johnson

2. Client   Unifications
   Designer   Gordon Cathey

3. Client   ProTab
   Designer   Gordon Cathey

4. Client   One Source
               Communications, Inc.
   Designer   Matt Westapher

5. Client   CBI Laboratory
   Designers   Susan Berson & Deirdre Tighe

6. Client   Unisunstar B.V., Inc.
   Designers   Phyllis Aragaki & Deirdre Tighe

7. Client   Leap Energy and Power Corp.
   Designers   Phyllis Aragaki & Natalie Jacobs

8. Client   BioNexus Foundation
   Designer   Stephen Loges

9. Client   ATCC
   Designer   Stephen Loges

10. Client   Electric Stock
    Designer   Stephen Loges

11. Client   Edison Brothers Stores (5•7•9)
    Designer   Danielle John

12. Client   Pearl Izumi/Greptile Grip
    Designer   Steve Wienke

13. Client   The Inferno Sound Room
    Designer   Kathy Wilkinson

14. Client   The Firehouse
    Designer   Kathy Wilkinson

15. Client   Edison Brothers Stores/
               Outrigger
    Designer   Jenny Anderson

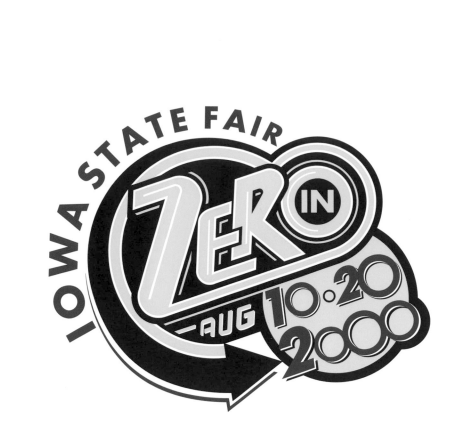

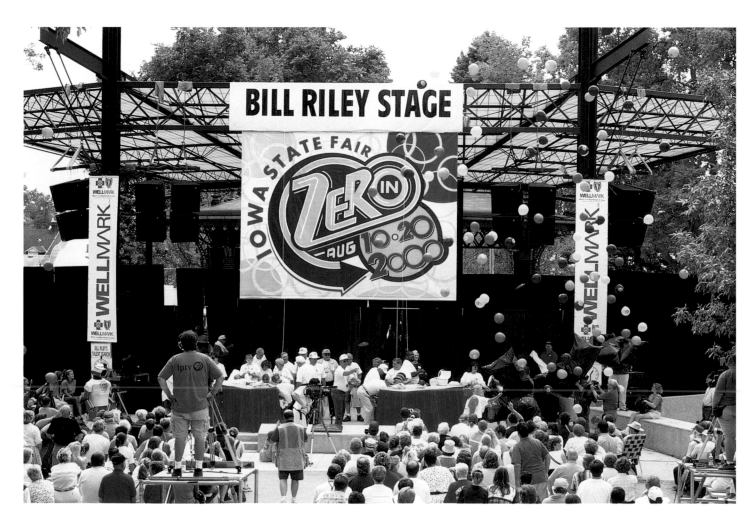

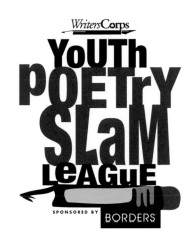

1.

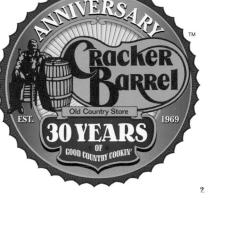

2.

3.

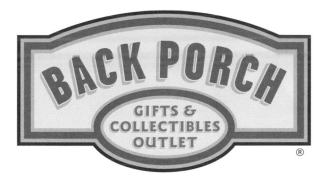

4.

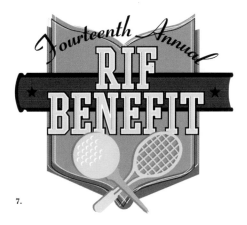

5.

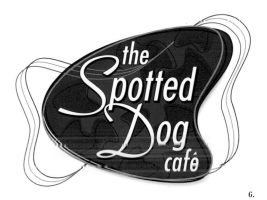

6.

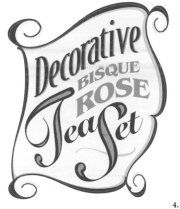

7.

(opposite)

Design Firm Sayles Graphic Design

Client   2000 Iowa State Fair
             "Zero In On Fun"
Designer   John Sayles

1 - 7
Design Firm Phoenix Creative

1. Client   Borders/Youth Poetry Slam
    Designers   Deborah Finkelstein
                 & Jenny Anderson

2. Client   Cracker Barrel Old Country
                 Store (30th Anniversary)
    Designer   Paul Jarvis

3. Client   Cracker Barrel Old Country
                 Store/Back Porch
    Designer   Kathy Wilkinson

4. Client   Cracker Barrel Old
                 Country Store (Tea Set)
    Designer   Curtis Potter

5. Client   Borders/Living Through Books
    Designer   Kathy Wilkinson

6. Client   The Spotted Dog Café
    Designer   Kathy Wilkinson

7. Client   WaldenBooks/RIF Benefit
    Designer   Tyler Small

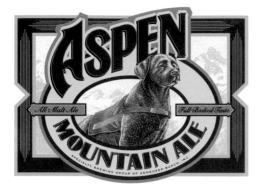

1.

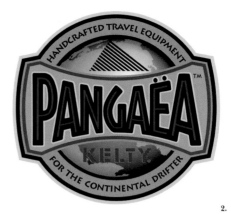

2.

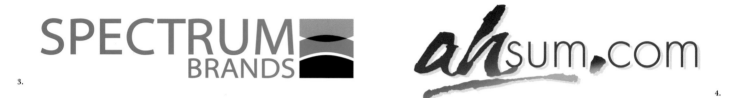

3.

4.

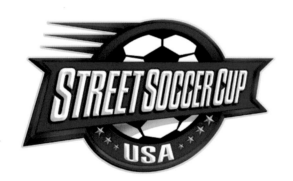

5.

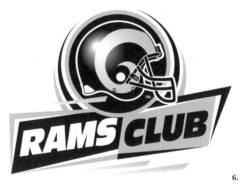

6.

INTERVENTIONS FOR BEHAVIORAL CHANGE

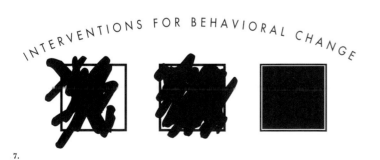

7.

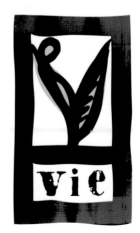

8.

40

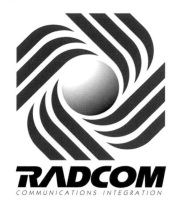

9.

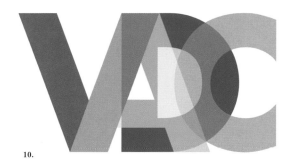

10.

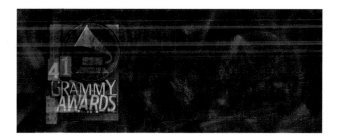

11.

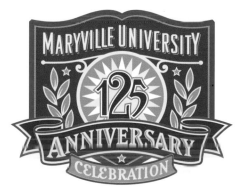

12.

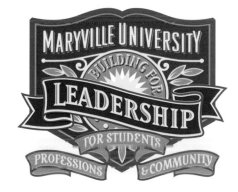

13.

MARYVILLE UNIVERSITY
125
ANNIVERSARY
CELEBRATION

14.

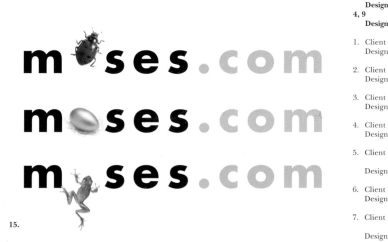

15.

1 - 3, 5 - 8, 10 - 15
  Design Firm **Phoenix Creative**
4, 9
  Design Firm **Cathey Associates, Inc.**

1. Client   Anheuser-Busch/Aspen Ale
    Designer   Kathy Wilkinson

2. Client   Kelty/Pangãea
    Designer   Kathy Wilkinson

3. Client   Spectrum Brands
    Designer   Tyler Small

4. Client   ahsum.com
    Designer   Matt Westapher

5. Client   Think Tank/
                Street Soccer Cup USA
    Designer   Steve Hicks

6. Client   St. Louis Rams
    Designer   Kathy Wilkinson

7. Client   Interventions for
                Behavioral Change
    Designer   Steve Morris

8. Client   Vie
    Designer   Jenny Anderson

9. Client   Radcom Communications
                Integration
    Designers   Matt Westapher
                & Gordon Cathey

10. Client   Washington University
                Visual Arts and Design Center
    Designer   Deborah Finkelstein

11. Client   Borders/National Association
                of Recording Merchandisers
    Designers   Deborah Finkelstein
                & Scott Ferguson

12. Client   Anne Ibur Creations
    Designer   Deborah Finkelstein

13, 14
    Client   Maryville University of St. Louis
    Designer   Ed Mantels-Seeker

15. Client   Moses.com
    Designer   Elizabeth Williams

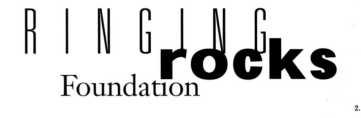

1.

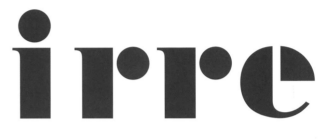

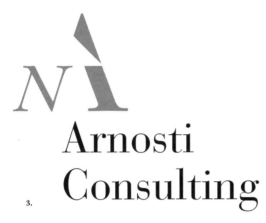

3.

irre

Institute for
Research and Reform
in Education

4.

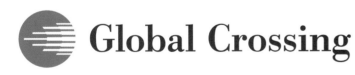

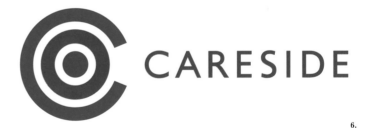

5.

6.

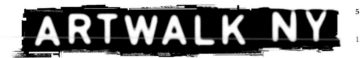

7.

1 - 4
Design Firm Joel Katz Design Associates
5 - 7
Design Firm Studio Morris

1. Client   Freire Charter School
   Designers Mary Torrieri & Joel Katz

2. Client   Ringing Rocks Foundation
   Designers Leslie Conner-Newbold
              & Jennifer Long

3. Client   Arnosti Consulting
   Designer   Joel Katz

4. Client   Institute for Research
              and Reform in Education
   Designers Dave Schpok & Joel Katz

5. Client   Global Crossing
   Designer   Jeff Morris

6. Client   Careside
   Designer   Hyun Lee

7. Client   Coalition for The Homeless
   Designers Jeff Morris & Kaoru Sato

(opposite)
Design Firm Lawson Design

   Client   Rubin Postaer & Assoc. for
              American Century
   Designers Jeff Lawson & Bob Francis

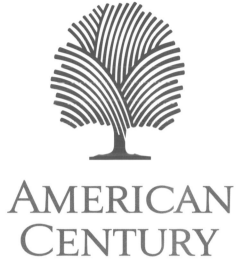

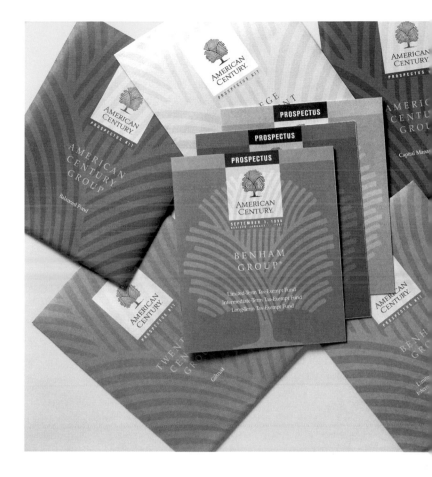

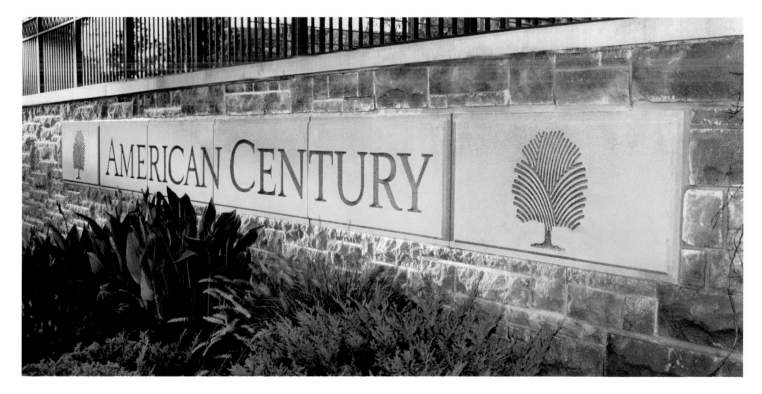

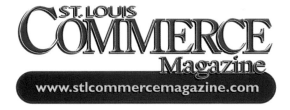

1.

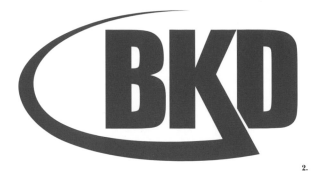

2.

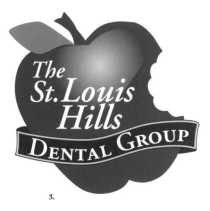

3.

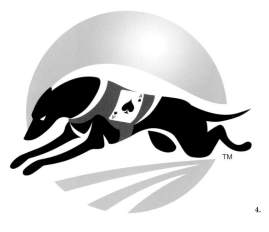

4.

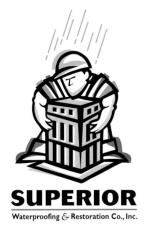

5.

6.

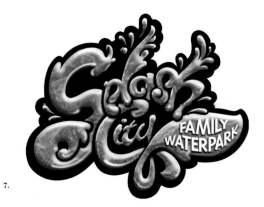

7.

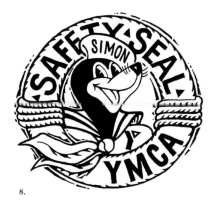

8.

44

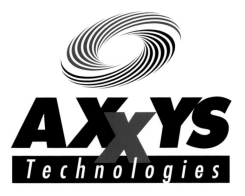

AXXYS *Technologies*

9.

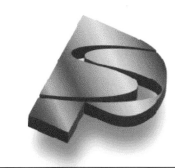

THE PRINTING SOURCE INC.

10.

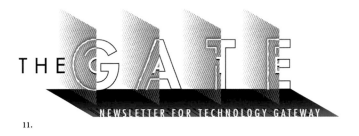

THE **GATE**

NEWSLETTER FOR TECHNOLOGY GATEWAY

11.

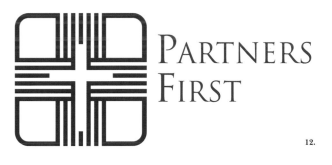

PARTNERS FIRST

12.

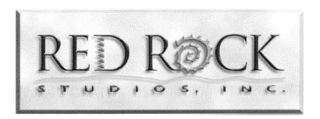

RED ROCK STUDIOS, INC.

13.

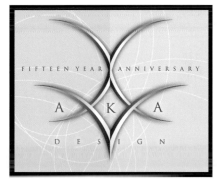

FIFTEEN YEAR ANNIVERSARY

AKA

DESIGN

14.

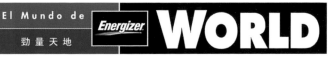

El Mundo de **Energizer** WORLD

动量天地

15.

1 - 8, 10 - 15
Design Firm AKA Design, Inc.

9
Design Firm Cathey Associates, Inc.

1. Client Designer	Commerce Magazine Stacy Lanier	8. Client Designer	YMCA of Greater St. Louis John Ahearn

1. Client   Commerce Magazine
   Designer   Stacy Lanier

2. Client   Baird, Kurtz & Dobson
   Designers   Stacy Lanier & John Ahearn

3. Client   St. Louis Hills Dental Group
   Designers   Jim Jarvis & John Ahearn

4. Client   Object Computing Inc.
   Designer   Mike Mullen

5. Client   Superior Waterproofing
               & Construction Related
               Restoration
   Designer   John Ahearn

6. Client   Parkcrest Surgical Associates
   Designer   Virginia Schneider

7. Client   Splash City Waterpark
   Designers   Craig Martin Simon
               & Mike Mullen

8. Client   YMCA of Greater St. Louis
   Designer   John Ahearn

9. Client   Axxys Technologies
   Designer   Matt Westapher

10. Client   The Printing Source
    Designer   Richie Murphy

11. Client   Technology Gateway
    Designer   Virginia Schneider

12. Client   Partners First
    Designer   Craig Martin Simon

13. Client   Red Rock Studios
    Designer   Richie Murphy

14. Client   AKA Design, Inc.
    Designer   Richie Murphy

15. Client   Energizer World
    Designer   Mike Mullen

45

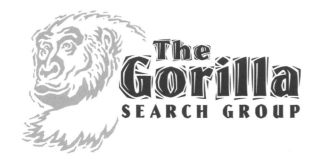

1.

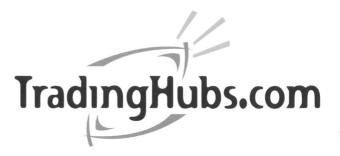

2.

Alche**media**

🌙 | 🌗 | ⚫ | ✦ | ✴

3.

☀ clevercontent.com

4.

ASTROBIOLOGY

5.

⬯ | Supply-Line.com

6.

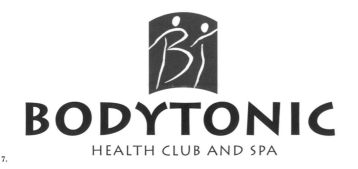

7.

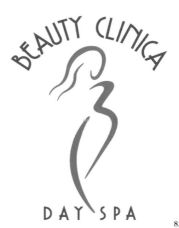

8.

46

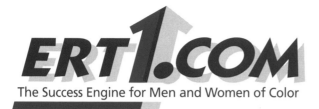

The Success Engine for Men and Women of Color

9.

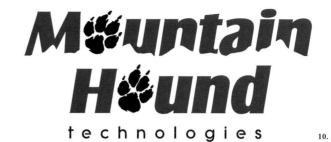

10.

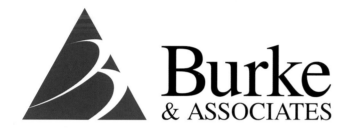

11.

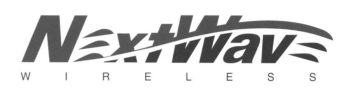

12.

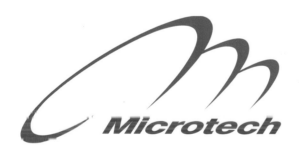

13.

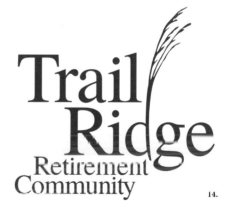

14.

15.

1 - 8, 10 - 15
Design Firm **The Visual Group**

9
Design Firm **Cathey Associates, Inc.**

1. Client   The Gorilla Search Group
   Designer   Ark Stein

2. Client   Hewlett-Packard Company
   Designer   Ark Stein

3. Client   Alchemedia, Inc.
   Designers   Lim Ng & Ark Stein

4. Client   Alchemedia, Inc.
   Designers   Ark Stein & Lim Ng

5. Client   NASA
   Designers   Lim Ng & Ark Stein

6. Client   Supply-Line.com
   Designer   Lim Ng

7. Client   Bodytonic
   Designer   Ark Stein

8. Client   Beauty Clinica
   Designer   Lim Ng

9. Client   ert1.com
   Designer   Gordon Cathey

10. Client   Mountain Hound Technologies
    Designer   Lim Ng

11. Client   Burke & Associates
    Designer   Lim Ng

12. Client   NextWave Wireless
    Designer   Lim Ng

13. Client   Microtech Systems
    Designer   Ark Stein

14. Client   Trail Ridge
    Designer   Lim Ng

15. Client   Jaffe Enterprises
    Designer   Ark Stein

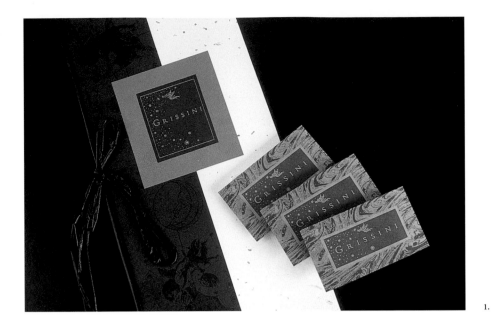

1.

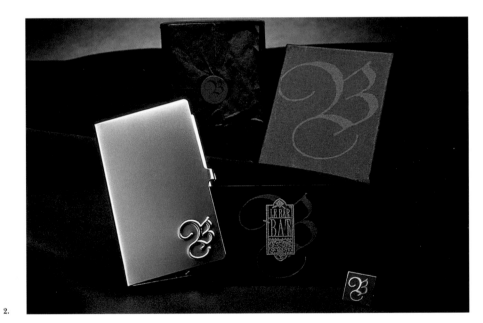

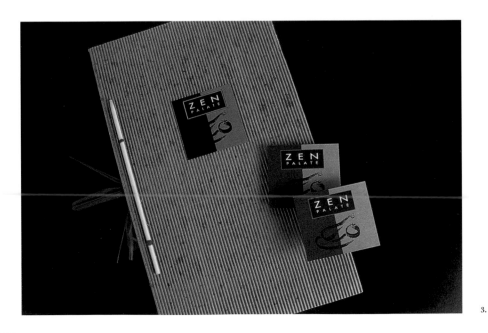

2.

3.

4.

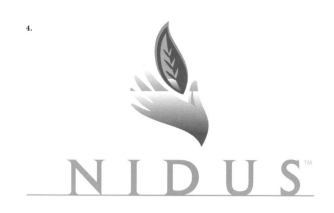

5.

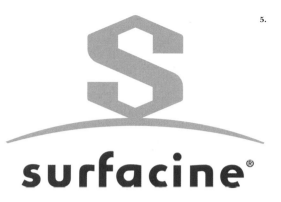

6.

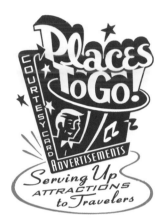

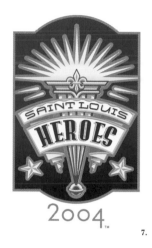

7.

8.

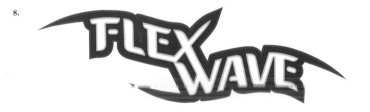

conceptual capital

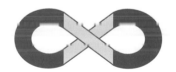

9.

10.

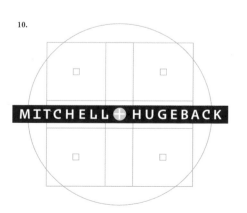

1 - 3
Design Firm Louey/Rubino
             Design Group, Inc.
4 - 10
Design Firm Phoenix Creative

1. Client   Grissini
   Designer Robert Louey

2. Client   Le Bar Bat
   Designer Robert Louey

3. Client   Zen Palate
   Designer Robert Louey

4. Client   Monsanto Company/
             Nidus Center
   Designer Ed Mantels-Seeker

5. Client   Surfacine Development
             Company
   Designer Ed Mantels-Seeker

6. Client   Places To Go
   Designer Ed Mantels-Seeker

7. Client   Saint Louis Heroes/
             St. Louis 2004
   Designer Ed Mantels-Seeker

8. Client   St. Louis Music/
             FlexWave Amplifiers
   Designers Ed Mantels-Seeker
             & Luke Partridge

9. Client   Conceptual Capital
   Designer Ed Mantels-Seeker

10. Client   Mitchell and Hugeback
             Architects
    Designer Ed Mantels-Seeker

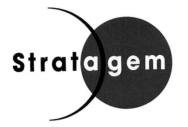

1.

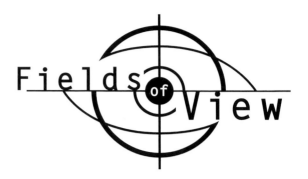

2.

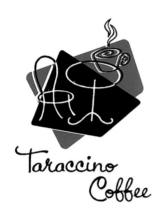

3.

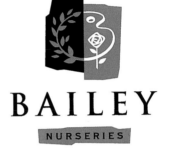

4.

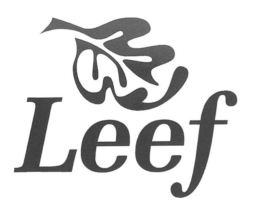

5.

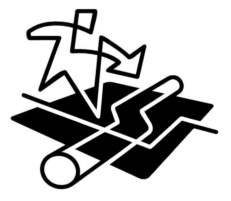

6.

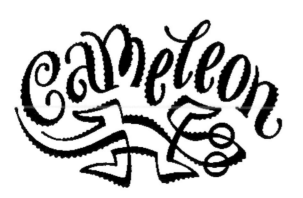

7.

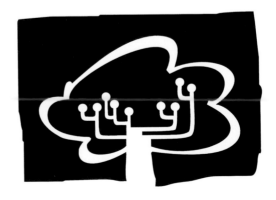

8.

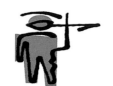

Systems Consulting Group, Inc.

9.

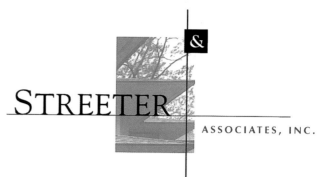

S TREETER

ASSOCIATES, INC.

10.

WELLSPRING

The Source for
Women's Health
and Fitness

11.

HOME
AND **GARDEN**
SHOWSM

12.

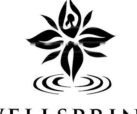

Living **Wise**

Choices for
Your Health

13.

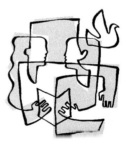

14.

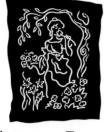

AVONLEA

FLORAL ARTS

15.

(all)

Design Firm Design Center

1. Client   Strategem
    Designers   John Reger
    Design Director:
                 Sherwin Schwartzrock

2. Client   Fields of View
    Designers   John Reger & Cory Dockew

3. Client   Taraccino Coffee
    Designers   John Reger & Todd Spichke

4. Client   Baileys Nursery
    Designers   John Reger
                 & Sherwin Schwartzrock

5. Client   Leef
    Designers   John Reger
                 & Sherwin Schwartzrock

6. Client   Noram
    Designers   John Reger
                 & Sherwin Schwartzrock

7. Client   Cameleon
    Designers   John Reger
                 & Sherwin Schwartzrock

8. Client   Oak Systems
    Designers   John Reger & Jon Erickson

9. Client   System Consulting Group
    Designers   John Reger, Sherwin
                 Schwartzrock & Jon Erickson

10. Client   Streeter & Associates
    Designers   John Reger
                 & Sherwin Schwartzrock

11. Client   Wellspring
    Designers   John Reger
                 & Sherwin Schwartzrock

12. Client   Home and Garden Show
    Designers   John Reger
                 & Sherwin Schwartztock

13. Client   Living Wise
    Designers   John Reger
                 & Sherwin Schwartzrock

14. Client   Resurrection Life Church
    Designers   John Reger
                 & Sherwin Schwartzrock

15. Client   Avonlea
    Designers   John Reger
                 & Sherwin Schwartzrock

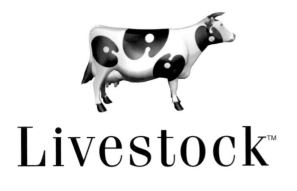

Livestock™

1.

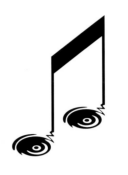

RIVERFRONT
CONCERTS

2.

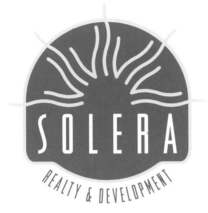

3.

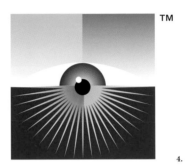

TM

4.

∧V∆NTIX
AVANTIX LABORATORIES, INC.

5.

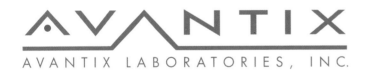

VERITY™
INVESTIGATION AND RESPONSE

6.

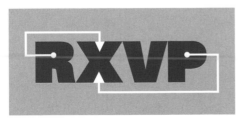

7.

1 - 7		
Design Firm	**Orbit Integrated**	
1. Client	Livestock	
Designer	Jack Harris	
2. Client	Delaware Theatre Company	
3. Client	Solera Realty + Development	
Designer	Mark Miller	
4. Client	New Media Insight	
Designer	Jack Harris	

5. Client	Avantix Laboratories, Inc.	
Designer	Jack Harris	
6. Client	Verity	
Designer	Jack Harris	
7. Client	RXVP	
Designer	Jack Harris	
(opposite)		
Design Firm	**Squires & Company**	
Client	Everlink	
Designer	Anna Magruder	

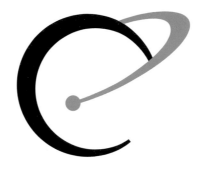

EverLink™

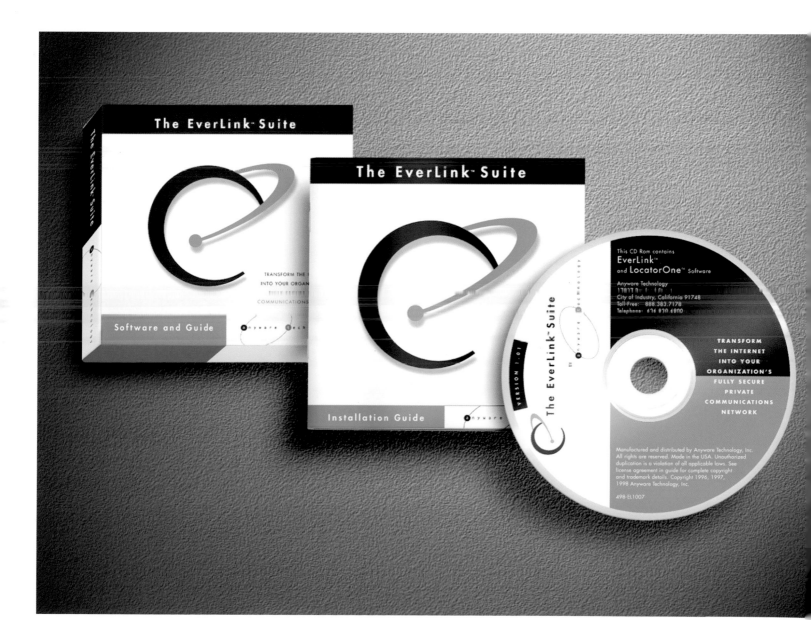

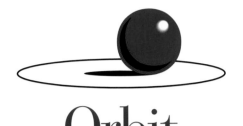

Orbit.
integrated

1.

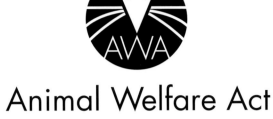

Animal Welfare Act

2.

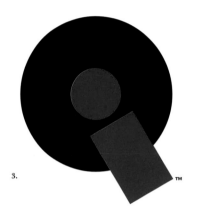

3.

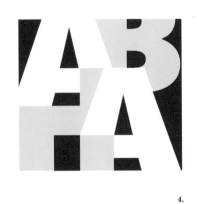

4.

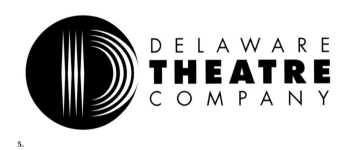

DELAWARE
THEATRE
COMPANY

5.

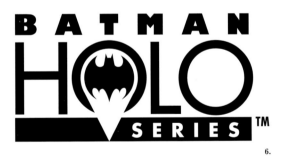

6.

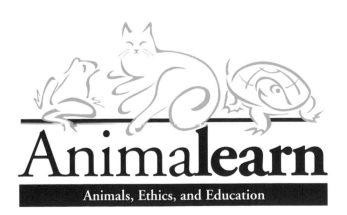

7.

American Anti-Vivisection Society

8.

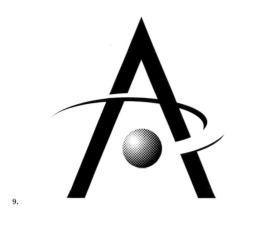

9.

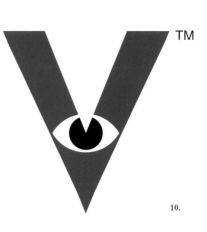

TM

10.

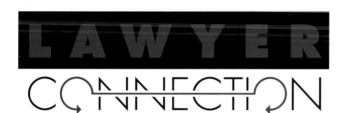

OF GREATER PHILADELPHIA

11.

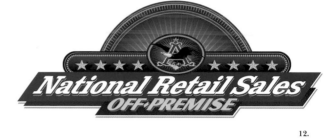

12.

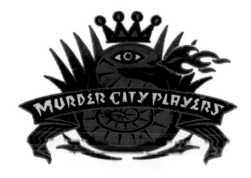

13.

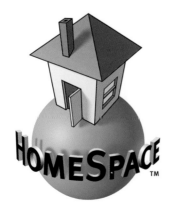

14.

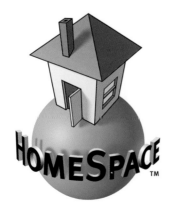

15.

1 - 11
Design Firm Orbit Integrated
12 - 14
Design Firm Phoenix Creative, St. Louis
15
Design Firm Studio Morris

1. Client   Orbit Integrated
    Designer   Jack Harris

2. Client   American Anti-Vivisection
                      Society
    Designer   Jack Harris

3. Client   Orbit Integrated
    Designer   Jack Harris

4. Client   ABHA
    Designer   Jack Harris

5. Client   Delaware Theatre Company
    Designer   Jack Harris

6. Client   DC Comics
    Designer   Jack Harris

7. Client   American Anti-Vivisection
                      Society
    Designer   Jack Harris

8. Client   American
                      Anti-Vivisection Society
    Designer   Jack Harris

9. Client   Environmental Alliance
    Designer   Jack Harris

10. Client   Visual Logic
    Designer   Jack Harris

11. Client   Lawyer Connection of
                      Gr. Philadelphia
    Designer   Jack Harris

12. Client   Anheuser-Busch
                      National Retail Sales
    Designer   Ed Mantels-Seeker

13. Client   Murder City Players
    Designer   Ed Mantels-Seeker

14. Client   Big Brothers Big Sisters
                      of Greater St. Louis
    Designer   Deborh Finkelstein

15. Client   Homespace
    Designer   Hyun Lee

1.

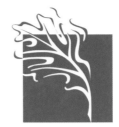

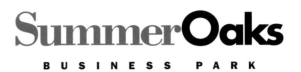

2.

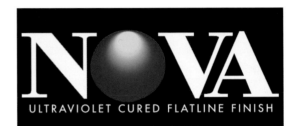

3.

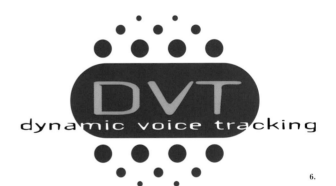

4.

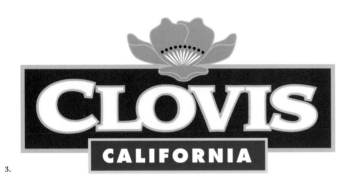

5.

6.

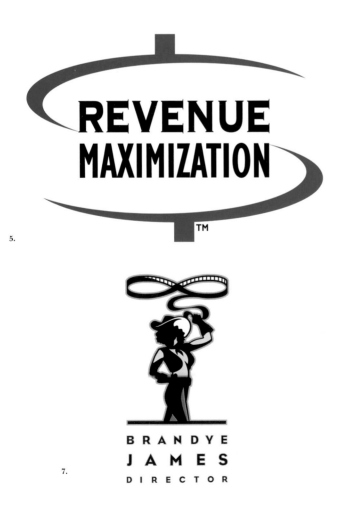

7.

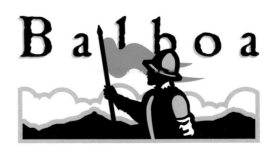

8.

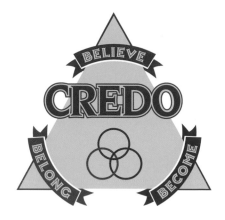

9.

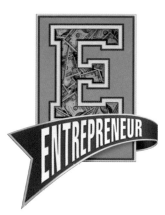

10.

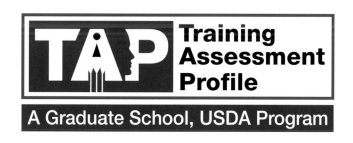

11.

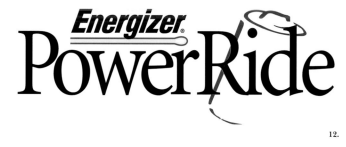

12.

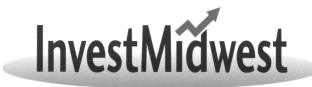

13

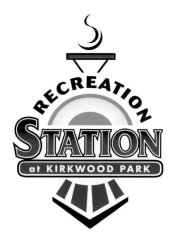

15.

Eastport BUSINESS CENTER

14

1 - 6
Design Firm Funk and Associates
7 - 8
Design Firm Squires & Company
9 - 15
Design Firm AKA Design, Inc.

1. Client   Eugene Public
                Library Foundation
    Designers   Beverly Soasey
                & Kathleen Heinz

2. Client   Dan Tucci
    Designers   Beverly Soasey
                & Christopher Berner

3. Client   City of Clovis, CA
    Designer   Christopher Berner

4. Client   States Industries
    Designer   Christopher Berner

5. Client   CBSI (Revenue Maximization)
    Designer   Krista Lippert

6. Client   CBSI (DVT)
    Designer   Krista Lippert

7. Client   Brandye James
    Designer   Paul Black

8. Client   Balboa
    Designer   Paul Black

9. Client   Credo
    Designers   John Ahearn & Sara Gries

10. Client   Collegiate Entrepreneur
                of the Year
    Designers   Richie Murphy & John Ahearn

11. Client   Graduate School, USDA
    Designer   Mike Mullen

12. Client   Energizer
    Designer   Richie Murphy

13. Client   Invest Midwest
    Designer   Richie Murphy

14. Client   Eastport Business Center
    Designers   Virginia Schneider
                & John Ahearn

15. Client   Recreation Station
    Designers   Stacy Lanier
                & Craig Martin Simon

57

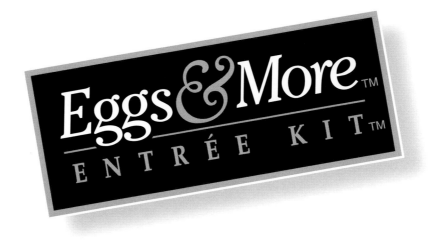

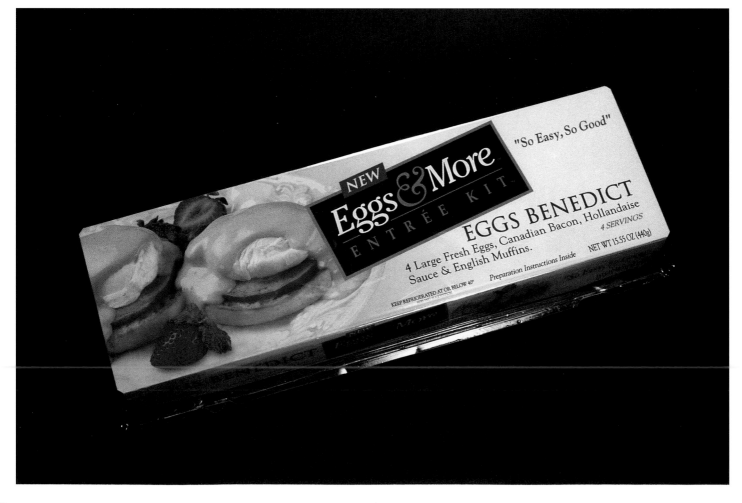

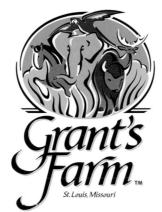

1.

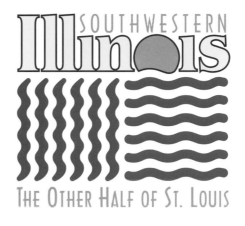

2.

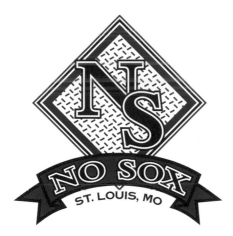

3.

KEHRS MILL
FAMILY DENTAL CARE

4.

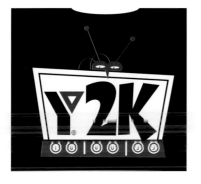

5.

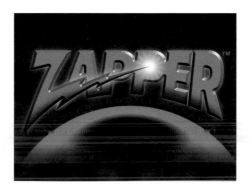

6.

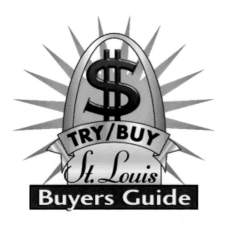

7.

(opposite)
Design Firm Dixon & Parcels Associates, Inc.

Client   Eggland's Best, Inc.

1 - 7
Design Firm AKA Design, Inc.

1. Client   Grant's Farm
    Designer   Mike Mullen

2. Client   Southwestern Illinois
                Tourism Bureau
    Designer   Craig Martin Simon

3. Client   No Sox Charity Ball Team
    Designer   Richie Murphy

4. Client   Kehrs Mill Dental
    Designers   Richie Murphy & John Ahearn

5. Client   Kirkwood/Webster YMCA
    Designer   John Ahearn

6. Client   Infinitech
    Designer   John Ahearn

7. Client   St. Louis Regional Chamber
                & Growth Association
    Designers   Richie Murphy & John Ahearn

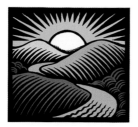

BANK OF PETALUMA

1.

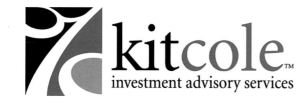

TamalpaisBank

2.

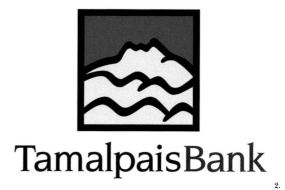

kitcole™
investment advisory services

3.

eaze∟

4.

myplay

5.

Call THE Sh ts

6.

handspring

7.

springboard

8.

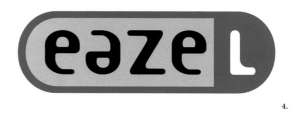
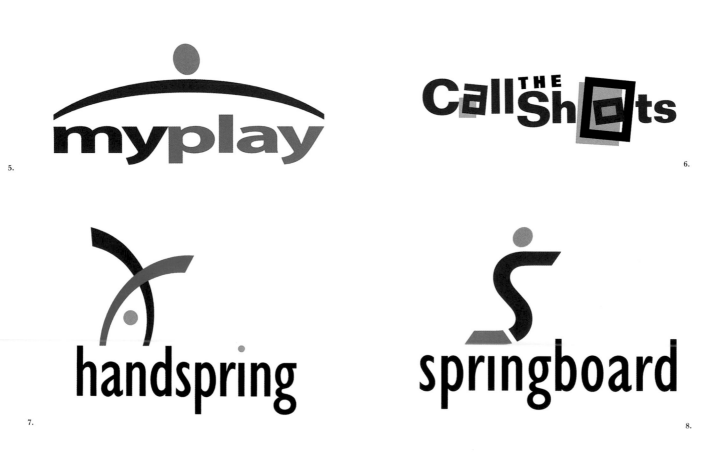

60

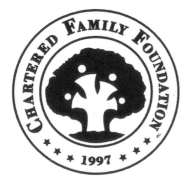

9.

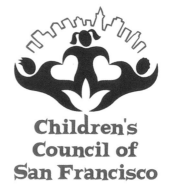

Children's
Council of
San Francisco

10.

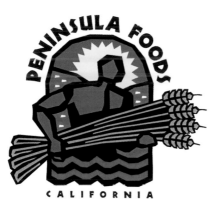

11.

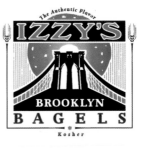

12.

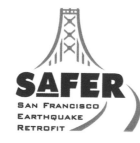

13.

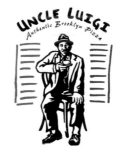

14.

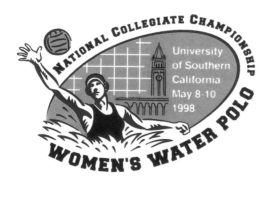

15.

1 - 8
Design Firm **Mortensen Design**
9 - 15
Design Firm **The Visual Group**

1. Client — Bank of Petaluma
   Designers — Gordon Mortensen,
   Wendy Chon, & Chris Gall

2. Client — Tamalpais Bank
   Designers — Wendy Chon
   & Gordon Mortensen

3. Client — Kit Cole Investment
   Advisory Services
   Designers — Gordon Mortensen
   & Wendy Chon

4. Client — Eazel
   Designers — PJ Nidecker
   & Gordon Mortensen

5. Client — MyPlay, Inc.
   Designers — PJ Nidecker
   & Gordon Mortensen

6. Client — CallTheShots
   Designers — Gordon Mortensen
   & Wendy Chon

7. Client — Handspring
   Designers — PJ Nidecker
   & Gordon Mortensen

8. Client — Handspring, Inc.
   Designers — PJ Nidecker
   & Gordon Mortensen

9. Client — Peninsula Community
   Foundation
   Designers — Lim Ng & Ark Stein

10. Client — Children Council
    of San Francisco
    Designer — Ark Stein

11. Client — Peninsula Foods
    Designer — Ark Stein

12. Client — Uncle Luigi Pizza
    Designer — Ark Stein

13. Client — Caltrans
    Designer — Ark Stein

14. Client — Izzy's Brooklyn Bagels
    Designers — Bill Mifsud & Ark Stein

15. Client — USC
    Designer — Ark Stein

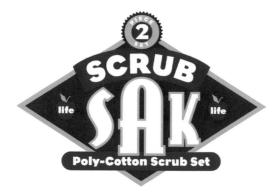

1.

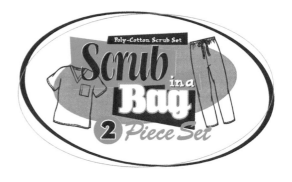

2.

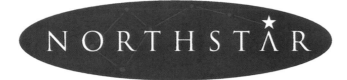

3.

SetRite™

4.

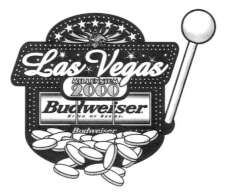

5.

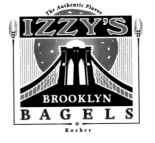

6.

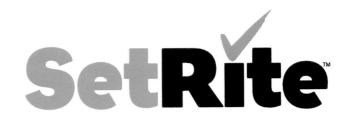

7.

(all)
Design Firm CUBE Advertising & Design

1. Client   Life Uniform
   Designer   David Chiow

2. Client   Life Uniform
   Designer   David Chiow

3. Client   Northstar Management Co.
   Designers   David Chiow & Matt Marino

4. Client   Crown Theraputics, Inc.
   Designer   David Chiow

5. Client   Anheuser-Busch, Inc.
   Designers   David Chiow & Kevin Hough

6. Client   The Natural Way
   Designer   David Chiow

7. Client   dreyfus + associates photography
   Designer   David Chiow

(opposite)
Design Firm CUBE Advertising & Design

   Client   St. Louis Zoo
   Designer   David Chiow

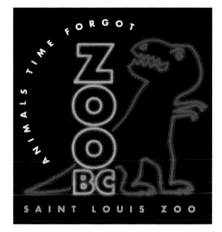

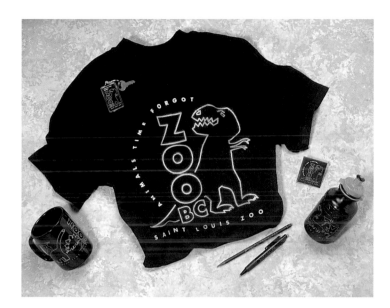

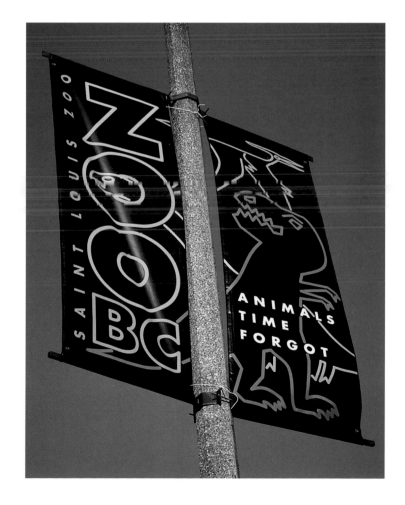

63

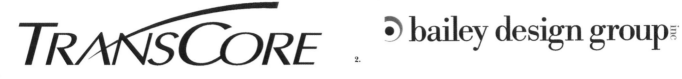

1.

2.

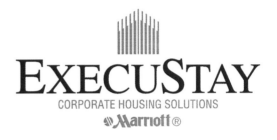

3.

4.

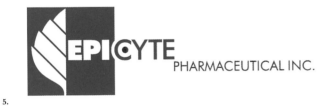

5.

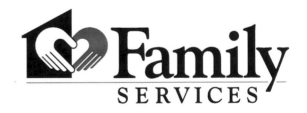

6.

7.

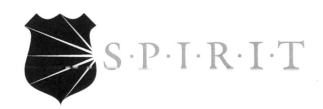

8.

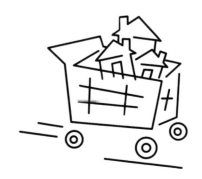

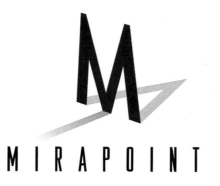

MIRAPOINT

9.

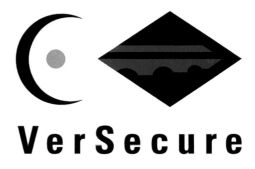

VerSecure

10.

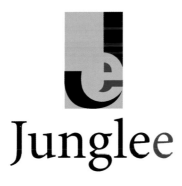

Junglee

11.

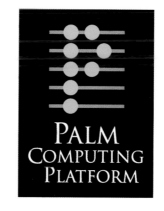

PALM
COMPUTING
PLATFORM

12.

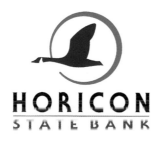

HORICON
STATE BANK

13.

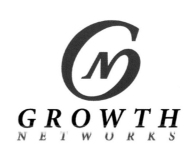

GROWTH
NETWORKS

14

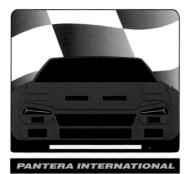

PANTERA INTERNATIONAL

15.

1 - 8					
Design Firm	**Bailey Design Group, Inc.**		8.	Client	Annabelle Properties
9 - 14				Designer	Steve Perry
Design Firm	**Mortensen Design**		9.	Client	Mirapoint, Inc.
15				Designers	PJ Nidecker
Design Firm	**Theodore C. Alexander, Jr.**				& Gordon Mortensen
1.	Client	Transcore	10.	Client	Hewlett-Packard
	Designer	Laura Markley		Designers	Diana Kauzlarich
					& Gordon Mortensen
2.	Client	Bailey Design Group, Inc.			
	Designer	Gary LaCroix	11.	Client	Junglee Corporation
				Designers	Diana Kauzlarich
3.	Client	Marriott Corporation			& Gordon Mortensen
	Designers	Wendy Slavish & Steve Perry			
			12.	Client	Palm Computing
4.	Client	Marriott Corporation		Designers	Gordon Mortensen
	Designer	David Fiedler			& Wendy Chon
5.	Client	Epicyte Pharmaceutical	13.	Client	Horicon Bank
	Designer	Steve Perry		Designers	Wendy Chon
					& Gordon Mortensen
6.	Client	Family Services			
	Designer	Steve Perry	14.	Client	Growth Networks
				Designers	Wendy Chon
7.	Client	Spirit			& Gordon Mortensen
	Designer	David Fiedler			
			15.	Client	Pantera International
				Designer	Theodore C. Alexander

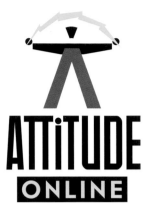

1.

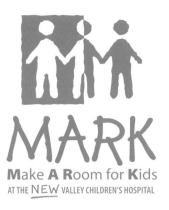

2.

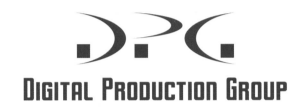

3.

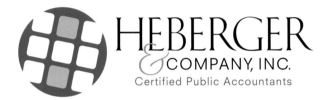

4.

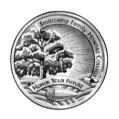

5.

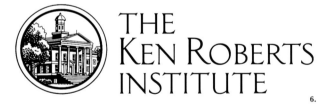

6.

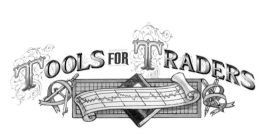

7.

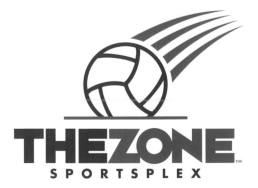

8.

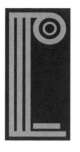

Paul E. Lerandeau
ATTORNEY AT LAW

9.

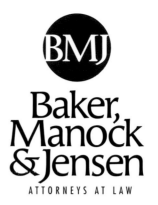

Baker, Manock & Jensen
ATTORNEYS AT LAW

10.

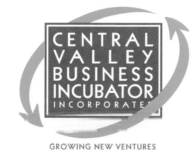

Phil Rudy

Photography

11.

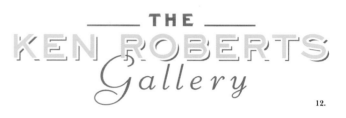

THE **KEN ROBERTS** *Gallery*

12.

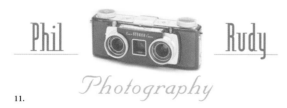

CENTRAL VALLEY BUSINESS INCUBATOR INCORPORATED

GROWING NEW VENTURES

13.

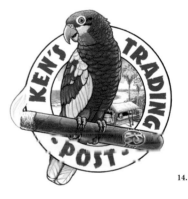

KEN'S TRADING POST

14.

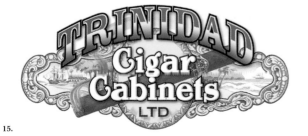

TRINIDAD Cigar Cabinets LTD

15.

(all)

	Design Firm	Shields Design

#			#		
1.	Client	Attitude Online	8.	Client	The Zone Sportsplex
	Designers	Juan Vega & Charles Shields		Designers	Charles Shields & Stephanie Wong
2.	Client	Valley Children's Hospital			
	Designers	Laura Thornton & Charles Shields	9.	Client	Paul E. Lerandeau
				Designers	Thoms Kimmelman & Charles Shields
3.	Client	Digital Production Group			
	Designers	Thomas Kimmelman & Charles Shields	10.	Client	Baker, Manock & Jensen
				Designer	Charles Shields
4.	Client	Heberger & Company	11.	Client	Phil Rudy Photography
	Designers	Charles Shields & Stephanie Wong		Designer	Charles Shields
			12.	Client	The Ken Roberts Company
5.	Client	Smittcamp Family Honors College		Designer	Charles Shields
	Designers	Charles Shields & Stephanie Wong	13.	Client	Central Valley Business Incubator
				Designer	Charles Shields
6.	Client	The Ken Roberts Company	14.	Client	The Ken Roberts Company
	Designer	Charles Shields		Designer	Charles Shields
7.	Client	Great Pacific Trading Company	15.	Client	The Ken Roberts Company
	Designer	Charles Shields		Designer	Charles Shields

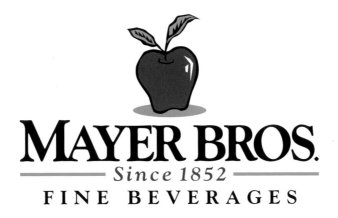

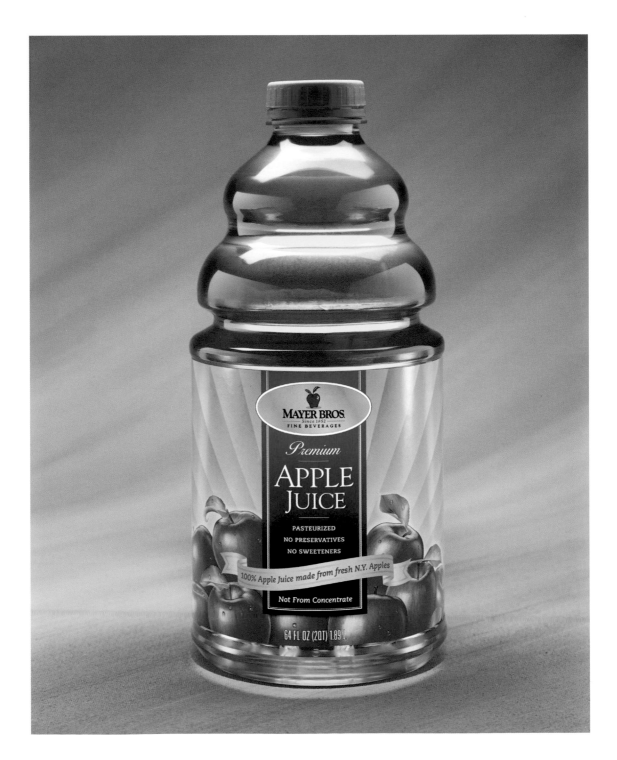

1.

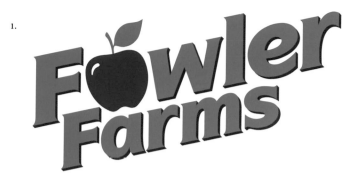

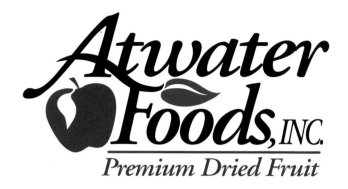

3.

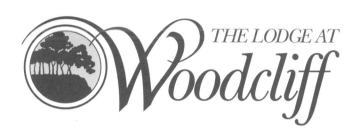

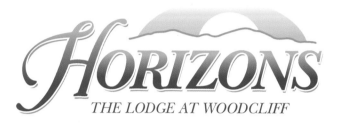

4.

5.

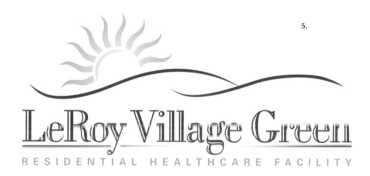

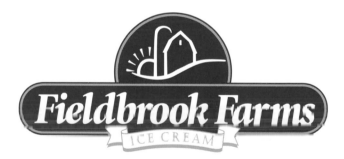

6.

7.

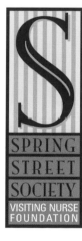

(opposite)
Design Firm **McElveney & Palozzi**
Design Group, Inc.

Client   Mayer Bros.
Designers   William McElveney
            & Lisa Parenti

1 - 7
Design Firm **McElveney & Palozzi**
Design Group, Inc.

1. Client   Fowler Farms
    Designers   William McElveney, Matt
                 Nowicki, & Jan Marie Gallagher

2. Client   Atwater Foods Inc.
    Designers   Bill McElveney
                 & Lisa Williamson

3. Client   The Lodge at Woodcliff
    Designers   William McElveney
                 & Ellen Johnson

4. Client   The Lodge at Woodcliff
    Designers   William McElveney
                 & Ellen Johnson

5. Client   LeRoy Village Green
    Designers   William McElveney, Lisa Parenti,
                 & Jan Marie Gallagher

6. Client   Fieldbrook Farms Inc.
    Designers   William McElveney
                 & Ellen Johnson

7. Client   Spring Street Society
    Designer   Steve Palozzi

ε

THE ELLIOTT

1.

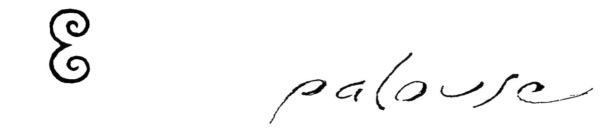

2.

 Starting Early
STARTING SMART

3.

ESM CONSULTING ENGINEERS

4.

redley

5.

iridio •••

6.

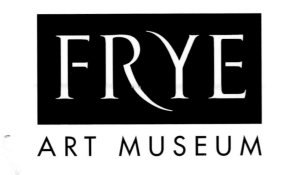

FRYE
ART MUSEUM

7.

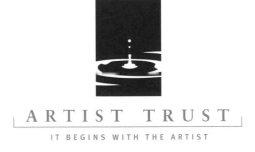

ARTIST TRUST
IT BEGINS WITH THE ARTIST

8.

70

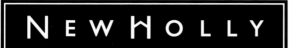

 HENRY M. JACKSON
FOUNDATION

9.

10.

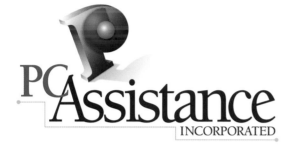

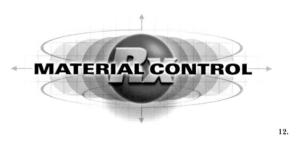

11.

12.

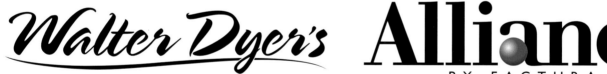

Walter Dyer's
SHOES & LEATHER

BY FACTURA

13.

14.

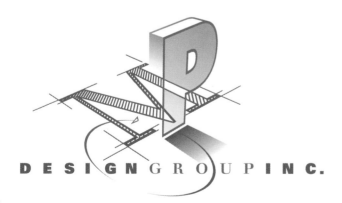

DESIGN GROUP INC.

15.

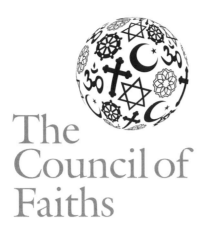

The
Council of
Faiths

1.

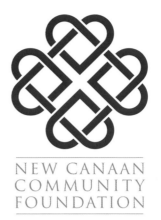

NEW CANAAN
COMMUNITY
FOUNDATION

2.

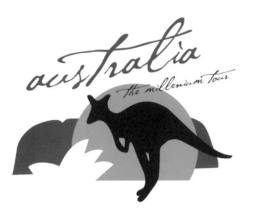

australia
the millenium tour

3.

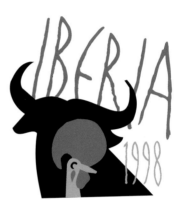

IBERIA
1998

4.

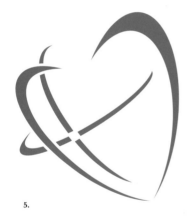

5.

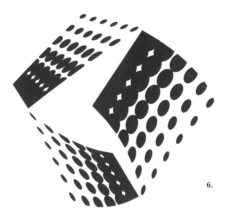

6.

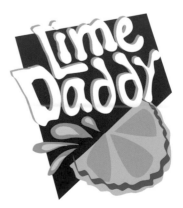

7.

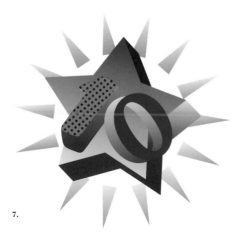

8.

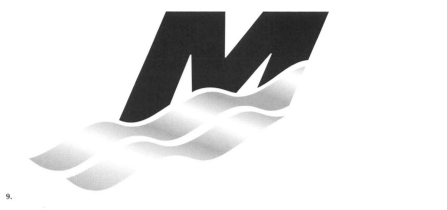

9.

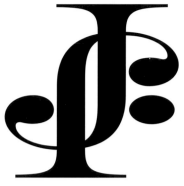

10.

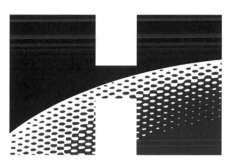

11.

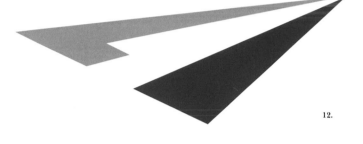

12.

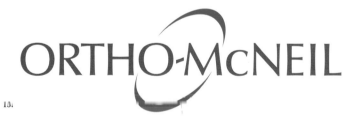

13.

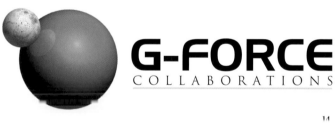

14.

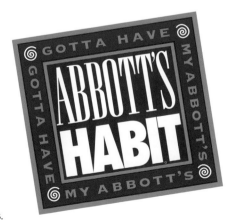

15.

1 - 13		7. Client	BMG
Design Firm	**Congdon & Company LLC**	Designer	Arthur Congdon
14 - 15			
Design Firm	**McElveney & Palozzi Design Group**	8. Client	Delaware Valley Distributing
		Designer	Arthur Congdon
1. Client	Council of Faiths of Southwestern Connecticut	9. Client	Mercury Marine
Designer	Arthur Congdon	Designer	Arthur Congdon
2. Client	New Canaan Connecticut Community Foundation	10. Client	Jeniam Foundation
Designer	Arthur Congdon	Designer	Athur Congdon
3. Client	New Canaan (Connecticut) High School Madrigal Ensemble	11. Client	Hypernex
Designer	Arthur Congdon	Designer	Arthur Congdon
4. Client	New Canaan (Connecticut) High School Madrigal Ensemble	12. Client	Corp Air
Designer	Arthur Congdon	Designer	Arthur Congdon
5. Client	Biosense Webster, Johnson & Johnson Co.	13. Client	Ortho-McNeil
Designer	Arthur Congdon	Designer	Arthur Congdon
6. Client	Novasource	14. Client	G-Force Collaborations
Designer	Arthur Congdon	Designers	William McElveney, Matt Nowicki, & Dillon Constable
		15. Client	Abbott's Frozen Custard
		Designers	Bill McElveney & Lisa Parenti

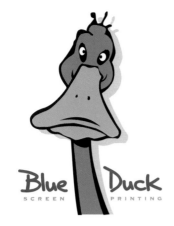

1.

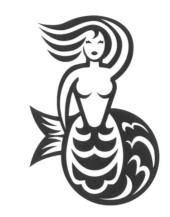

2.

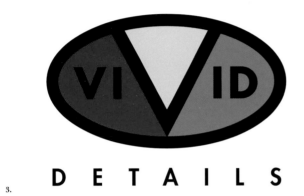

3.

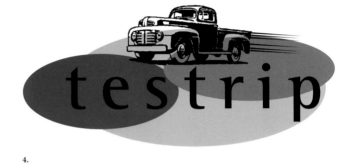

4.

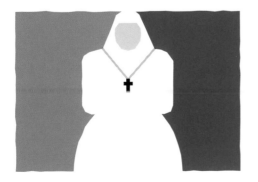

5.

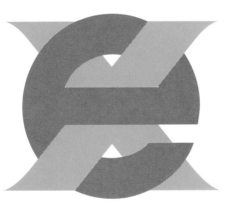

6.

7.

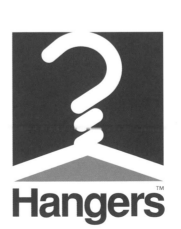

8.

Hangers™

74

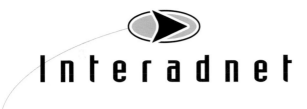

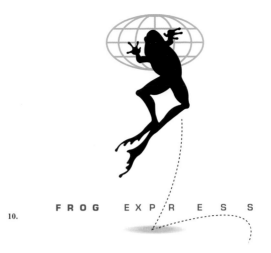

FROG EXPRESS

10.

9.

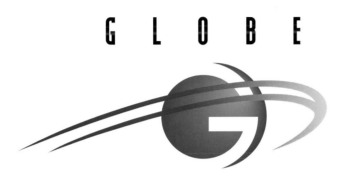

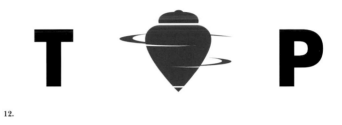

12.

11.

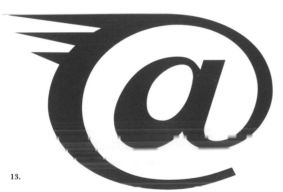

ST. PATRICK
PARTNERSHIP CENTER

14.

13.

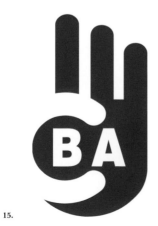

15.

(all)
Design Firm   Bartels & Company, Inc.

1. Client   Blue Duck Screen Printing
    Designers   David Bartels
                 & Ron Rodemacher

2. Client   Blue Deep, Ltd.
    Designers   David Bartels, Mary Flock,
                 & Chris Schott

3. Client   UI

4. Client   Testrip
    Designers   David Bartels
                 & Ron Rodemacher

5. Client   Executive Expression
    Designers   Ron Rodemacher
                 & David Bartels

6. Client   American Manicure
    Designers   Ron Rodemacher, David Bartels,
                 & Don Strander

7. Client   Sacred Heart Villa
    Designer   Bob Thomas

8. Client   Micell Technologies, Inc.
    Designers   Ron Rodemacher
                 & David Bartels

9. Client   Interadnet
    Designers   Chris Schott & David Bartels

10. Client   Frog Express
    Designers   David Bartels &
                 Ron Rodemacher

11. Client   The Sandcastle
    Designers   Ron Rodemacher &
                 David Bartels

12. Client   Top Graphics
    Designers   Ron Rodemacher &
                 David Bartels

13. Client   Generalife Insurance Company
    Designers   David Bartels &
                 Ron Rodemacher

14. Client   St. Patrick Partnership Center
    Designers   Ron Rodemacher &
                 David Bartels

15. Client   Ceci Bartels Associates
    Designer   Ron Rodemacher

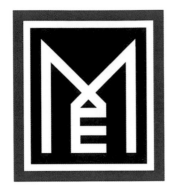

1.

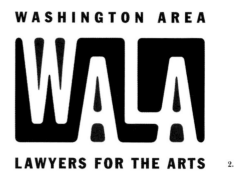

LAWYERS FOR THE ARTS

2.

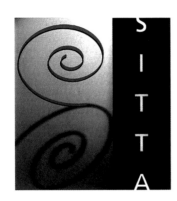

3.

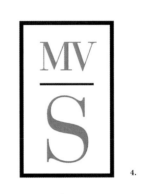

4.

WiNK

5.

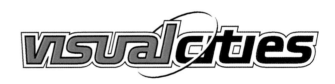

6.

A E R I E

networks

7.

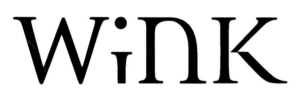

all kinds of minds

A NON-PROFIT INSTITUTE FOR THE
UNDERSTANDING OF DIFFERENCES IN LEARNING

8.

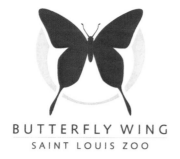

BUTTERFLY WING
SAINT LOUIS ZOO

9.

10.

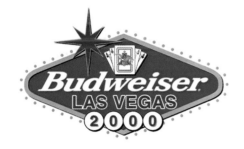

11.

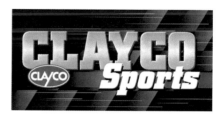

12.

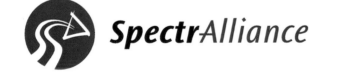

13.

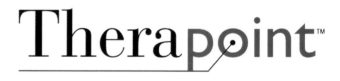

14.

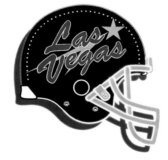

15.

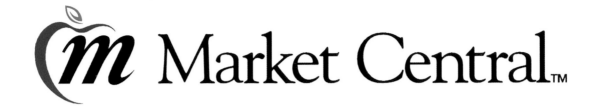

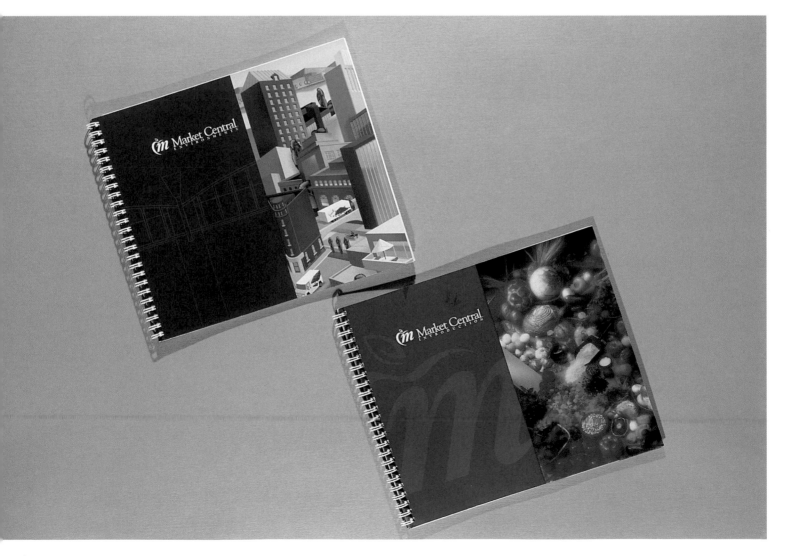

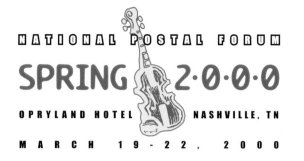

1.

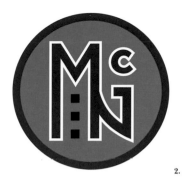

2.

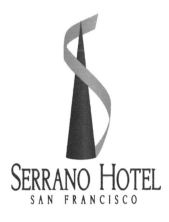

SERRANO HOTEL
SAN FRANCISCO

3.

Costanoa

4.

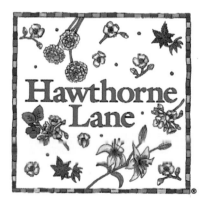

5.

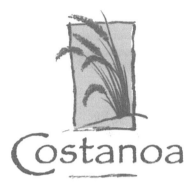

6.

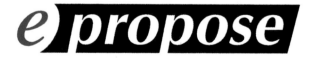

7.

(opposite)
Design Firm Bailey Design Group, Inc.

Client   Compass Group of America

3 -4
Design Firm McGaughy Design
5 -9
Design Firm Hunt Weber Clark
             Associates, Inc.

1. Client   National Postal Forum
    Designer   Malcolm McGaughy

2. Client   McGaughy Design
    Designer   Malcolm McGaughy

3. Client   Kimpton Hotel
                 & Restaurant Group
    Designers   Jim Deeken
                 & Nancy Hunt-Weber

4. Client   Joie deVivre Hospitality
    Designers   Nancy Hunt-Weber
                 & Christine Chung

5. Client   Hawthorne Lane
    Designers   Nancy Hunt-Weber & Jason Bell

6. Client   Denny Eye + Laser Center
    Designers   Christine Chung
                 & Nancy Hunt-Weber

7. Client   epropose
    Designers   Jason Bell & Nancy Hunt-Weber

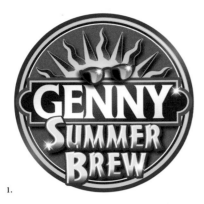

1.

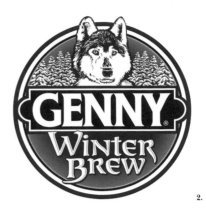

2.

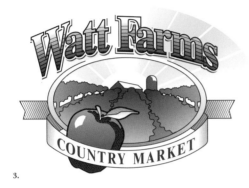

3.

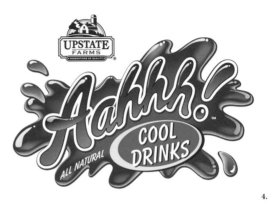

4.

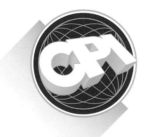

BUSINESS GROUPS

5.

TWO THOUSAND

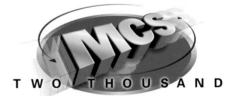

6.

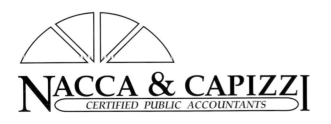

CERTIFIED PUBLIC ACCOUNTANTS

7.

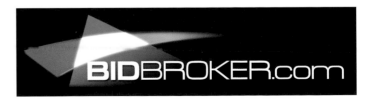

8.

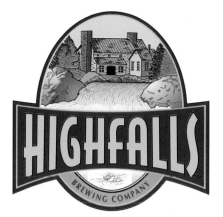

9.

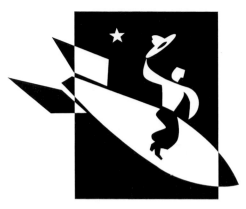

10.

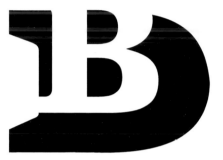

11.

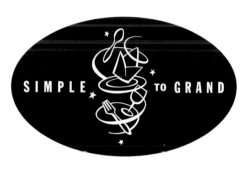

12.

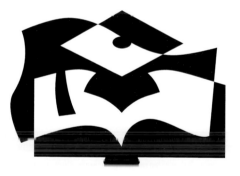

13.

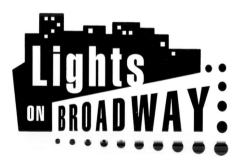

14.

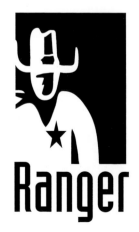

15.

1 - 9
Design Firm McElvency & Palozzi
             Design Group, Inc.

10 - 15
Design Firm Design Center

1. Client   Genessee Brewing Company
    Designers   Steve Palozzi & Lisa Parenti

2. Client   Genessee Brewing Compant
    Designers   Steve Palozzi & Matt Garrity

3. Client   Watt Farms Country Market
    Designers   Jon Westfall
                & William McElveney

4. Client   Upstate Farms Inc.
    Designers   Bill McElveney, Steve Palozzi
                & Ellen Johnson

5. Client   CPI Business Groups
    Designers   William McElveney
                & Jon Westfall

6. Client   Auto-Soft
    Designers   Jon Westfall & Steve Palozzi

7. Client   Nacca & Capizzi
    Designer   William McElveney

8. Client   LPA Software
    Designers   Matt Nowicki, Paul Reisinger, Jr.,
                & Steve Palozzi

9. Client   Genessee Brewing Company
    Designers   Steve Palozzi & Matt Nowicki

10. Client   Scimed
    Designers   John Reger & Cory Docken

11. Client   Determan Brownie
    Designers   John Reger & Jon Erickson

12. Client   Simple To Grand
    Designers   John Reger
                & Sherwin Schwartzrock

13. Client   Citizens Scholarship Fund
    Designers   John Reger
                & Sherwin Schwartzrock

14. Client   Lights on Broadway
    Designers   John Reger & Cory Docken

15. Client   Scimed
    Designers   John Reger & Cory Docken

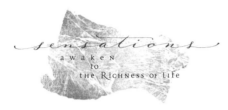

LifeSongs
GIVING VOICE TO THE SPIRIT WITHIN

1.

Fresh Air
2.

sensations
awaken
to
the Richness of life

scent
how often we associate the warmth
of a place or event with the memory
of a scent. scent is nostalgia's best
friend. the impression of smell lingers
in us longer and evokes reflection
more than any other sense.

3.

Gardens
and
MEMORIES

4.

Portfolio
BY HALLMARK

5.

Symbolic Notions

6.

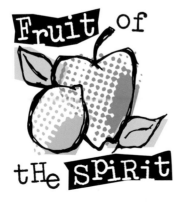

Fruit of
tHe SPIRIT

7.

1 - 7
Design Firm Hallmark Cards, Inc.

1. Client   Hallmark Cards
    Designer   Peg Carlson-Hoffman

2. Client   Hallmark Cards
    Designer   Peg Carlson-Hoffman

3. Client   Hallmark Cards
    Designer   Sean Branagan

4. Client   Hallmark Cards
    Designer   Barb Mizik

5. Client   Hallmark Cards
    Designer   John Marak

6. Client   Hallmark Cards
    Designer   Erica Becker

7. Client   Hallmark Cards
    Designer   Jake Mikolic

(opposite)
Design Firm Bailey Design Group, Inc.

    Client   Cultivations
    Designers   Tisha Armour, David Fiedler,
                 & Christian Williamson

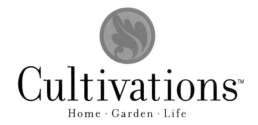

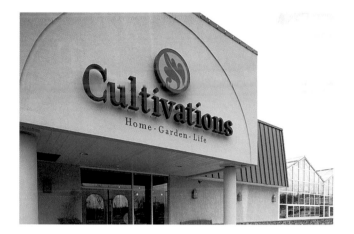

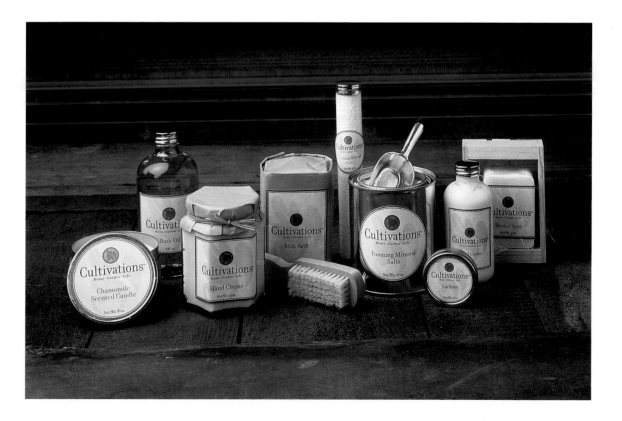

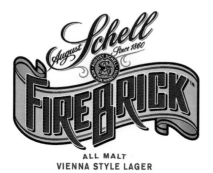

ALL MALT
VIENNA STYLE LAGER

1.

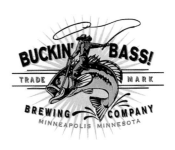

KÖLSCH STYLE
SUMMER MALT ALE

2.

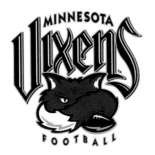

MINNESOTA

FOOTBALL

3.

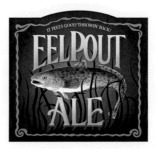

TRADE   MARK

BREWING   COMPANY
MINNEAPOLIS   MINNESOTA

4.

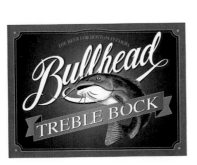

5.

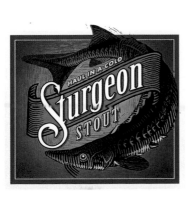

6.

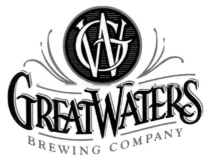

7.

GREATWATERS
BREWING COMPANY

8.

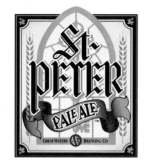

9.

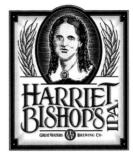

10.

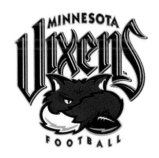

11.

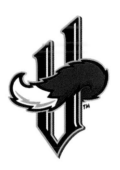

12.

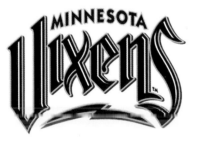

13.

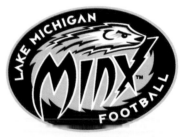

14.

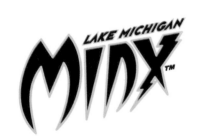

15.

(all)
Design Firm Compass Design

1 - 3
Client   August Schell Brewing Co.
Designers   Mitchell Lindgren, Tom Arthur,
              & Rich McGowen

4 - 7
Client   Buckin' Bass Brewing Co.
Designers   Mitchell Lindgren, Tom Arthur,
              & Rich McGowen

8 - 10
Client   Great Waters Brewing Co.
Designers   Mitchell Lindgren, Tom Arthur,
              & Rich McGowen

11 - 15
Client   World Wide Sports
Designers   Mitchell Lindgren, Tom Arthur,
              & Rich McGowen

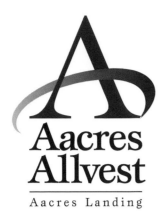

1.

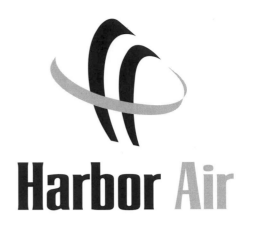

Harbor Air

2.

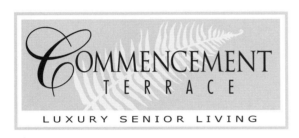

LUXURY SENIOR LIVING

3.

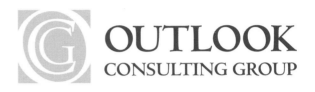

OUTLOOK
CONSULTING GROUP

4.

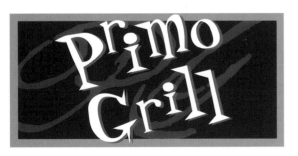

5.

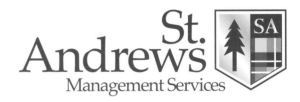

6.

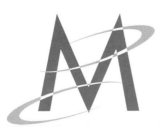

MILLENNIUM
RESTAURANT
CONSULTANTS

7.

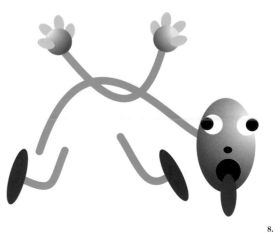

8.

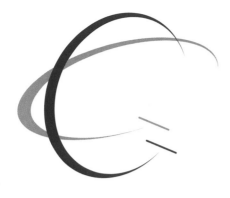

9.

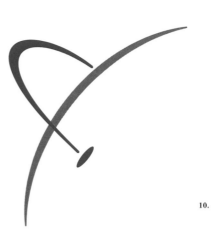

10.

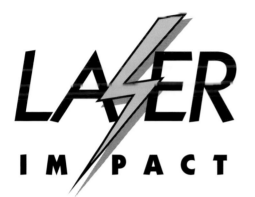

11.

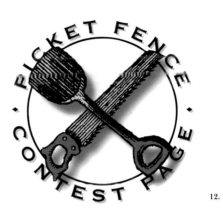

12.

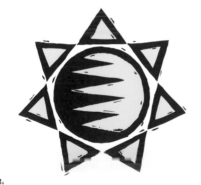

13.

14.

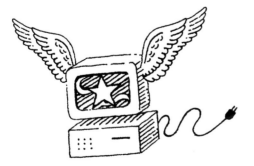

15.

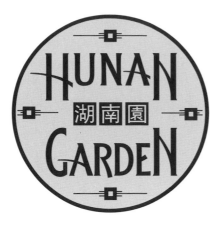

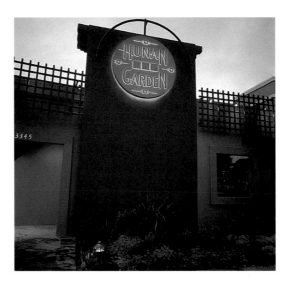

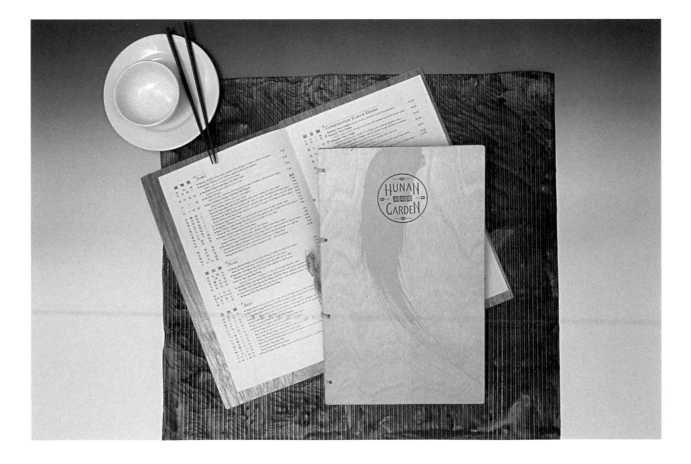

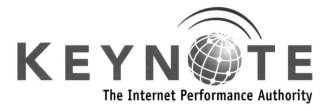

1.

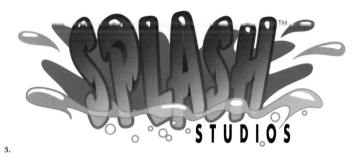

2.

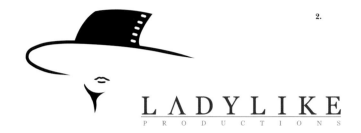

3.

4.

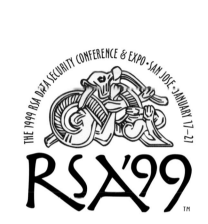

5.

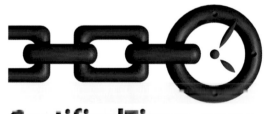

6.

7.

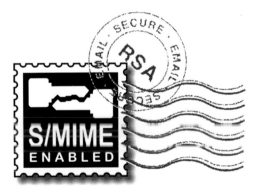

überbabe™ media, inc.

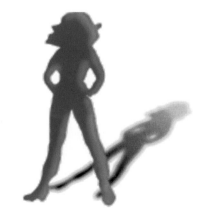

(opposite)
Design Firm   **Bruce Yelaska Design**

Client   Hunan Garden
Designer   Bruce Yelaska

1 - 7
Design Firm   **Coda Creative, Inc.**

1. Client   Keynote Systems
   Designers   Paola Coda &
                 Kurt Stammberger

2. Client   Ladylike Productions
   Designers   Pavida Hoparsatsuk &
                 Kurt Stammberger

3. Client   Splash Studios
   Designers   Mark Deamer & Paola Coda

4. Client   RSA Data
                 Security Conference 1999
   Designers   Paola Coda &
                 Kurt Stammberger

5. Client   Certified Time
   Designers   Paola Coda &
                 Kurt Stammberger

6. Client   RSA Data Security
   Designers   Paola Coda &
                 Kurt Stammberger

7. Client   überbabe media, inc.
   Designers   Lisa Voldeng & Ashley Phelps

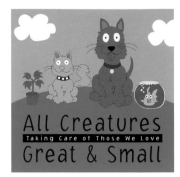

1.

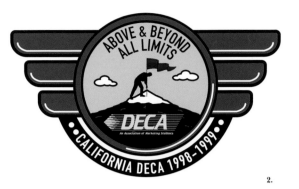

2.

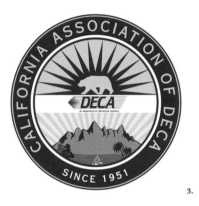

3.

4.

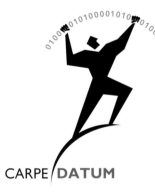

CARPE DATUM

5.

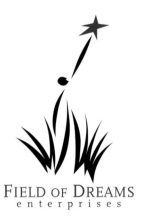

FIELD OF DREAMS
enterprises

6.

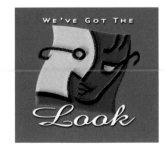

7.

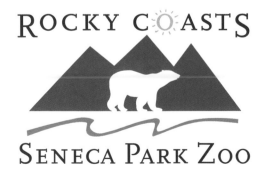

8.

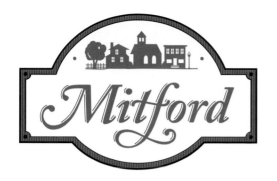

9.

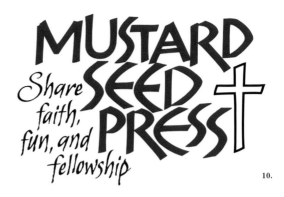

10.

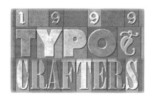

11.

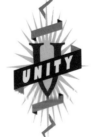

12.

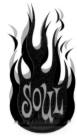

13.

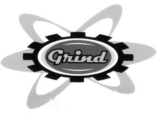

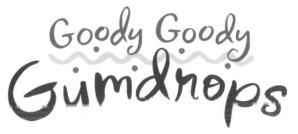

14.

15.

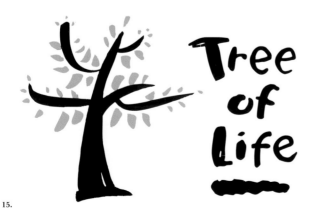

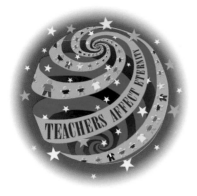

1.

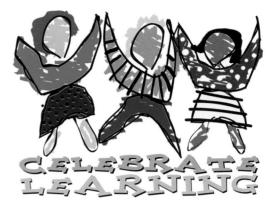

2.

DREAM WIZARDS

3.

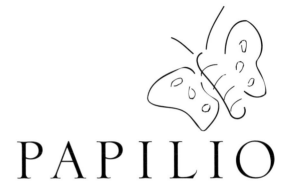

PAPILIO

4.

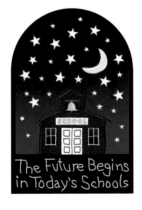

5.

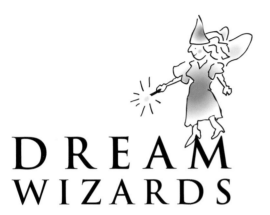

SANS SOUCI PRESS

6.

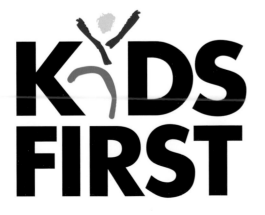

7.

1 - 7

Design Firm Designsmith

1. Client   Teachers Affect Eternity/
                The Education People
    Designer   Richard Smith

2. Client   Celebrate Learning/
                The Education People
    Designer   Richard Smith

3. Client   Dream Wizards
    Designer   Richard Smith

4. Client   Papilio
    Designer   Richard Smith

5. Client   The Future Begins/
                The Education People
    Designer   Richard Smith

6. Client   Sans Souci Press
    Designer   Richard Smith

7. Client   Kids First/
                The Education People
    Designer   Richard Smith

(opposite)
Design Firm Bailey Design Group, Inc.

    Client   Compass Group of America
    Designer   Steve Perry

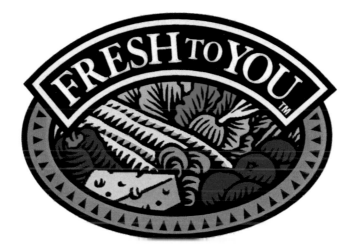

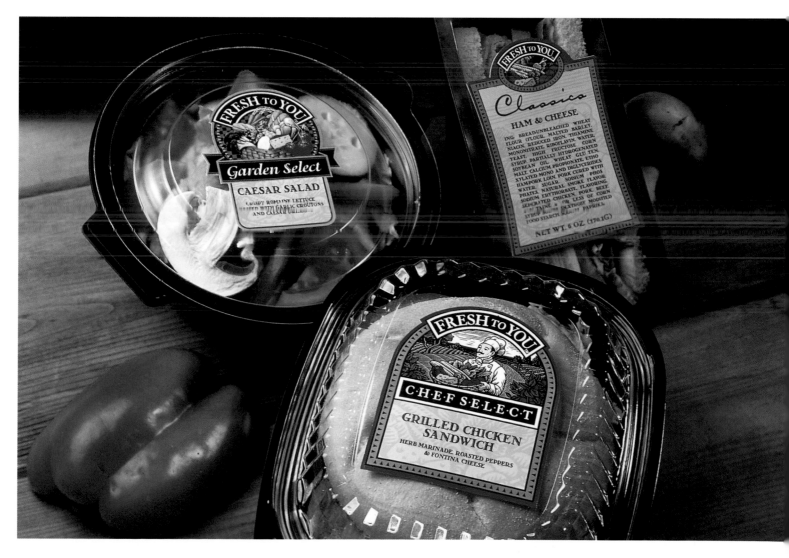

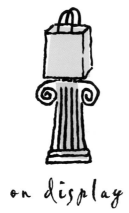

on display

1.

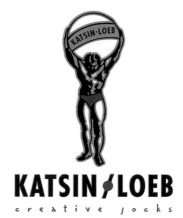

KATSIN/LOEB
creative jocks

2.

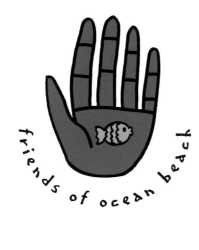

big Score big Score big Score

3.

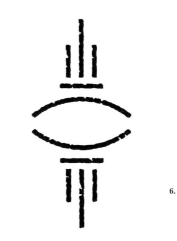

BOOST WORKS

4.

friends of ocean beach

5.

6.

TELL·GET
LOYALTY LOOP
KEEP·BUILD

7.

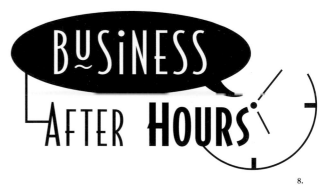

8.

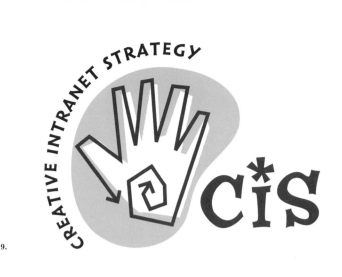

CREATIVE INTRANET STRATEGY

cis

9.

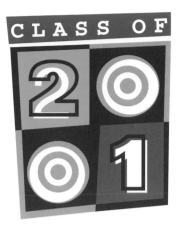

CLASS OF 20 01

10.

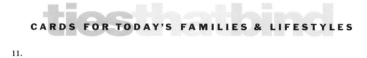

CARDS FOR TODAY'S FAMILIES & LIFESTYLES

11.

SPECIaLTY DESIGN StUDIO

12.

13.

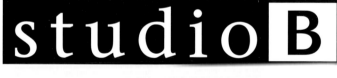

studio B

14.

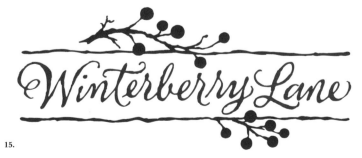

15.

1 - 2
Design Firm Rubber Design
3 - 5
Design Firm Duncan/Channon
6 - 7
Design Firm Griffith Phillips Creative
8
Design Firm double entendre
9 - 15
Design Firm Hallmark Cards, Inc.

1. Client   Stoneridge Shopping Center
    Designer   Jacquie VanKeuren

2. Client   Katsin-Loeb Advertising
    Designer   Jacquie VanKeuren

3. Client   Big Score
    Designer   Jacquie VanKeuren

4. Client   Boostworks
    Designer   Jacquie VanKeuren

5. Client   California Coastal Commission
    Designer   Jacquie VanKeuren

6. Client   Craig Varjabedian Photography
    Designer   Alan Benest

7. Client   GPCInteractive -
                Loyalty Loop Program
    Designer   Brian Niemann

8. Client   Greater Seattle
                Chamber of Commerce
    Designers   Daniel P. Smith
                & Richard A. Smith

9. Client   Hallmark Cards
    Designer   Jake Mikolic

10. Client   Specialty Design
    Designer   Jake Mikolic

11. Client   Hallmark Cards
    Designer   Sean Branagan

12. Client   Specialty Design
    Designer   Barb Mizik

13. Client   Specialty Design
    Designer   Jake Mikolic

14. Client   Specialty Design
    Designer   Jake Mikolic

15. Client   Specialty Design
    Designer   Lee Stork

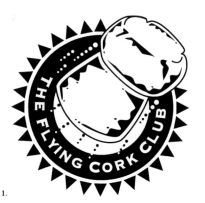

1.

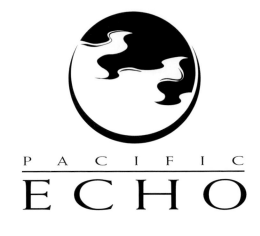

2.

Committed to Excellence

3.

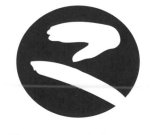

·ROR·

4.

BURKE WILLIAMS

5.

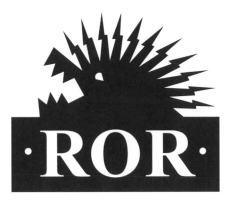

ZINERA

6.

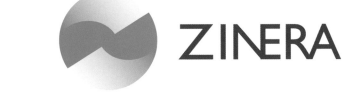

ZIG ZIGLAR NETWORK

7.

THE
METROPOLITAN
OPERA

8.

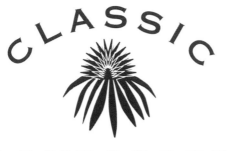

CLASSIC

LANDSCAPE

9.

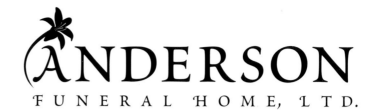

ANDERSON

FUNERAL HOME, LTD.

10.

SASAir, Inc.

11.

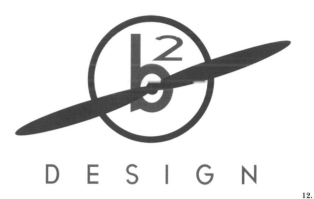

DESIGN

12.

school of

THEATRE & DANCE

13.

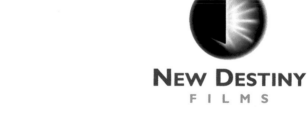

NEW DESTINY

FILMS

14.

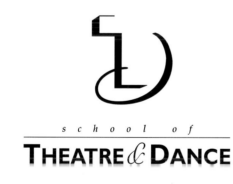

15.

1 - 3					
Design Firm	**Designsmith**		7. Client	Zig Ziglar Network	
4 - 7			Designers	Mamory Shimokochi	
Design Firm	**Shimokochi/Reeves**			& Anne Reeves	
8					
Design Firm	**World Studio**		8. Client	The Metropolitan Opera	
9 - 13			Designers	David Sterling, Mark Randall,	
Design Firm	**B² Design**			Jeroen Jas, Stefan Hengst, Klaus	
14 - 15				Kempenaars & Michael Samuels	
Design Firm	**Dotzler Creative Arts**				
			9. Client	Classic Landscape	
1. Client	The Flying Cork Club/		Designer	Carol M. Benthal-Bingley	
	Pacific Echo Cellars				
Designer	Richard Smith		10. Client	Anderson Funeral Home	
			Designers	Julie Wojak & Carol	
2. Client	Pacific Echo			Benthal-Bingley	
Designer	Richard Smith				
			11. Client	SASAir, Inc.	
3. Client	Committed to Excellence/		Designer	Carol M. Benthal-Bingley	
	The Education People				
Designer	Richard Smith		12. Client	B² Design	
			Designer	Carol Benthal-Bingley	
4. Client	ROR				
Designers	Mamoru Shimokochi, Anne		13. Client	Northern Illinois University	
	Reeves, & Eugene Bustillos			School of Theatre and Dance	
			Designer	Carol Benthal-Bingley	
5. Client	Burke Williams				
Designers	Mamoru Shimokochi		14. Client	New Destiny Films	
	& Anne Reeves				
			15. Client	Trinity Church	
6. Client	Zig Ziglar Network				
Designers	Mamoru Shimokochi				
	& Anne Reeves				

e.

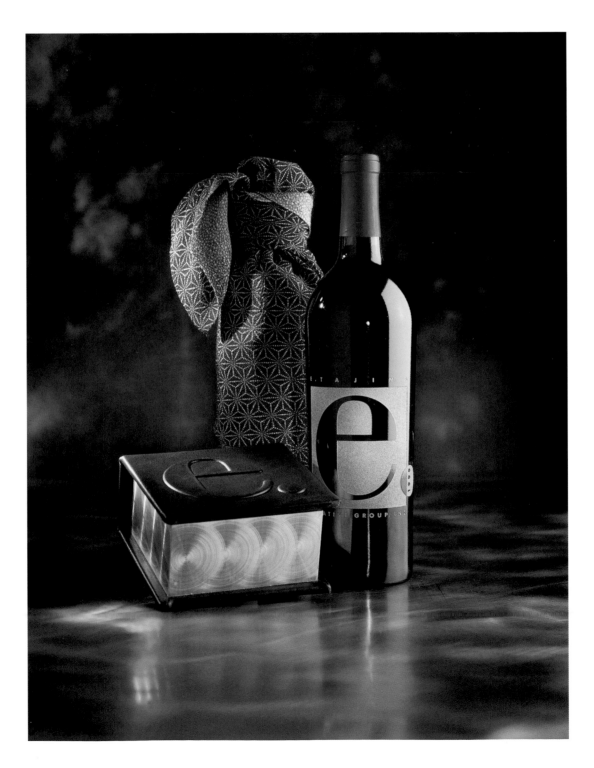

1.

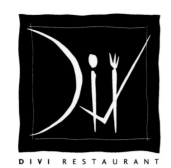

DIVI RESTAURANT

2.

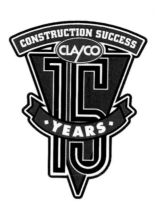

3.

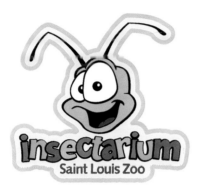

insectarium
Saint Louis Zoo

4.

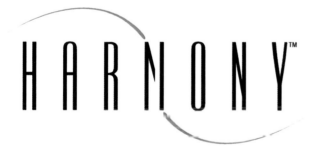

314 434 7237

5.

HARMONY™

6.

  LABARGE CLAYCO WIRELESS, LLC

7.

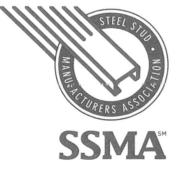

STEEL STUD MANUFACTURERS ASSOCIATION

SSMA℠

(opposite)
  Design Firm   E. Tajima Creative Group, Inc.

  Client   E. Tajima Creative Group, Inc.
  Designers   Roz Roos Designs for the
                  E. Tajima Creative Group, Inc.

1 - 8
  Design Firm   CUBE Advertising & Design
9
  Design Firm   J G M Design

1.   Client   Divi Restaurant
     Designer   David Chiow

2.   Client   Clayco Construction Company
     Designers   David Chiow & Kevin Hough

3.   Client   Saint Louis Zoo
     Designer   David Chiow

4.   Client   Retail Results
     Designer   David Chiow

5.   Client   Crown Therapeutics, Inc.
     Designer   David Chiow

6.   Client   LaBarge Clayco Wireless, LLC
     Designers   Steve Wienke & David Chiow

7.   Client   Steel Stud Manufacturers
                  Association
     Designer   Joan Gilbert Madsen

1.

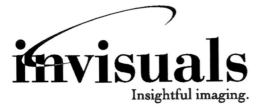

2.

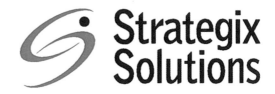

3.

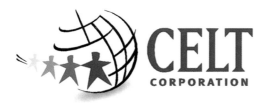

4.

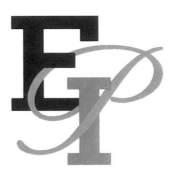

5.

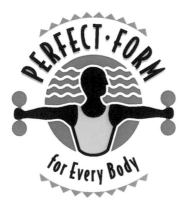

6.

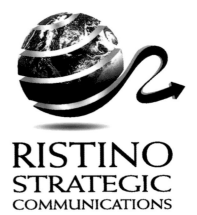

7.

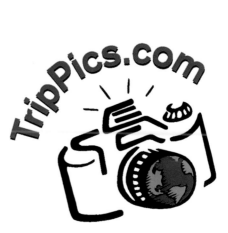

8.

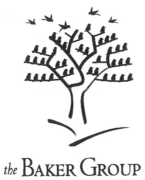

9.

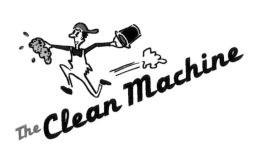

10.

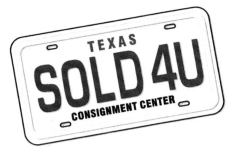

11.

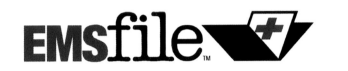

12.

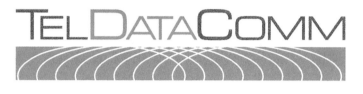

14.

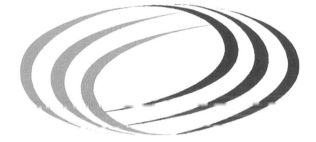

13.

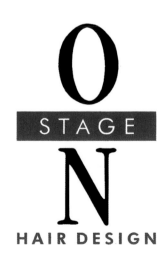

15.

1 - 9		
Design Firm	**Hess Design Inc.**	

10 - 15		
Design Firm	**Michael Lee Advertising**	
	& Design, Inc.	

1.	Client	Invisuals
	Designer	Karyn Goba

2.	Client	Strategix Solutions
	Designer	Karyn Goba

3.	Client	CELT Corp.
	Designer	Kim Daly

4.	Client	Equity Industrial Partners
	Designer	Kim Daly

5.	Client	Perfect Form
	Designer	Kim Daly

6.	Client	Ristino Strategic
		Communications
	Designer	Jim Harrington

7.	Client	the Baker Group
	Designers	Kim Daly & Karyn Goba

8.	Client	Trippics.Com
	Designers	Kim Daly & Melissa Meinhold

9.	Client	The Clean Machine
	Designers	Hannah Gilmore
		& Heather Knopf

10.	Client	SOLD4U
	Designer	Michael Lee

11.	Client	EMSfile
	Designer	Michael Lee

12.	Client	TelDataComm
	Designer	Michael Lee

13.	Client	Wester Landscape Management
	Designer	Michael Lee

14.	Client	Efficient Systems
	Designer	Michael Lee

15.	Client	On Stage Hair Design
	Designer	Michael Lee

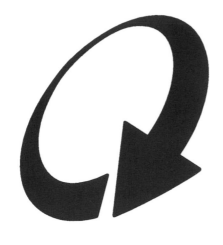

1.

EL'E MEN TAL'

2.

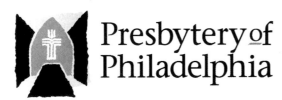

3.

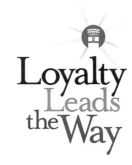

Loyalty
Leads
the Way

4.

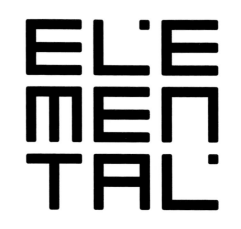
Presbytery of Philadelphia

5.

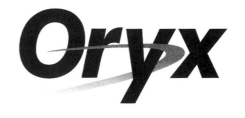
Oryx

6.

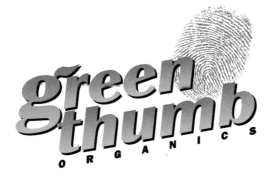
green thumb ORGANICS

7.

1 - 3
Design Firm EAI
4 - 6
Design Firm Art 270, Inc.
7
Design Firm Schlatter Design

1. Client   The Coca-Cola Company
    Designer   Todd Simmons

2. Client   Elemental Interactive Design
                 & Development
    Designer   Matt Rollins

3. Client   Human Arts Gallery
    Designer   Matt Rollins

4. Client   Beaver College
    Designer   John Opet

5. Client   Presbytery of Philadelphia
    Designers   Carl Mill, Sean Flanagan,
                 & Holly Kempf

6. Client   LHS Priority Call
    Designer   Holly Kempf

7. Client   Green Thumb Organics, Inc.
    Designer   Richard Schlatter

(opposite)
    Design Firm Bailey Design Group, Inc.

    Client   Marriott Corporation
    Designer   David Fiedler

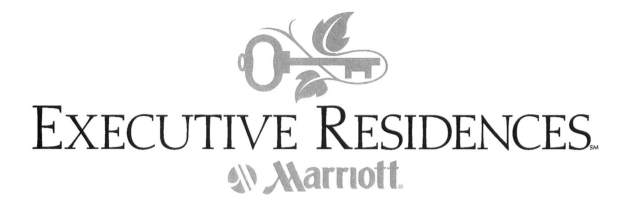

EXECUTIVE RESIDENCES℠

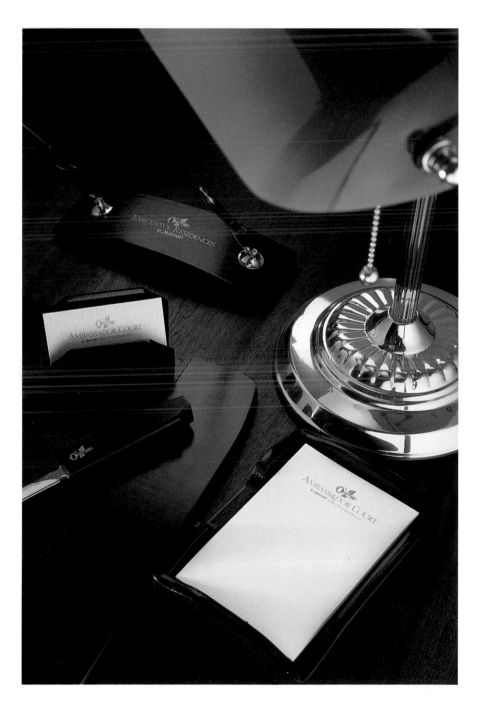

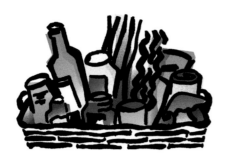

1.

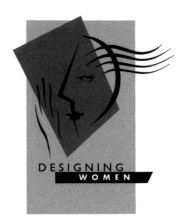

2.

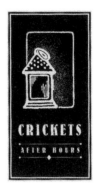

RESOURCE

3.

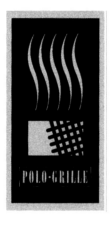

CATHOLIC
SOCIAL
SERVICES
OF SOUTHWESTERN OHIO

4.

5.

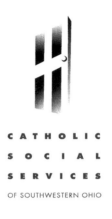

6.

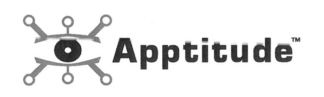

7.

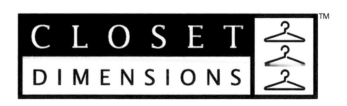

8.

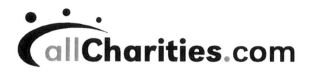

9.

10.

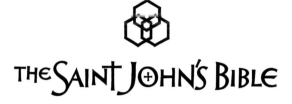

11.

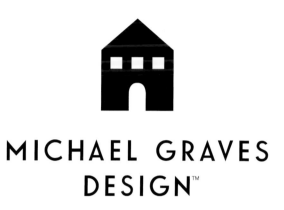

12.

THEATER ZERO

13.

ORGANIC COTTON

14.

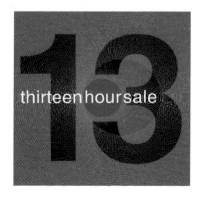

15.

1.

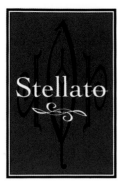

Stellato

2.

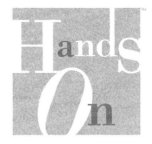

A Spa for Hands and Feet

3.

cybergourmet.

4.

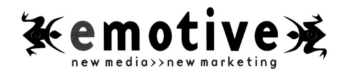

emotive

new media >> new marketing

5.

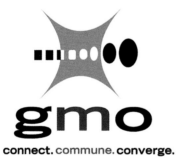

gmo

connect. commune. converge.

6.

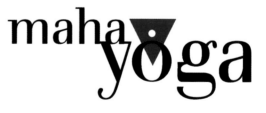

maha yoga

7.

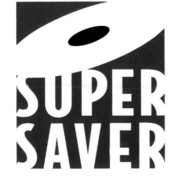

SUPER SAVER

8.

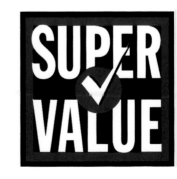

SUPER VALUE

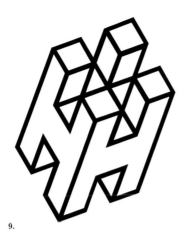

9.

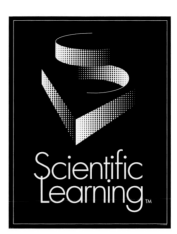

Scientific Learning™

10.

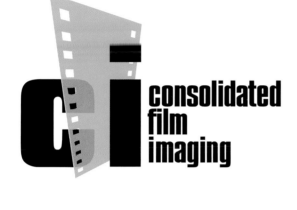

consolidated film imaging

11.

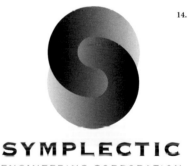

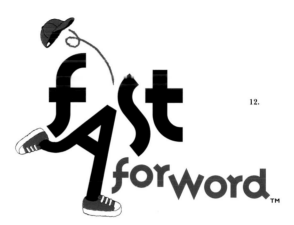

fast forword™

12.

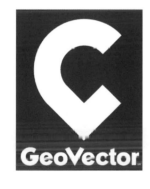

GeoVector™

13.

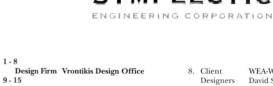

SYMPLECTIC
ENGINEERING CORPORATION

14.

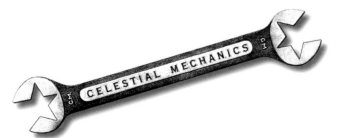

15.

1 - 8
Design Firm Vrontikis Design Office
9 - 15
Design Firm Linden Design/LogoGuy

1. Client   Global-Dining, Inc.
   Designers   Tammy Kim & Petrula Vrontikis

2. Client   Hands On Day Spas
   Designers   Peggy Woo & Petrula Vrontikis

3. Client   William Jackson/Cybergourmet
   Designer   Petrula Vrontikis

4. Client   Global Music One
   Designers   Marilyn Prado
               & Petrula Vrontikis

5. Client   Global Music One
   Designers   Laura Leiman
               & Petrula Vrontikis

6. Client   Steve Ross/Maha Yoga
   Designer   Petrula Vrontikis

7. Client   Warner/Elektra/Atlantic-WEA
   Designers   Peggy Woo & Petrula Vrontikis

8. Client   WEA-Warner/Elektra/Atlantic
   Designers   David Schweiger
               & Petrula Vrontikis

9. Client   Harold Hedelman
   Designer   Stephen Linden

10. Client   Scientific Learning
    Designer   Stephen Linden

11. Client   CFI
    Designer   Stephen Linden

12. Client   Scientific Learning
    Designer   Stephen Linden

13. Client   GeoVector
    Designer   Stephen Linden

14. Client   Symplectic Engineering
    Designer   Stephen Linden

15. Client   Celestial Mechanics
    Designer   Stephen Linden

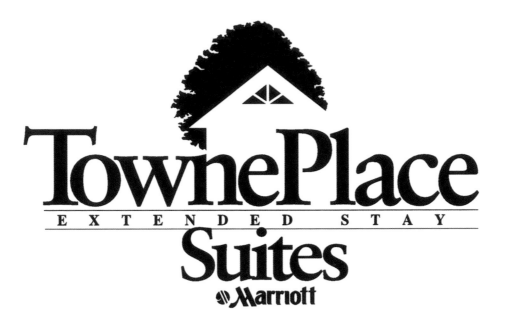

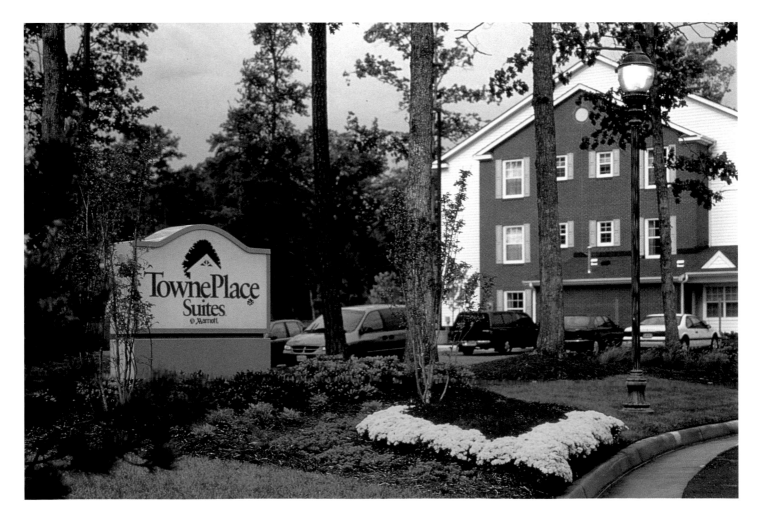

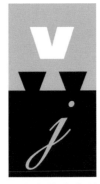

1.

VILLAGE

V

j

JOINERY

2.

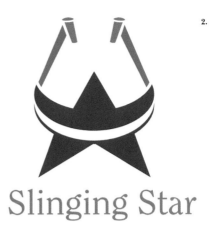

Slinging Star

3.

icf

4.

SUS

5.

BEALS MARTIN

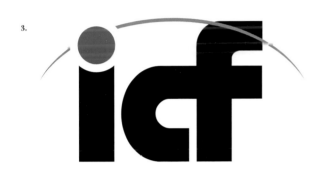

6.

CiscoRemote™

The Remote Access Software Solution!

7.

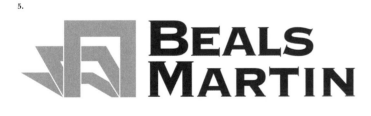

kindercotton.com

(opposite)
Design Firm Bailey Design Group, Inc.

Client   Marriott Corporation
Designer   Gary LaCroix

1 - 7
Design Firm Stratford Design Associates

1. Client   Village Joinery
    Designer   Silvia Stephenson

2. Client   Slinging Star
    Designer   Tim Gerould

3. Client   ICF
    Designer   Silvia Stephenson

4. Client   SUS
    Designer   Tim Gerould

5. Client   Beals Martin
    Designers Gerald Stratford, Sr.
                   & Tim Gerould

6. Client   Cisco
    Designers Gerald Stratford, Sr.
                   & Rebecca Lambing

7. Client   Kindercotton
    Designer   Silvia Stephenson

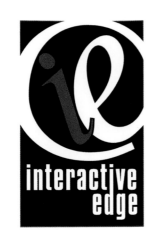

1.

interactive edge

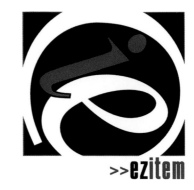

2.

>>ezitem

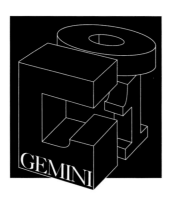

GEMINI

3.

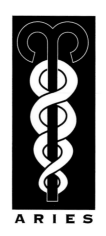

4.

ARIES

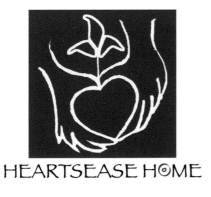

HEARTSEASE HOME

5.

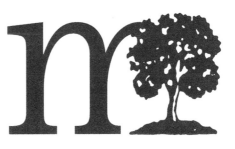

6.

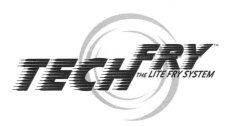

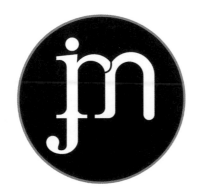

7.

8.

TECH FRY
THE LITE FRY SYSTEM

9.

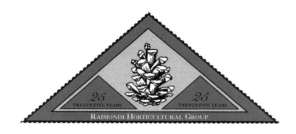

10.

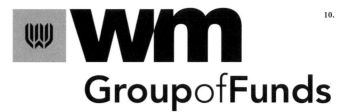

11.

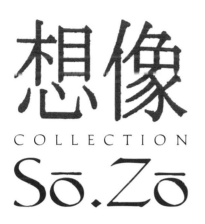

12.

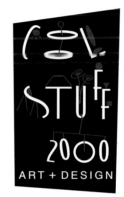

13.

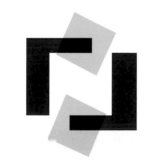

nSite Software, Inc.

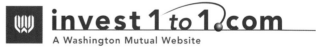

14.

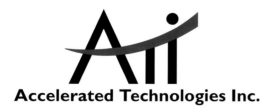

15.

1 - 5, 7 - 9
Design Firm John R. Mongelli & Assoc. Inc.
6
Design Firm Nightlight Design
10 - 14
Design Firm E. Tajima Creative Group, Inc.
15
Design Firm Guy Design

1, 2
Client   Interactive Edge
Designers   John Mongelli & Dara Mongelli

3, 4
Client   Paramount Capital
              Financial Investment
Designer   Dara Mongelli

5. Client   Heartsease Home, Inc.
   Designer   Dara Mongelli

6. Client   Morgan Management
   Designers Lisa Haim & Dara Mongelli

7. Client   John R. Mongelli & Assoc., Inc.
   Designer   Dara Mongelli

8. Client   Techfoods USA
   Designer   Dara Mongelli

9. Client   Raimondi Horticultural Group
   Designer   Dara Mongelli

10. Client   Washington Mutual
              Group of Funds
    Designer Janice Wong

11. Client   SÒ-ZÒ - Collection SÒ-ZÒ
    Designer George Hoehn

12. Client   San Jose Museum of Art
    Designer Daniel Tiburcio

13. Client   nSite Software Inc.—Paul Tabet
    Designer Janice Wong

14. Client   Washington Mutual Bank
    Designer Rich Nelson

15. Client   ATI
    Designer Debbie Guy

1.

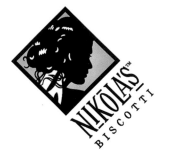

2.

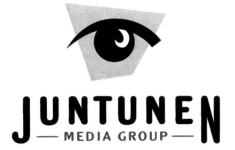

3.

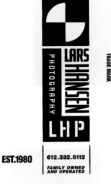

4.

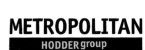

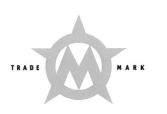

5.

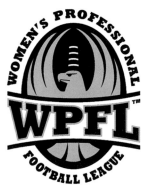

6.

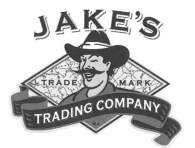

7.

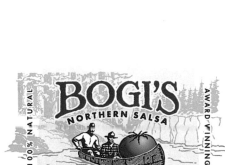

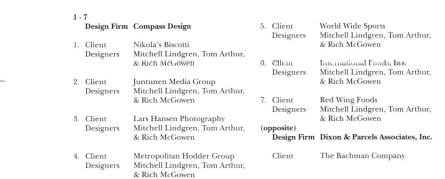

1 - 7

Design Firm Compass Design

1. Client   Nikola's Biscotti
    Designers   Mitchell Lindgren, Tom Arthur,
                  & Rich McGowen

2. Client   Juntunen Media Group
    Designers   Mitchell Lindgren, Tom Arthur,
                  & Rich McGowen

3. Client   Lars Hansen Photography
    Designers   Mitchell Lindgren, Tom Arthur,
                  & Rich McGowen

4. Client   Metropolitan Hodder Group
    Designers   Mitchell Lindgren, Tom Arthur,
                  & Rich McGowen

5. Client   World Wide Sports
    Designers   Mitchell Lindgren, Tom Arthur,
                  & Rich McGowen

6. Client   International Foods, Inc.
    Designers   Mitchell Lindgren, Tom Arthur,
                  & Rich McGowen

7. Client   Red Wing Foods
    Designers   Mitchell Lindgren, Tom Arthur,
                  & Rich McGowen

(opposite)
Design Firm Dixon & Parcels Associates, Inc.

    Client   The Bachman Company

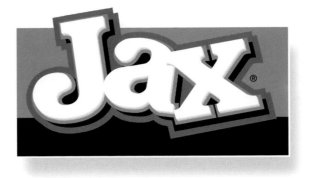

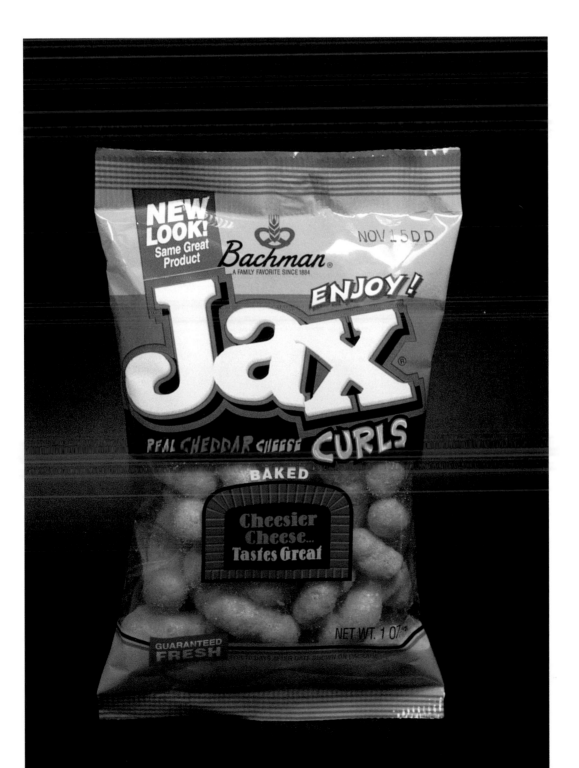

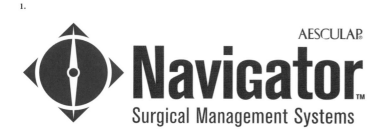

1.

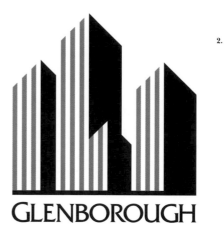

2.

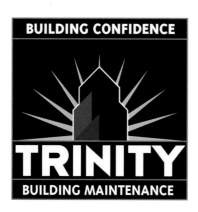

3.

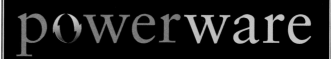

4.

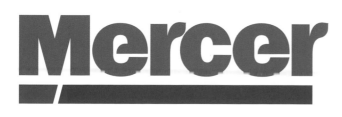

5.

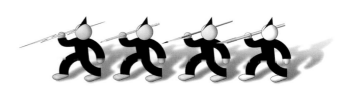

6.

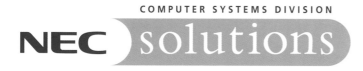

7.

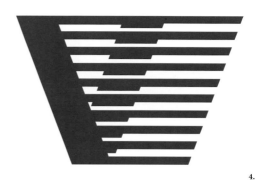

8.

Crawford & Associates
I N T E R N A T I O N A L

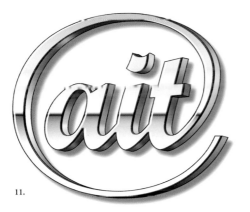

The Power of Creative Learning℠

9.

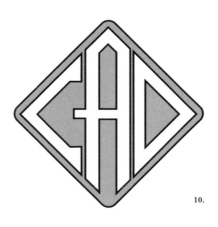

10.

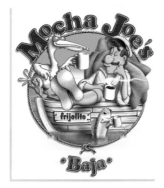

11.

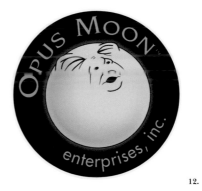

12.

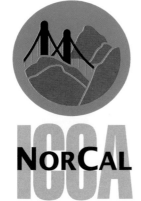

13.

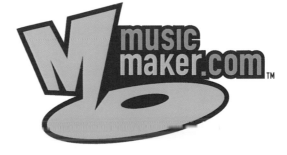

14.

15.

1 - 7		
Design Firm	**Stratford Design Associates**	
8 - 13		
Design Firm	**Electric Illustration + Design**	
14		
Design Firm	**Doublespace**	
15		
Design Firm	**Square Peg Graphics**	

1.	Client	Aesculap
	Designer	Tim Gerould
2.	Client	Glenborough
	Designer	Tim Gerould
3.	Client	Trinity Building Maintenance
	Designer	John F. Morgan
4.	Client	Valley Communications
	Designer	Tim Gerould
5.	Client	NEC
	Designer	Tim Gerould
6.	Client	Powerware Solutions
	Designer	Tim Gerould

7.	Client	Mercer
	Designer	Tim Gerould
8.	Client	Electric Illustration & Design
	Designer	Jeff Flower
9.	Client	Crawford & Associates, Int'l
	Designers	Jeff Flower & Karen Allison
10.	Client	Cindy Diamond Attorney @ Law
	Designer	Jeff Flower
11.	Client	Advanced Integrated Training
	Designer	Jeff Flower
12.	Client	Opus Moon Enterprises
	Designers	Jeff Flower & Jim Brown
13.	Client	Mocha Joe's
	Designer	Jeff Flower
15.	Client	Independent Computer Consultants Assoc. Northern California Chapter
	Designer	Jack Jackson

1.

2.

health quarters

your source for sexuality education and medical care

3.

C R E S C E N T
networks

4.

XyEnterprise™

5.

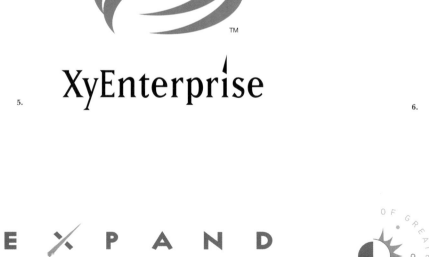

kallix

6.

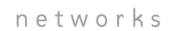

E X P A N D
networks

7.

LEAGUESCHOOL

8.

9.

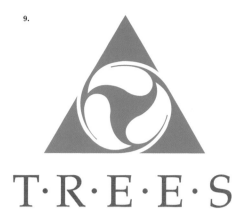

T·R·E·E·S

10.

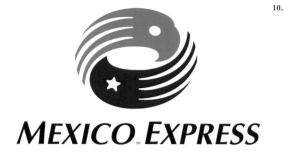

MEXICO EXPRESS

12.

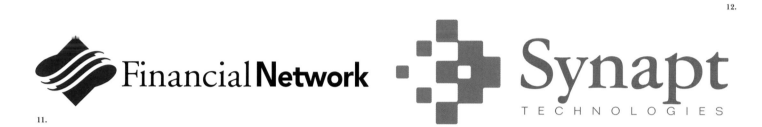

Financial **Network**

Synapt
TECHNOLOGIES

11.

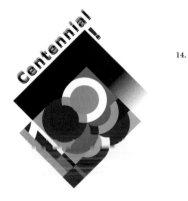

CEATECH USA

13.

14.

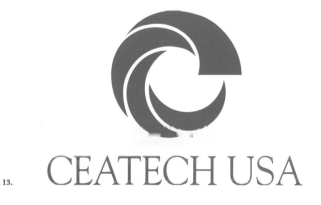

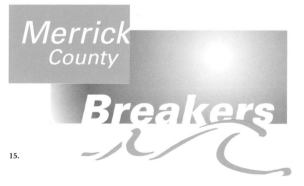

Merrick
County

Breakers

15.

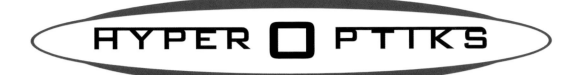

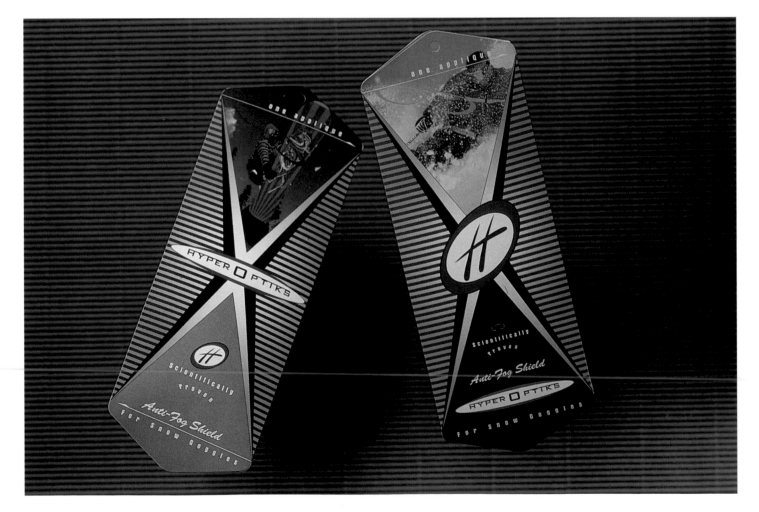

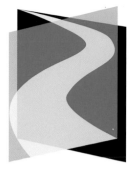

GRAEBE, DANNA & ASSOCIATES

THE RIGHT PATH FOR YOUR FINANCIAL FUTURE

1.

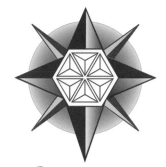

CENTER FOR LEADERSHIP DEVELOPMENT

2.

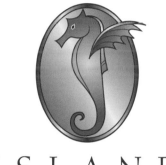

ISLAND
COMMUNICATIONS

3.

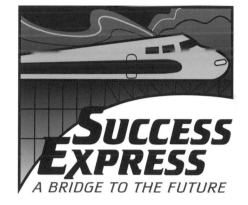

SUCCESS EXPRESS
A BRIDGE TO THE FUTURE

4.

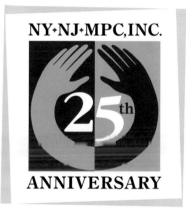

NY·NJ·MPC,INC.

25th

ANNIVERSARY

5.

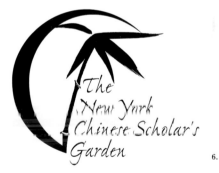

The New York Chinese Scholar's Garden

6.

singlish™

7.

(opposite)
Design Firm Onyx Design Inc.

Client   Modern World Ventures Inc.
Designer   Paul Morales

1 - 6
Design Firm Island Communications

7
Design Firm Philbrook & Associates

1. Client   Graebe, Danna & Associates
   Designer Linda E. Danaher

2. Client   Center for Leadership
             Development at Bristol-Myers
             Squibb Company
   Designer Linda E. Danaher

3. Client   Island Communications
   Designer Linda E. Danaher

4. Client   Success Express at Bristol-Myers
             Squibb Company
   Designer Linda E. Danaher

4. Client   NY, NJ Minority
             Purchasing Council, Inc.
   Designer Linda E. Danaher

6. Client   New York Chinese
             Scholar's Garden
   Designer Linda E. Danaher

7. Client   Singlish Enterprises, Inc.
   Designer Bill Philbrook

119

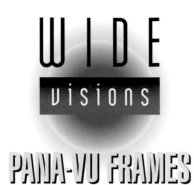

1.

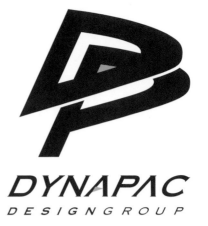

2.

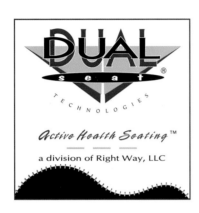

3.

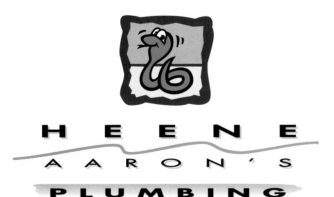

4.

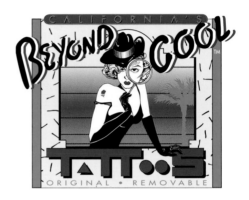

5.

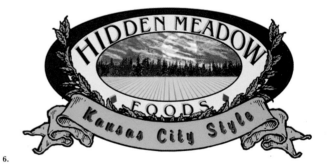

6.

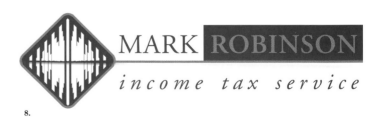

7.

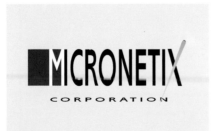

8.

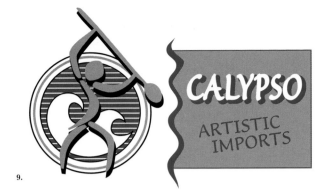

9.

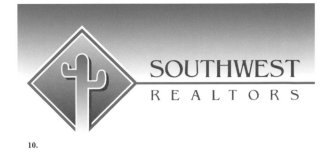

10.

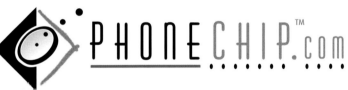

11.

ProServices, Inc.
Professional HVAC/R Service
♦
Commercial • Industrial
Air Conditioning • Heating • Refrigeration

12.

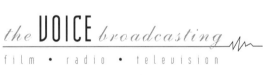

13.

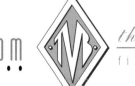

the VOICE broadcasting
film • radio • television

14.

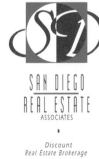

Discount
Real Estate Brokerage

15.

(all)
Design Firm DYNAPAC Design Group

1. Client   Advance Plastics
   Designers Lee A. Aellig & Elsa Valdez

2. Client   DYNAPAC Design Group
   Designers Lee A. Aellig, Marland Chow ,
        & Angus R. Colson

3. Client   Dual Seat Technologies
   Designer Lee A. Aellig

4. Client   Beyond Cool Tattoos
   Designer Lee A. Aellig

5. Client   Heene Aaron's Plumbing
   Designer Lee Aellig

6. Client   Hidden Meadow Foods
   Designer Lee A. Aellig

7. Client   Micronetix Corporation
   Designer Lee A. Aellig

8. Client   Mark Robinson
        Income Tax Service
   Designer Lee A. Aellig

9. Client   Calypso Artistic Imports
   Designers Lee A. Aellig &
        Robert Alexander

10. Client   Southwest Realtors
   Designer Lee A. Aellig

11. Client   Mt. Helix Pest &
        Termite Control
   Designer Lee A. Aellig

12. Client   ProServices, Inc.
   Designer Lee A. Aellig

13. Client   PhoneChip.com
   Designer Lee A. Aellig

14. Client   The Voice Broadcasting
   Designer Lee A. Aellig

15. Client   San Diego Real Estate Associates
   Designer Lee A. Aellig

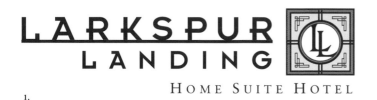

1.

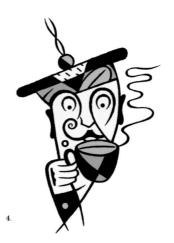

2.

Gilroy FOODS

3.

4.

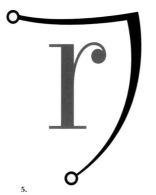

5.

visto.com™
life on the dot

6.

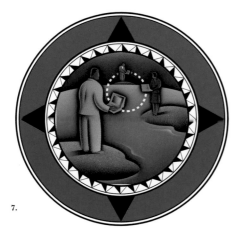

7.

1 - 6
Design Firm Onyx Design Inc.

7
~~Design Firm Primo Angeli Inc.~~

1. Client   Larkspur Hospitality Hotels
   Designers   Paul Morales & Dean Alvarez

2. Client   La Raza Centro legal
   Designer   Paul Morales

3. Client   Gilroy Foods/Con Agra
   Designers   Paul Morales & Dean Alvarez

4. Client   Caffe Marseille
   Designer   Paul Morales

5. Client   Riscorian Enterprise
   Designers   Dean Alvarez & Paul Morales

6. Client   Visto Corporation
   Designers   Dean Alvarez, Paul Morales,
               & Wendy McPhee

7. Client   Informix/Software
   Designers   Paul Morales & Jeff Keogel

(opposite)
Design Firm Dynapac Design Group

   Client   C & H International
   Designers   Lee A. Aellig & Paula Hong

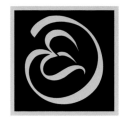

EUROPEAN
AVANTÁGE™

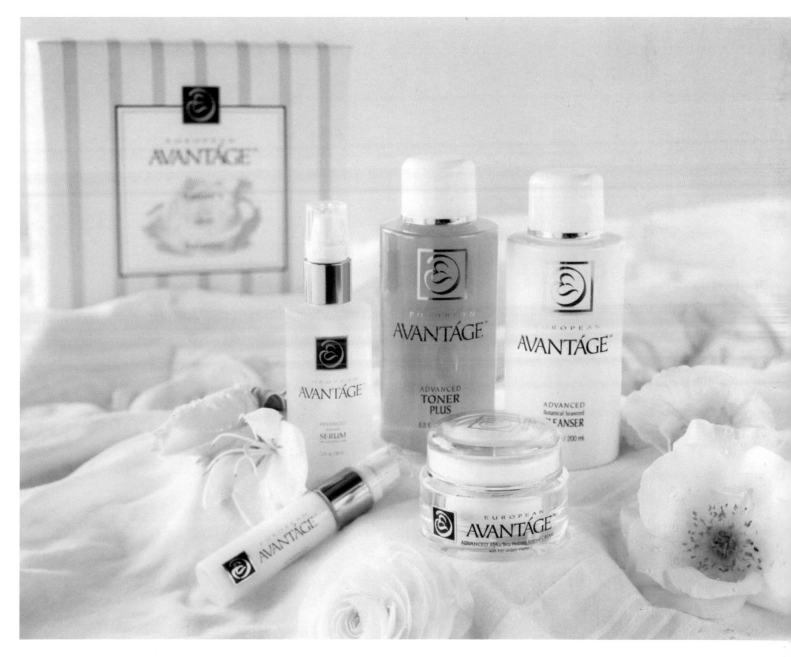

1.

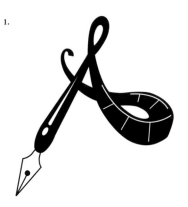

2.

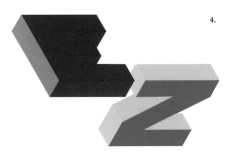

3.

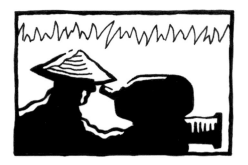

4.

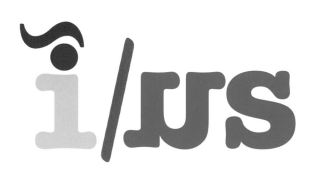

EZ • METRICS

5.

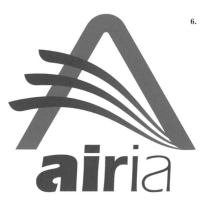

6.

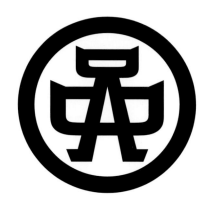

7.

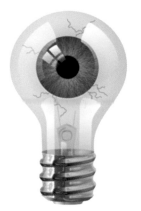

8.

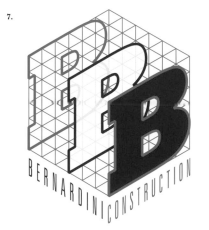

9.

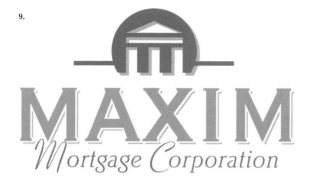

10.

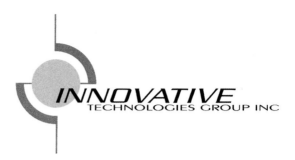

11.

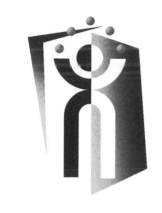

12.

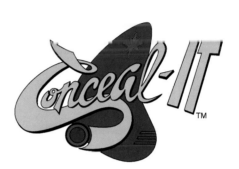

13.

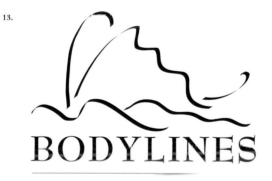

14.

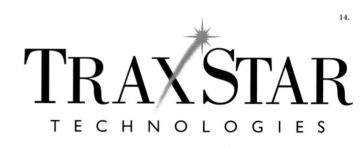

15.

1 - 3		
Design Firm	**Dean Alvarez Design**	
4 - 8		
Design Firm	**The Black Point Group**	
9		
Design Firm	**Shields Design**	
10 - 12		
Design Firm	**Balderman Creative Services**	
13 - 15		
Design Firm	**Creative Edge Design**	

1.	Client	Kimberly Aoki
	Designer	Dean Alvarez
2.	Client	Dean Alvarez Design
	Designer	Dean Alvarez
3.	Client	Plantation Pictures
	Designer	Dean Alvarez
4.	Client	EZ Metrics, Foster Coburn
	Designers	Gary W. Priester & Foster Coburn
5.	Client	i/us Corp., Arlen Bartch, Chris Dickman
	Designers	Gary W. Priester & Chris Dickman

6.	Client	Airia A Division of Flanders Filters
	Designers	Gary W. Priester & Mark Husa
7.	Client	Bernardini Construction
	Designers	Gary W. Priester & Steve Bernardini
8.	Client	The Black Point Group
	Designer	Gary W. Priester
9.	Client	Maxim Mortgage Corporation
	Designer	Charles Shields
10.	Client	Innovative Technologies
	Designer	Bobbi Balderman
11.	Client	Balderman Creative Services
	Designer	Bobbi Balderman
12.	Client	Conceal-it
	Designer	Bobbi Balderman
13.	Client	Bodylines
	Designer	Cynthia Bancale
14.	Client	TraxStar Technologies
	Designer	Chris Mohler
15.	Client	Healthtrac
	Designer	Cynthia Bancale

1.

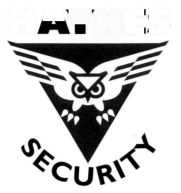

HAYNES
SECURITY

2.

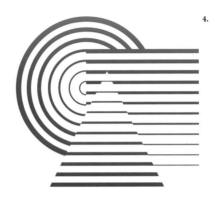
W

3.

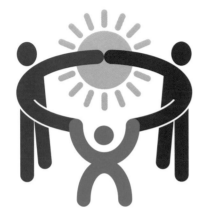

4.

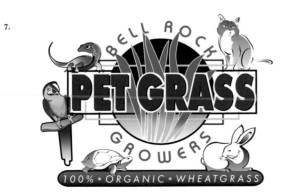

5.

HORIZON
NETWORK SOLUTIONS, INC.

6.

H1

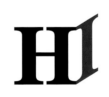

HamiltonInk

7.

BELL ROCK
PET GRASS
GROWERS
100% · ORGANIC · WHEATGRASS

8.

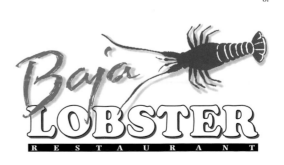

Baja
LOBSTER
RESTAURANT

9.

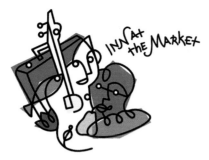

10.

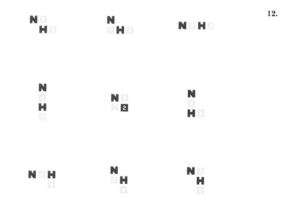

F I S H E R

TACOMA **POWER**
TACOMA PUBLIC UTILITIES

12.

TACOMA **WATER**
TACOMA PUBLIC UTILITIES

TACOMA **RAIL**
TACOMA PUBLIC UTILITIES

11.

plan B™
(LEVONORGESTREL)

13.

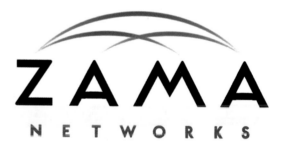

ZAMA
N E T W O R K S

14.

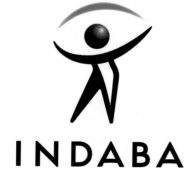

INDABA

15.

1 - 6
Design Firm De Martino Design
7 - 8
Design Firm DYNAPAC Design Group
9 - 15
Design Firm The Leonhardt Group

1. Client	Haynes Security	
Designer	Erick De Martino	
2. Client	Whitehall Capital Association	
Designer	Erick De Martino	
3. Client	Family Connections	
Designer	Erick De Martino	
4. Client	T.J. Willard & Assoc.	
Designer	Erick De Martino	
5. Client	Horizon Network Solutions	
Designer	Erick De Martino	
6. Client	Hamilton Ink	
Designer	Erick De Martino	
7. Client	Bell Rock Growers	
Designer	Lee A. Aellig	

8. Client	Baja Lobster Restaurant
Designer	Lee A. Aellig
9. Client	Inn at the Market
Designer	Janee Kreinheder
10. Client	Fisher Companies, Inc.
Designer	Steve Watson
11. Client	Tacoma Public Utilities
Designers	Ben Graham, John Cannell, & Greg Morgan
12. Client	N2H2
Designer	Thad Boss
13. Client	Elgin DDB
Designer	Jon King
14. Client	ZAMA
Designer	Janee Kreinheder
15. Client	INDABA
Designer	Janee Kreinheder

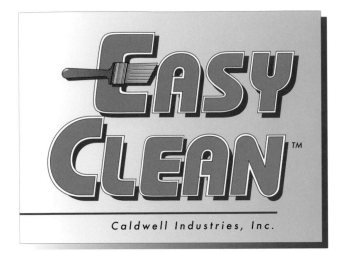

Caldwell Industries, Inc.

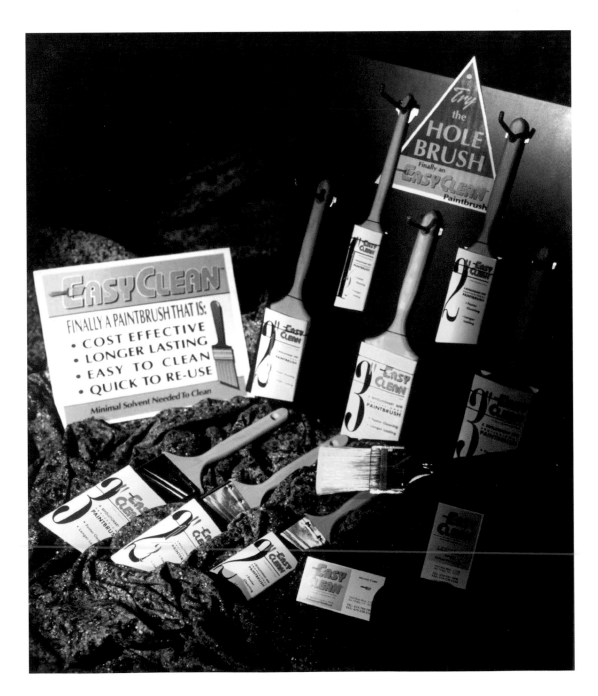

1.

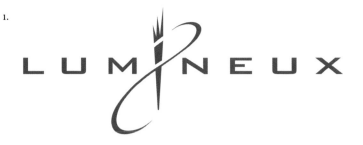

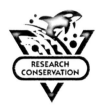

2.

3.

4.

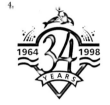

5.

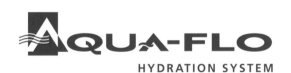

6.

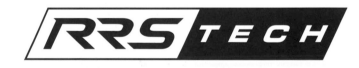

7.

(opposite)
Design Firm DYNAPAC Design Group

Client   Caldwell Industries, Inc.
Designer   Lee A. Aellig

1 - 7
Design Firm Laura Coe Design Assoc.

1. Client   Lumineux
    Designers Laura Coe Wright
               & Leanne Leveillee

2. Client   Active Motif
    Designers Ryoichi Yotsumoto
               & Laura Coe Wright

3. Client   Dataquick
    Designer   Ryoichi Yotsumoto

4. Client   Sea World of California
    Designers Leanne Leveillee
               & Ryoichi Yotsumoto

5. Client   Taylor Made Golf Co.
    Designer   Ryoichi Yotsumoto

6. Client   Road Runner Sports
    Designer   Darryl Glass

7. Client   Road Runner Sports
    Designer   Ryoichi Yotsumoto

1.

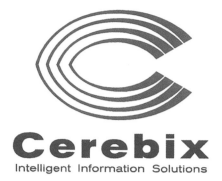

2.

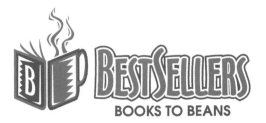

3.

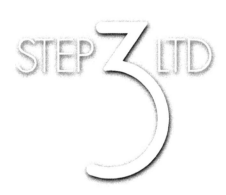

4.

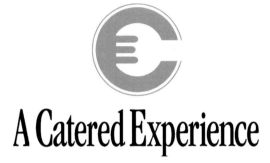

5.

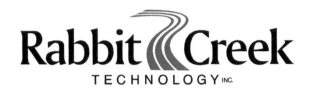

6.

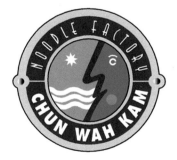

7.

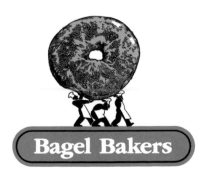

8.

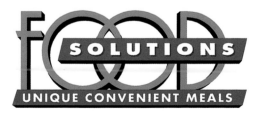

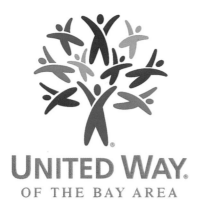

UNITED WAY®
OF THE BAY AREA

9.

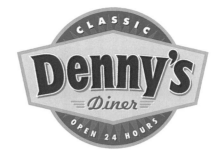

10.

UCSF STANFORD
HEALTH CARE

Stanford Hospital and Clinics

11.

Purple Moon™

12.

E*x*ponent™

13.

Cheskin
Research

14.

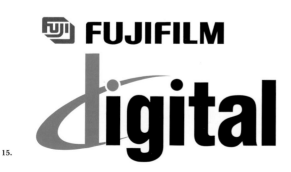

15.

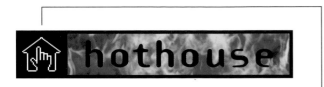

1.

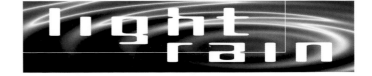

2.

inhaus

eliptica

3.

4.

SOLARIAN

KARMA

5.

6.

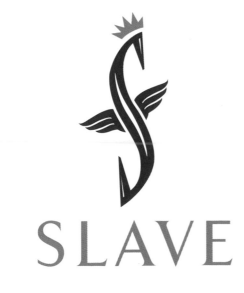

7.

SLAVE

1 - 7
Design Firm be.

1. Client   Hot House
   Designers Eric Read & Enrique Gaston

2. Client   Light Rain
   Designers Coralie Russo & Eric Read

3. Client   In Haus
   Designer Eric Read

4. Client   Eliptica
   Designer Yubuke Asaka

5. Client   Armstrong Solarian
   Designer Will Burke

6. Client   Karma
   Designer Eric Read

7. Client   Slave
   Designer Eric Read

(opposite)
Design Firm DYNAPAC Design Group

   Client   ClassMate, Inc.
   Designer Lee A. Aellig

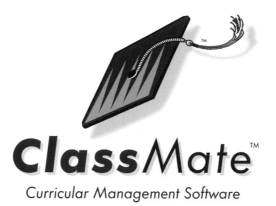

ClassMate™

Curricular Management Software

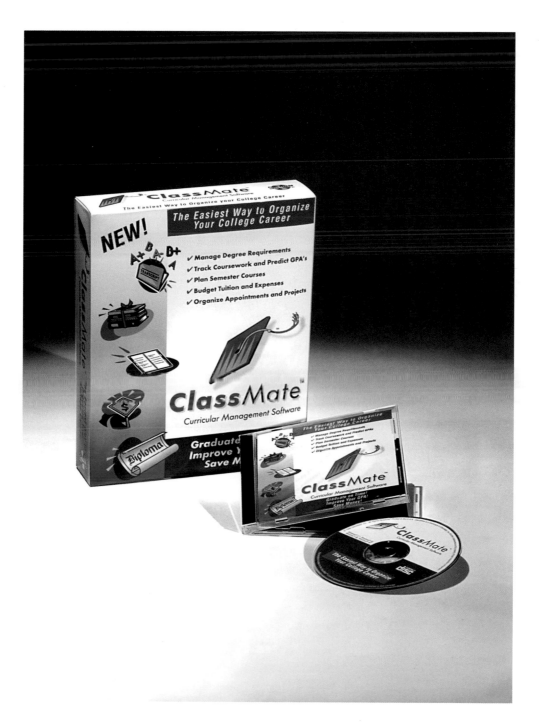

1.

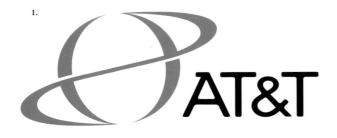

AT&T

2.

HAL's

bar & grill

3.

NOMADIX

4.

medschool.com

5.

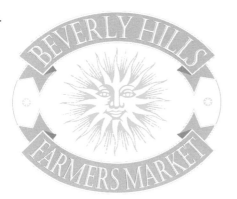

6.

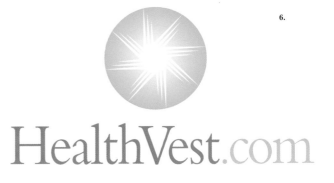

HealthVest.com

7.

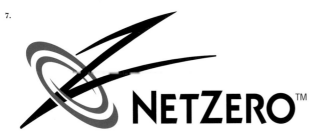

NetZero™

8.

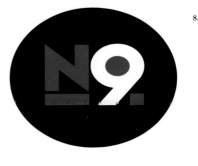

NO. 9 RECORDS

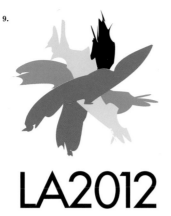

9.

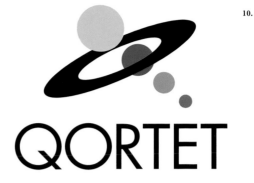

10.

LA2012

QORTET

11.

shipper.com

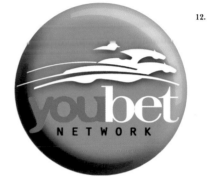

12.

13.

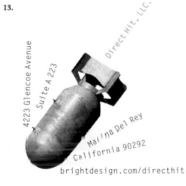

4223 Glencoe Avenue
Suite A 223

Direct Hit, LLC.

Marina Del Rey
California 90292

brightdesign.com/directhit

14.

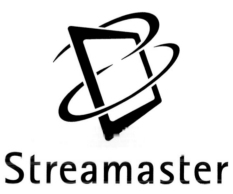

Streamaster

15.

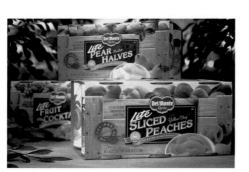

1.
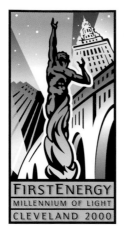

2.
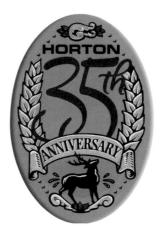

3.
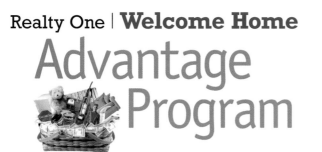

4.
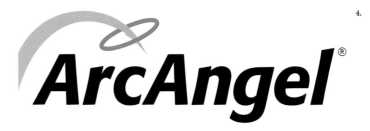

5.
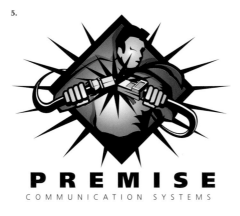

6.
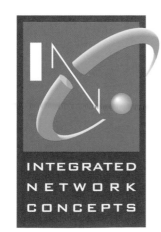

7.
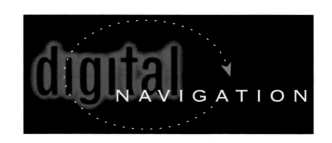

8.
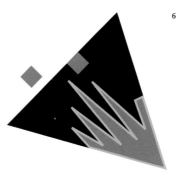

9.

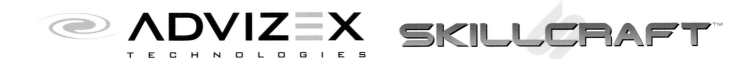

10.

11.

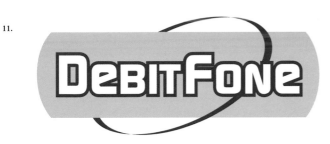

12.

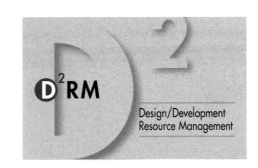

13.

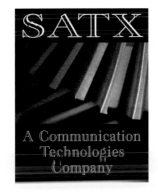

14.

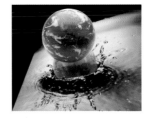

FURUTANI
USA · INC.

15.

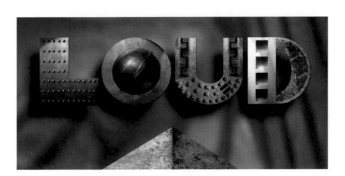

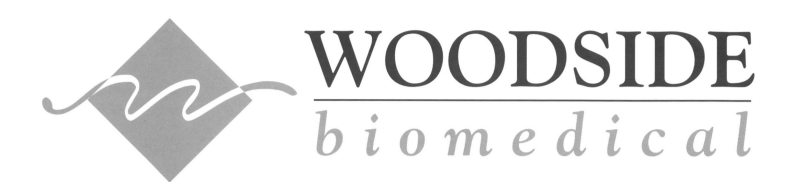

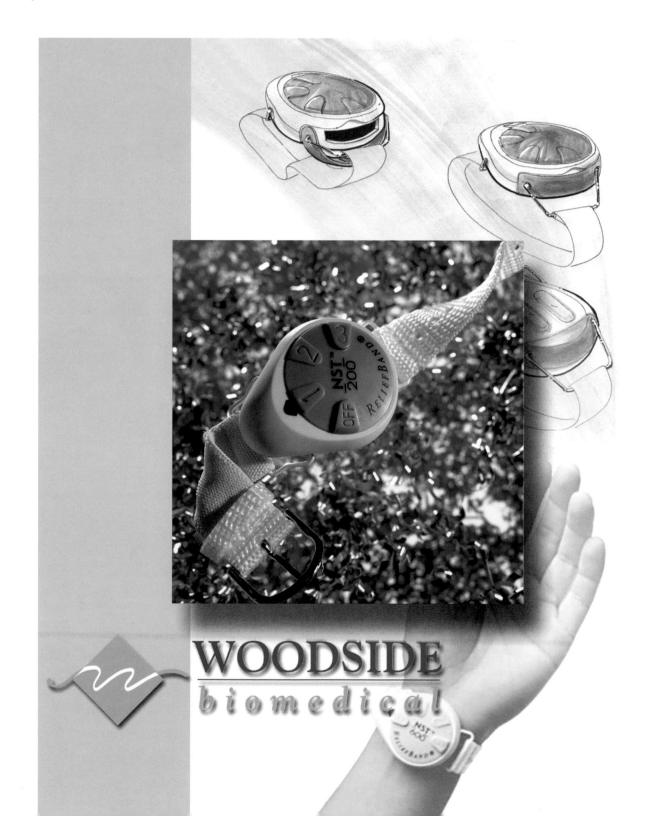

1.

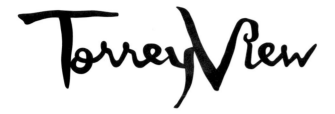

Fine Furnishings and Design

CLASSIC INTERIORS

2.

3.

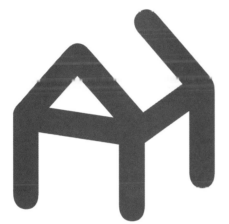

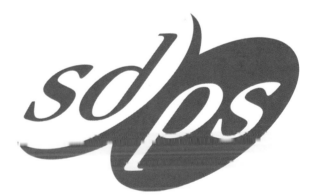

DOUBLE EAGLE

GOLF CENTER

4.

5.

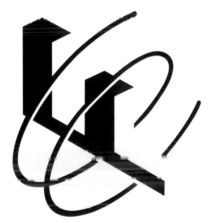

sdps

6.

7.

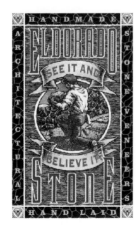

(opposite)
Design Firm   **DYNAPAC Design Group**

Client   Woodside Biomedical, Inc.
Designer   Lee A. Aellig

1 - 7
Design Firm   **Conover**

1. Client   Torrey View
    Designer   David Conover

2. Client   Classic Interiors
    Designers Amy Williams & David Conover

3. Client   Addison Homes
    Designer   David Conover

4. Client   Double Eagle
    Designer   David Conover

5. Client   Fraseworks
    Designer   David Conover

6. Client   Sejersen Digital
                Processing Services
    Designer   Carlos Avina

7. Client   El Dorado Stone
    Designers David Conover, Carlos Avina,
                & Amy Williams

1.

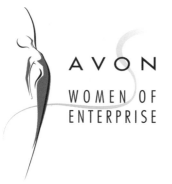

AVON
WOMEN OF ENTERPRISE

AVON the company for women

2.

AVON

worldwide fund for
women's health

AVON the company for women

3.

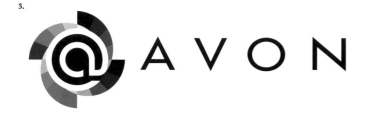

@AVON

4.

AVON
the company for women

5.

AVON

Women

inSight

Data base

6.

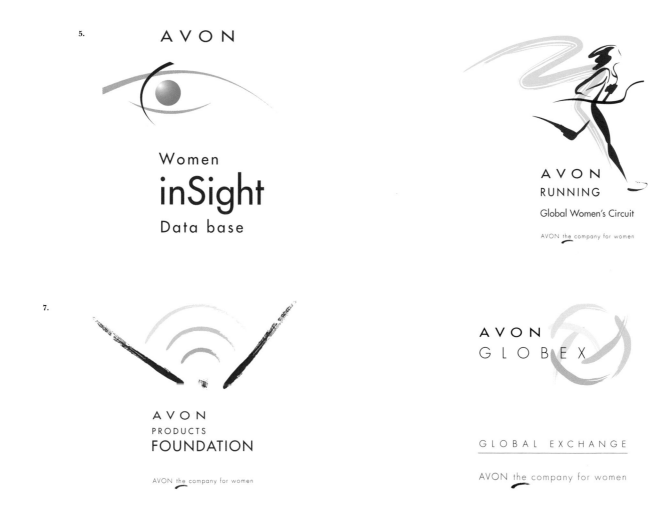

AVON
RUNNING

Global Women's Circuit

AVON the company for women

7.

AVON
PRODUCTS
FOUNDATION

AVON the company for women

8.

AVON
GLOBEX

GLOBAL EXCHANGE

AVON the company for women

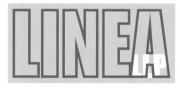 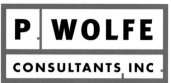

9.

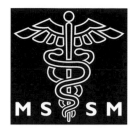

10.

MOUNT SINAI
SCHOOL OF
MEDICINE

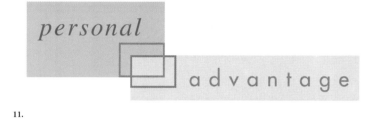

11.

○ ● ● ●

the acme **idea** company LLC

12.

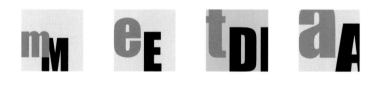

CCG meta**MEDIA** inc

13.

CONSUMERS
INTERSTATE
CORPORATION

Revolutionizing
The Buying Process™

14.

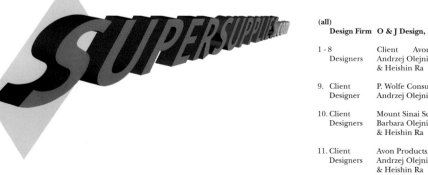

15.

(all)				
Design Firm	**O & J Design, Inc.**		12. Client	The Acme Idea Company
			Designers	Barbara Olejniczak
1 - 8	Client	Avon Products, Inc.		& Heishin Ra
	Designers	Andrzej Olejniczak		
		& Heishin Ra	13. Client	CCG MetaMedia, Inc.
			Designers	Andrzej Olejniczak
9. Client	P. Wolfe Consultants, Inc.			& Christina Mueller
	Designer	Andrzej Olejniczak		
			14. Client	Consumers Interstate
				Corporation
10. Client	Mount Sinai School of Medicine		Designers	Andrzej Olejniczak
	Designers	Barbara Olejniczak		& Lia Camara-Mariscal
		& Heishin Ra		
			15. Client	Consumer Interstate
11. Client	Avon Products, Inc.			Corporation
	Designers	Andrzej Olejniczak		Designers	Andrzej Olejniczak
		& Heishin Ra		& Lia Camara-Mariscal

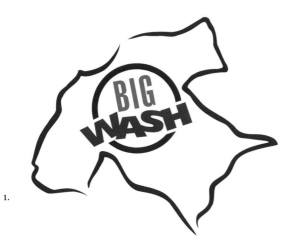

1.

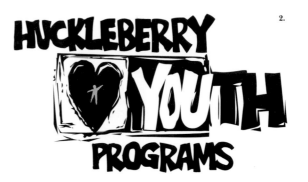

2.

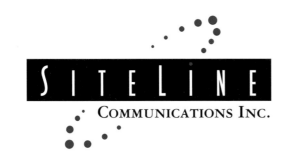

3.

SITELINE
COMMUNICATIONS INC.

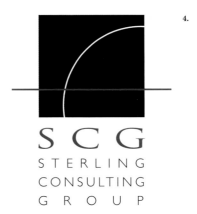

4.

S C G
STERLING
CONSULTING
GROUP

5.

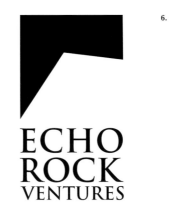

6.

ECHO
ROCK
VENTURES

7.

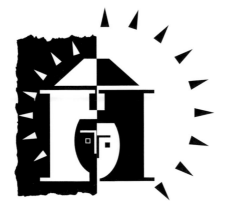

1 - 7

Design Firm Clark Creative Group

1. Client   Big Wash
   Designers   Annemarie Clark & Craig Stout

2. Client   HuckleberryYouth Programs
   Designers   Annemarie Clark &
                   Ozzie Patton

3. Client   Siteline Communications Inc.
   Designers   Annemarie Clark & Craig Stout

4. Client   Sterling Consulting Group
   Designers   Annemarie Clark
                   & Thurlow Washam

5. Client   J. Eiting & Co.
   Designers   Annemarie Clark
                   & Carol Piechocki

6. Client   Echo Rock Ventures
   Designers   Annemarie Clark
                   & Thurlow Washam

7. Client   Hope Housing
   Designers   Annemarie Clark
                   & Hiroko Chastain

(opposite)
Design Firm DYNAPAC Design Group

   Client   Experience Coffee
   Designer   Lee A. Aellig

142

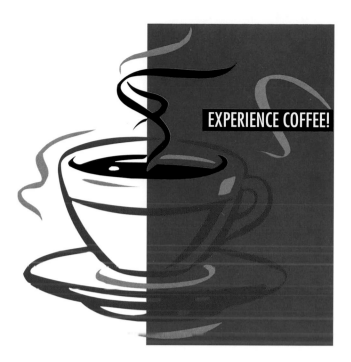

EXPERIENCE COFFEE!

Allow me to further detail what I cover:

The INVESTMENT section

BUSINESS PLAN
• I'll show you what mine contains
• How I developed it
• How I used it to secure a Loan (which I never used), from a small local lender.

CAPITAL
• What I used it for:
- Deposits
- Construction
- Inventory
- Permits
- Fixtures
- Marketing
- Licenses & fees
- Equipment
• Details of permits required • Breakdown of construction costs

SWEAT EQUITY
• Insight on required amount of sweat equity

MONEY MANAGEMENT
• How I managed to live while business grew • When to expect a profit

KEEPING EQUIPMENT COST DOWN
• How to invest in equipment at a low cost

INDUSTRY TRENDS
• Viability of this business • What the future holds

DEFINING TARGETS
• What numbers constitute a successful operation
- How many transactions per day • Average transaction amount

Before OPENING A BUSINESS section

HOW I STARTED
• Identifying & detailing Key Factors

LOCATION
• Identifying a good location
• Applying demographic formulas to identify potential market

LEASE
• Different types
• Free rent
• NNN
• What's negotiable
• Lease duration
• Escape clauses
• TI's
• Importance of realty advisors & lawyers
• Options & their importance
• Exclusivity clause
• Merchants Association

STORE DESIGN
• Pictures of my store
• Bean & tea sales area
• Menus
• The backroom
• Entertainment
• Why setup is important
• Behind the counter
• Blueprints
• Following ordinances
• Customer service & seating
- Interior & exterior

PRE-OPENING
• Time frame
• Effective design
• Floors, counters & cabinets
• Permits/Ordinances
• Interior/exterior signs
• Sweat equity
• Plumbing & Electrical

FIXTURES
• Lighting considerations
• Installing sinks
• Security system
• Water filtration system
• Water heater
• Requirements; length & costs

EQUIPMENT
• What Brewers to use • Espresso machine considerations
• Equipment support necessary for a diversified menu
• Misc. supplies used such as; janitorial, operating, etc.

INVENTORY
• Valuable supplier criteria
• Variety & regular blends
• Bulk teas used
• Kind of baked goods sold
• Stocking accessories
• Finding whole bean suppliers
• Dark roasts & decaffeinated blends
• Flavored beans used & why
• Food items found necessary

THE DRINK MENU
• What basic drinks to offer • Which variations work well

After OPENING A BUSINESS section

HOW I OPERATE (My experiences)

INTANGIBLES
• Importance of passion • Personality • Individuality
• Organizational Skills • People Skills
• Review the necessity of basic business knowledge
• How Owner/Operator relates to success in business

MARKETING
• Budget • Using "Direct Mail" to increase sales
• "Grand Opening" • Publicity • "Word of Mouth"
• Details of "Community Involvement" • Events
• Quantity & store discounts • "Free drink" policy
• Introductory specials • Success stories

OPERATION
• "Working the store myself; I'm my best employee."
• Costs
• Policies
• Hours of operation
• Procedures
• Prices
• Employees

HIRING
• How "Intuition" helps to hire good employees • Interviewing with a purpose
• Identifying potential candidates • Build a responsible, reliable staff
• Explain expectations • Listening • Prior experience

TRAINING
• The importance of "The time spent in the training period."
• Flexibility
• Self motivation
• Empowerment
• Team effort
• Communication
• Expect mistakes
• Praise!
• "Train employees to do everything;"
• Consistency
• Personal responsibility
• Keep it fun!
• "Show 'em, help 'em, watch 'em and let 'em go!"

MOTIVATION
• After training, how to keep them motivated
• Flexibility
• Levity
• Benefits & salary
• Communication
• Honesty & trust
• Bonuses
• Justifying your decisions

SOME SUCCESS STORIES
• I'll tell you about some of the many things I have done.
• How success and failure have impacted my business and decision making.

Learn all the KEY FACTORS
necessary
for Entreprenuerial Success!

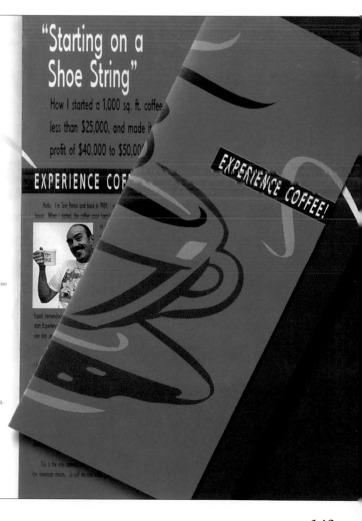

"Starting on a Shoe String"

How I started a 1,000 sq. ft. coffee

less than $25,000, and made

profit of $40,000 to $50,00

EXPERIENCE COF

Hello, I'm Tom Ferrus and back in 1989,

found tremendous

start Experienc

one day

EXPERIENCE COFFEE!

1.
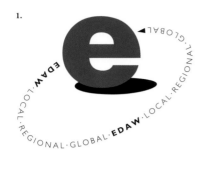

2.
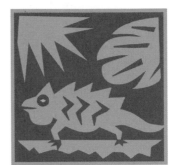

3.

4.
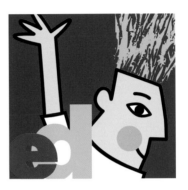

5.
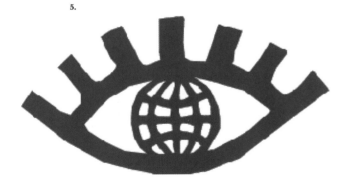

6.
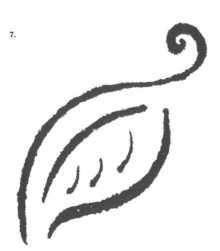

7.

8.
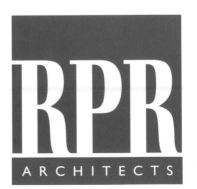

144

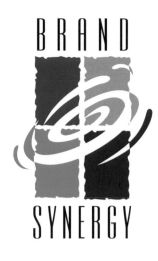

9.

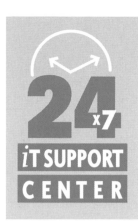

10.

11.

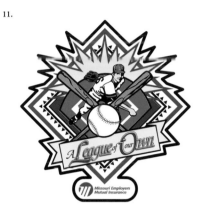

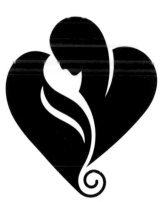

12.

14.

13.

Goldenleaf

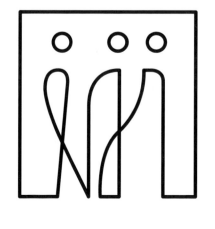

15.

1 - 8
Design Firm **EDAW, Inc.**
9 - 11
Design Firm **Ervin Marketing Creative Communications**
12 - 13
Design Firm **Julie Johnson Design**
14
Design Firm **Mires Design**
15
Design Firm **Doppelgänger, Inc.**

1. Client   EDAW Corporate Logo
   Designer   Marty McGraw

2. Client   EDAW Principals Meeting 1998
   Designer   Marty McGraw

3. Client   EDAW Summer Student Program
   Designer   Marty McGraw

4. Client   EDAW Intranet
   Designer   Marty McGraw

5. Client   EDAW Human Resources Eye
   Designer   Marty McGraw

6. Client   EDAW Human Resources Hand
   Designer   Marty McGraw

7. Client   Kate Stickley Landscape Architect
   Designer   Marty McGraw

8. Client   RPR Architects
   Designer   Marty McGraw

9. Client   Brand Synergy
   Designer   Erica Schwan

10. Client   Visteon Information Technology/ Ford Motor Company
    Designer   Erica Schwan

11. Client   Missouri Employers Mutual Insurance
    Designer   Jean Corea

12. Client   Mclean County Prenatal Clinic
    Designer   Julie Johnson

13. Client   Goldenleaf
    Designer   Julie Johnson

14. Client   Deleo Clay Tile Company
    Designer   José Serrano, Miguel Perez, & Dan Thoner

15. Client   Amana Corporation
    Designer   Otto Steininger

1.

Cellar Ideas

2.

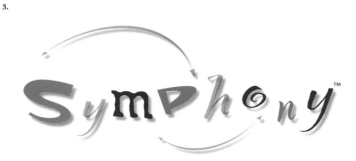

3.

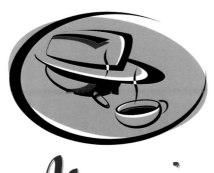

4.

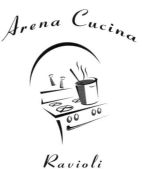

5.

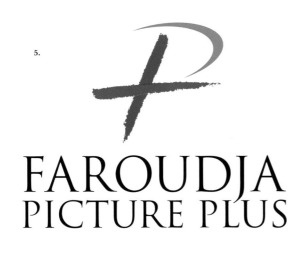

FAROUDJA
PICTURE PLUS

6.

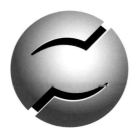

7.

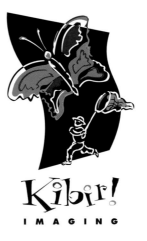

8.

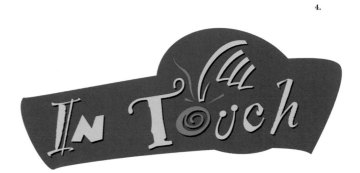

SiliconExchange

146

9.

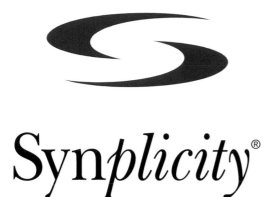

Syn*plicity*®

10.

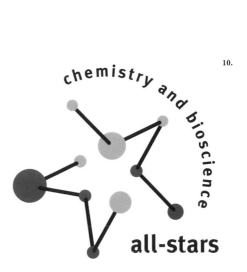

chemistry and bioscience all-stars

11.

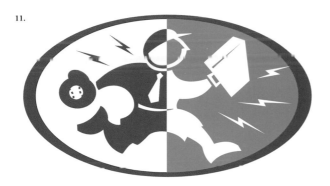

12.

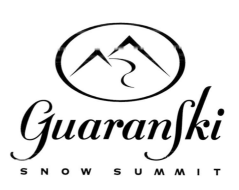

Guaranski

S N O W   S U M M I T

13.

 People**Support**

14.

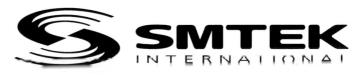 SMTEK
INTERNATIONAL

15.

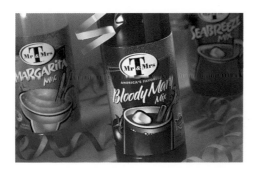

1 - 11
Design Firm Cellar Ideas
12 - 14
Design Firm McNulty & Co.
15
Design Firm SBG Enterprise

1.	Client	Cellar Ideas	8. Client	SGI: Silicon Exchange
	Designer	Don Barnes	Designer	Don Barnes
2.	Client	Arena Cucina	9. Client	Synplicity
	Designer	Don Barnes	Designer	Don Barnes
3.	Client	Proxim Symphony	10. Client	SGI: CBS all-stars
	Designer	Don Barnes	Designer	Don Barnes
4.	Client	Applied Materials: In Touch	11. Client	SGI: Don 2 work
	Designer	Don Barnes	Designer	Don Barnes
5.	Client	Faroudja Picture Plus	12. Client	Snow Summit
	Designer	Don Barnes	Designer	Dan McNulty
6.	Client	Kibir!	13. Client	People Support
	Designer	Don Barnes	Designers	Brian Jacobson & Dan McNulty
7.	Client	Mugsy's	14. Client	SMTEK International
	Designer	Don Barnes	Designers	Eugene Bustillos & Dan McNulty
			15. Client	Cadbury Beverages, Inc.
			Designers	Mark Bergman & Jessie McAnulty

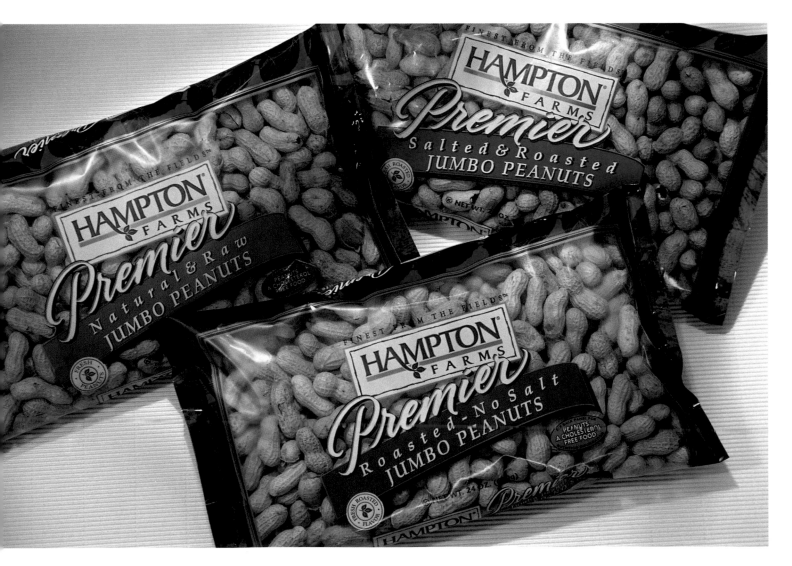

1.

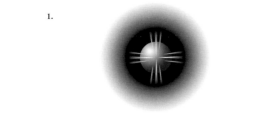

CYTOVIA

2.

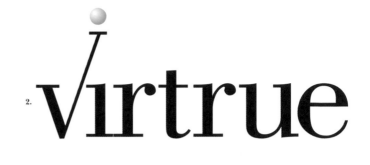

virtrue

3.

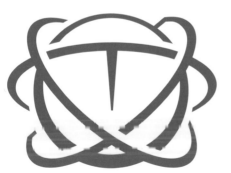

StellarRoad

4.

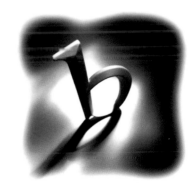

5.

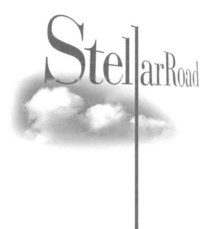

6.

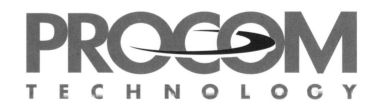

PROCOM
TECHNOLOGY

7.

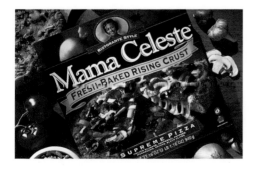

(opposite)
Design Firm Kollberg/Johnson

Client   Hampton Farms
Designer   Eileen Strauss

1 - 6
Design Firm Stoyan Design
7
Design Firm SBG Enterprise

1. Client   Cytovia
    Designer   Michael Stinson

2. Client   Virtrue
    Designer   Michael Stinson

3. Client   Stellar Road
    Designer   Michael Stinson

4. Client   Bell Photography
    Designer   Michael Stinson

5. Client   Global Technology
               Distribution Council
    Designer   Michael Stinson

6. Client   Procom Technology
    Designer   Michael Stinson

7. Client   Van de Kamp's
    Designers Mark Bergman & Phillip Ting

1.

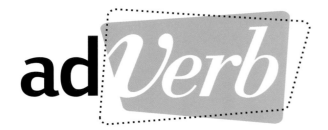

2.

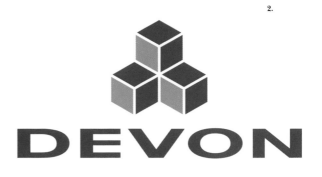

3.

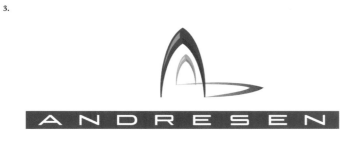

4.

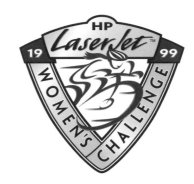

5.

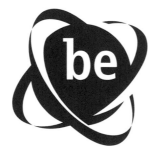

6.

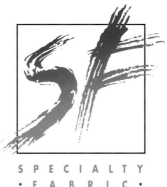

7.

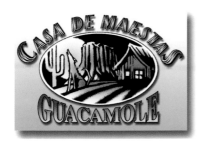

8.

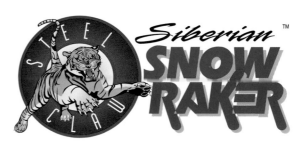

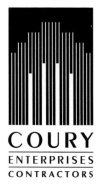

COURY
ENTERPRISES
CONTRACTORS

9.

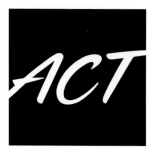

NETWORKS

10.

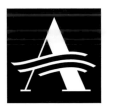

Alberstone Enterprises

11.

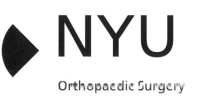

DiPrima
Insurance Specialists

12.

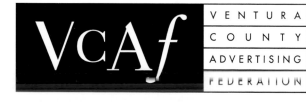

VENTURA
COUNTY
ADVERTISING
FEDERATION

13.

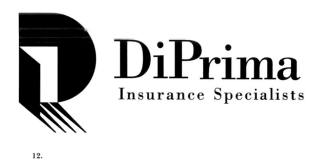

NYU

Orthopaedic Surgery

14.

NEW YORK UNIVERSITY
School of Continuing and
Professional Studies

15.

1 - 5
   Design Firm be.
6 8
   Design Firm DYNAPAC Design Group
9 - 13
   Design Firm McNulty & Co.
14 - 15
   Design Firm O & J Design, Inc.

1. Client	AdVerb	
Designer	Eric Read	
2. Client	Devon	
Designers	Enrique Gaston & Eric Read	
3. Client	Andresen	
Designer	Eric Read	
4. Client	HP LaserJet Women's Challenge	
Designers	Will Burke & Yusuke Asaka	
5. Client	be.	
Designers	Will Burke, Eric Read & Coralie Russo	
6. Client	Specialty Fabric & Accessories	
Designer	Lee A. Aellig	
7. Client	Casa De Maestas	
Designers	Lee A. Aellig & Jeff Maestas	

8. Client	Innotech, LLC	
Designer	Lee A. Aellig	
9. Client	Coury Enterprises	
Designers	Kristen Borg & Dan McNulty	
10. Client	ACT Networks	
Designers	Mark Luscombe & Dan McNulty	
11. Client	Alberstone Enterprises	
Designers	Mark Luscombe & Dan McNulty	
12. Client	Di Prima Insurance	
Designers	Eugene Bustillos & Dan McNulty	
13. Client	Ventura County Advertising Federation	
Designer	Dan McNulty	
14. Client	New York University, Hospital for Joint Diseases	
Designers	Barbara Olejniczak & Heishin Ra	
15. Client	New York University, School of Continuing & Professional Studies	
Designers	Andrzej Olejniczak, Christina Mueller & Leslie Nayman	

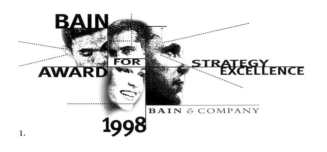

1.

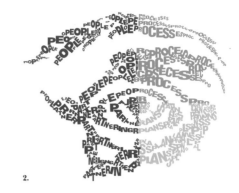

2.

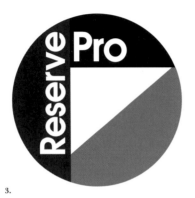

3.

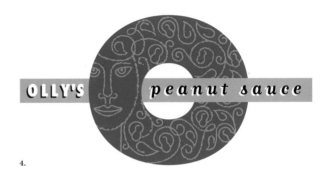

4.

6.

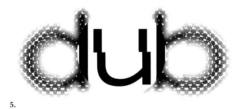

5.

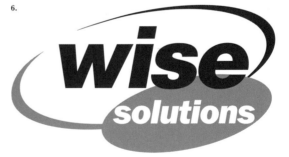

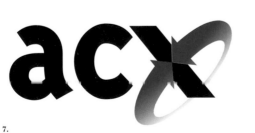

7.

1 - 7
    Design Firm Edward Walter Design, Inc.
8
    Design Firm Kym Abrams Design
9
    Design Firm Icon Graphics Inc.
10
    Design Firm Louey/Rubino
                Design Group, Inc.
11
    Design Firm Misha Design Studio
12
    Design Firm Festive Arts
13
    Design Firm Deutsch Design Works
14
    Design Firm Pisarkiewicz Mazur & Co., Inc.
15
    Design Firm Mickelson Design

1. Client   Bain & Co.
    Designers Edward Walter
             & Yuly Monsanto

2. Client   Coopers & Lybrand's
             Human Resource Advisory
    Designer   Yuly Monsanto

3. Client   Coopers & Lybrand ReservePro
    Designer   Martin Brynell

4. Client   South Pacific Foods
    Designer   Edward Walter

5. Client   Dub Rogers
    Designer   Edward Walter

6. Client   Wise Solutions, Inc.
    Designer   Edward Walter

7. Client   American Collectronix
    Designer   Edward Walter

8. Client   Lovell & Whyte
    Designers Amy Nathan & Kym Abrams

9. Client   Wild Bird Center of America
    Designers Icon Graphics Inc.

10. Client   Tutto Bene
    Designer   Robert Louey

11. Client   Temple Israel Synagogue
    Designer   Misha Lenn

12. Client   Miziker & Company
    Designer   Lee Storey

13. Client   Bammie Awards
    Designers Barry Deutsch & Jess Biambroni

14. Client   Town & Country Living Corp.
    Designer   Mary F. Pisarkiewicz
    Calligrapher Genevieve Cerasoli

15. Client   Anderson Auto
    Designer   Alan Mickelson

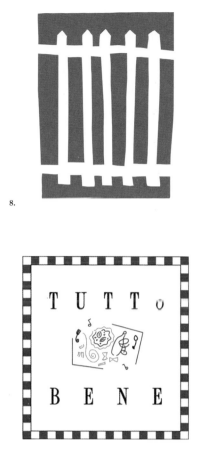

8.

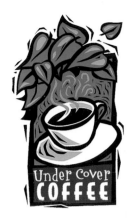

9.

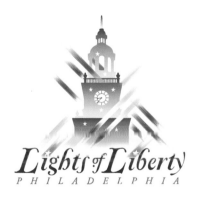

10.

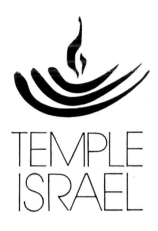

11.

12.

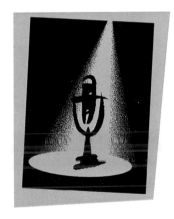

13.

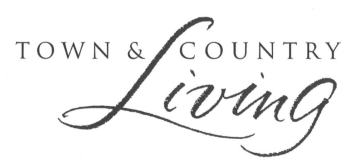

14.

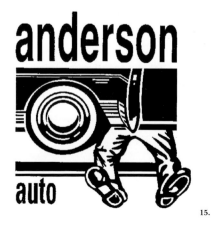

15.

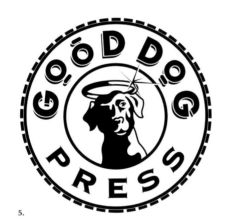

1.

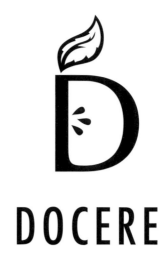

DOCERE

2.

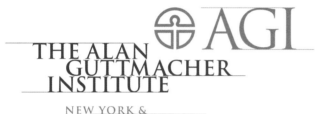

THE ALAN GUTTMACHER INSTITUTE
NEW YORK & WASHINGTON

3.

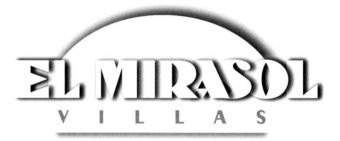

4.

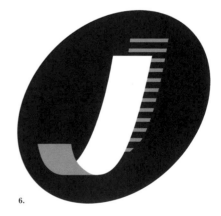

5.

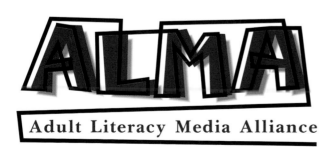

6.

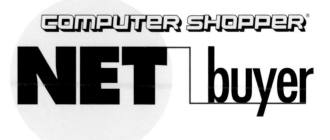

Adult Literacy Media Alliance

7.

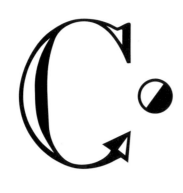

8.

154

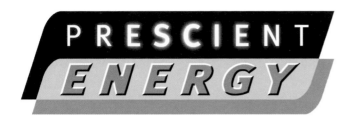

9.

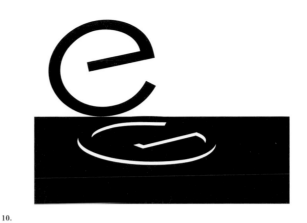

10.

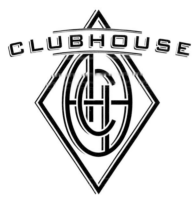

OAKBROOK

11.

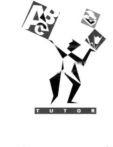

12.

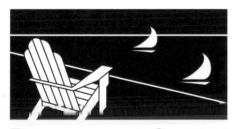

DENTAL CARE

13.

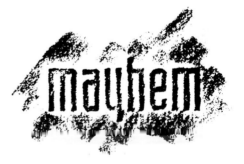

14.

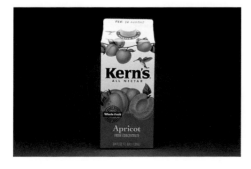

15.

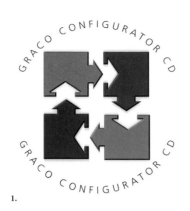

1.

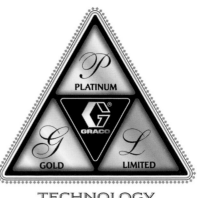

2.

TECHNOLOGY
DISTRIBUTOR PROGRAM

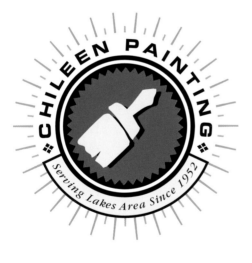

3.

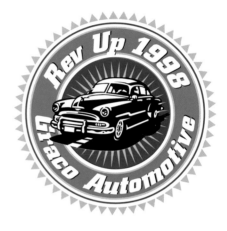

4.

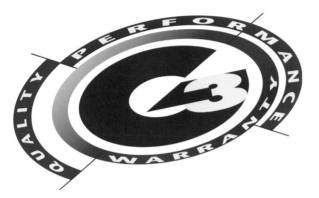

5.

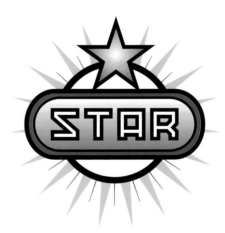

6.

7.

8.

156

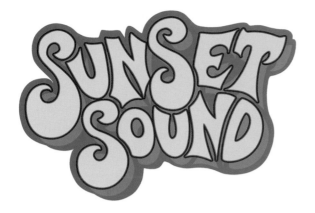

9.

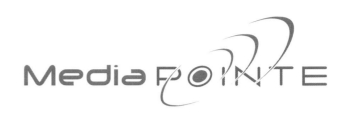

10.

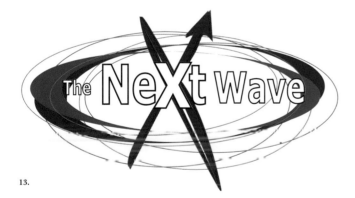

11.

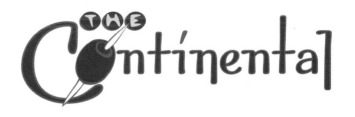

12.

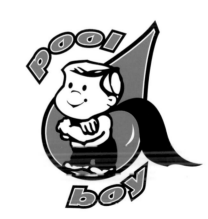

13.

14.

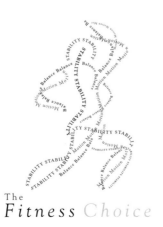

The *Fitness* Choice

15.

1 - 4
Design Firm Graco Advertising
5 - 8
Design Firm Imagine That Design
9 - 15
Design Firm [i]e design

1, 2
Client   Graco Industrial Division
Designer   Gary Schmidt

3. Client   Contractor Equip Division,
             Graco Inc
    Designer Gary Schmidt

4. Client   Graco Automotive Division
    Designer Gary Schmidt

5. Client   Chileen Painting
    Designer Terry Austin

6. Client   Star Cleaning
    Designer Terry Austin

7. Client   Imagine That Design
    Designer Gary Schmidt

8. Client   Scharacon General Contractors
    Designer   Terry Austin

9. Client   Sunset Sound
    Designers   Marcie Carson, Mirjam Selmi,
               & David Gilmour

10. Client   MediaPointe
    Designers   Cya Nelson & Marcie Carson

11. Client   The Continental
    Designer   Cya Nelson

12. Client   The Continental Olive Restaurant
    Designer   David Gilmour

13. Designer   David Gilmour

14. Client   Pool Boy
    Designer   Marcie Carson

15. Client   Fitness Choice
    Designers   Marcie Carson & David Gilmour

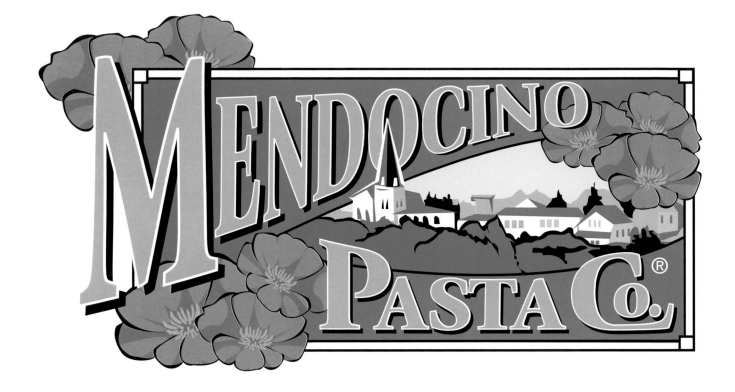

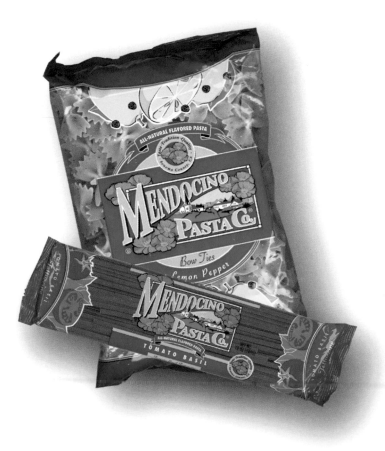

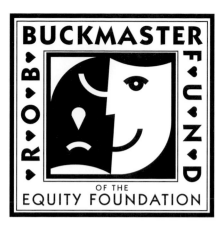

1.

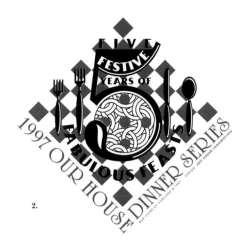

2.

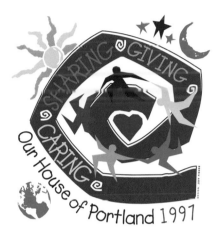

3.

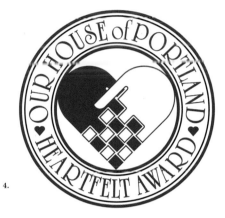

4.

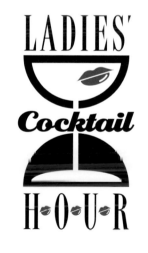

5.

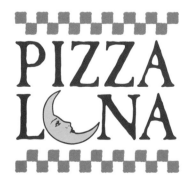

6.

7.

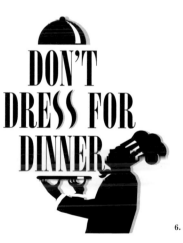

(opposite)
Design Firm JC Design

Client   Mendocino Pasta Inc.
Designer   James Cardell

1 - 7
Design Firm Jeff Fisher LogoMotives

1. Client   Rob Buckmaster Fund
    Designer   Jeff Fisher

2. Client   Our House of Portland
    Designer   Jeff Fisher

3 - 4
    Client   Our House of Portland
    Designer   Jeff Fisher

5. Client   Ladies' Cocktail Hour
    Designer   Jeff Fisher

6. Client   triangle productions!
    Designer   Jeff Fisher

7. Client   Pizza Luna
    Designer   Jeff Fisher

1.

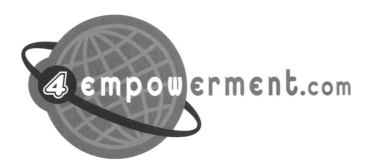

2.

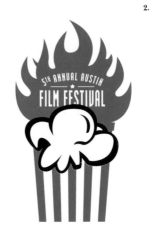

3.

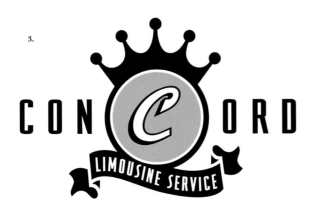

4.

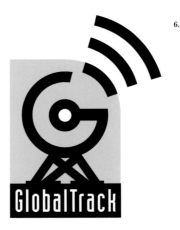

CYBERWAYSWATERWAYS

5.

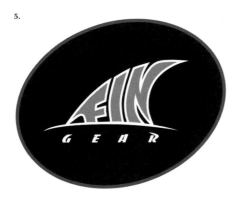

6.

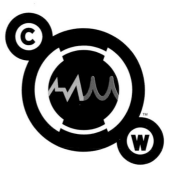

7.

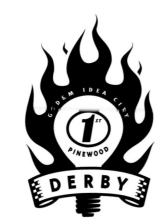

8.

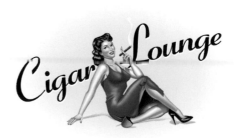

9.

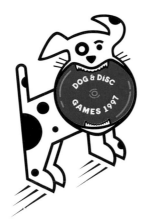

10.

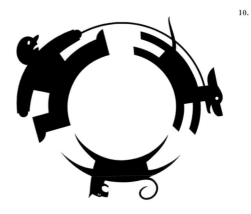

11.

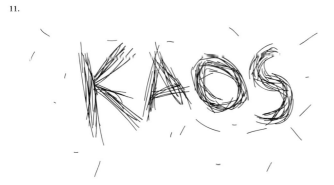

12.

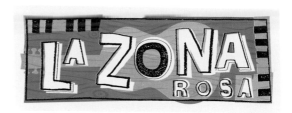

13.

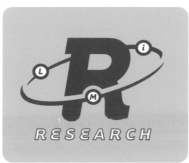

14.

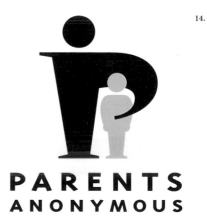

PARENTS
ANONYMOUS

15.

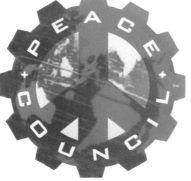

(all)
Design Firm	**GSD&M**		
1. Client	4empowerment.com	8. Client	Heroes & Legacies
Designer	Brett Stiles		Cigar Lounge
		Designer	Brett Stiles
2. Client	Austin Film Festival	9, 10	
Designer	Brett Stiles	Client	Humane Society of Austin
		Designer	Brett Stiles
3. Client	Concord Limousine Service	11. Client	KAOS Hair Salon
Designer	Brett Stiles	Designer	Brett Stiles
4. Client	Cyberway Waterways	12. Client	La Zona Rosa
Designer	Brett Stiles	Designer	Brett Stiles
5. Client	Fin Gear	13. Client	LIM Research
Designer	Brett Stiles	Designer	Brett Stiles
6. Client	GlobalTrack	14. Client	Parents Anonymous
Designer	Brett Stiles	Designer	Brett Stiles
7. Client	GSD&M	15. Client	Peace Council
Designer	Brett Stiles	Designer	Brett Stiles

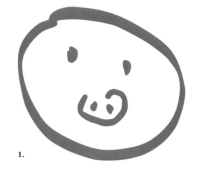

1.

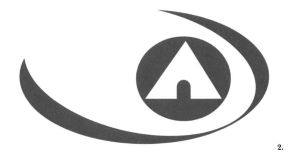

2.

sportzine

3.

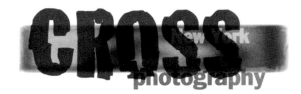

4.

5.

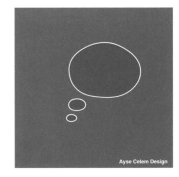

6.

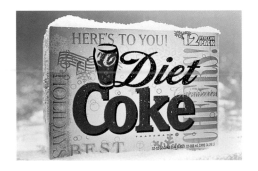

7.

1, 4
Design Firm Product 101
2, 3
Design Firm Rowan & Martin Design
5, 6
Design Firm Ayse Celem
7
Design Firm SBG Enterprises

1. Client   Happy Capitalist Productions
    Designer   Ayse Celem

2. Client   Airwalk-WalMart
    Designer   Ayse Celem

3. Client   Sportzine
    Designer   Ayse Celem

4. Client   Dave Cross Photography
    Designer   Ayse Celem

5. Client   Atwood Day Sail
    Designer   Ayse Celem

6. Client   Ayse Celem Design
    Designer   Ayse Celem

7. Client   The Coca-Cola Company
    Designers Mark Bergman, Margaret Lee,
               & Laura Cramer

(opposite)
Design Firm Cathey Associates, Inc.

    Client   Jwana Juice
    Designer   Isabel Campos

Jwana Juice

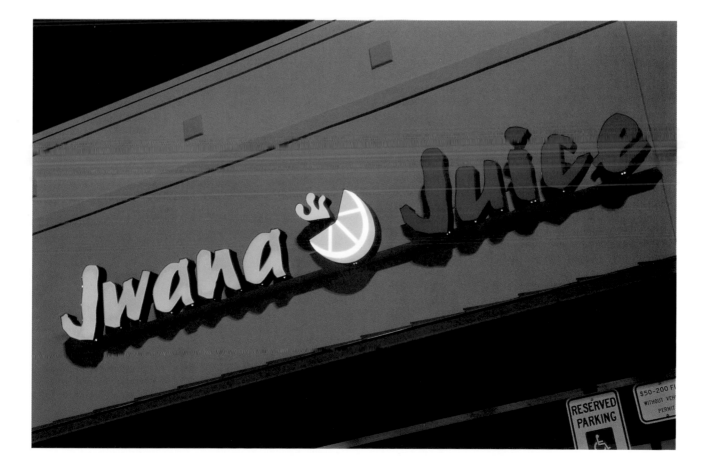

1.

belyea.

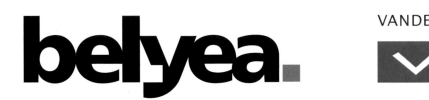

2.

3.
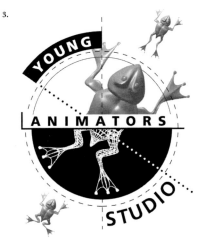

4.
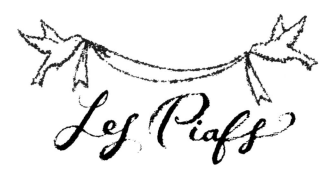

Les Piafs

5.
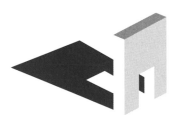

veenendaal**cave**

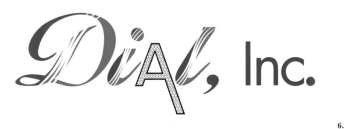
DiAl, Inc.

6.

7.
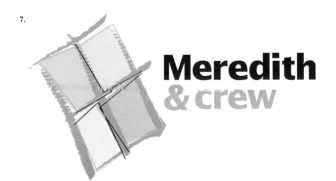
Meredith & crew

8.
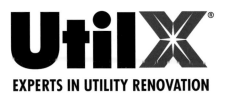
UtilX®
EXPERTS IN UTILITY RENOVATION

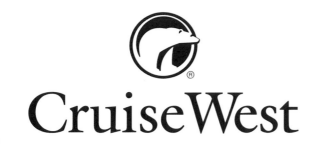

9.

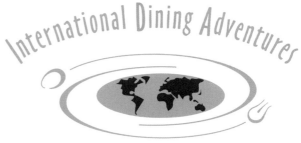

10.

11.

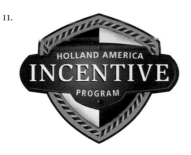

12.

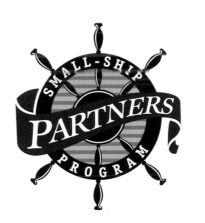

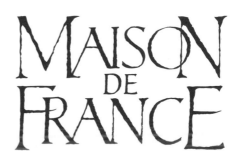

13.

14.

15.

GeoTrust SM

1 - 5, 7 - 15
Design Firm Belyea
6
Design Firm Corporate Multimedia Design

1. Client   Belyea
   Designers   Patricia Belyea
               & Ron Lars Hansen

2. Client   VHPR
   Designers   Patricia Belyea
               & Ron Lars Hansen

3. Client   Academy of Realist Art
   Designers   Patricia Belyea & Christian Salas

4. Client   Les Piafs
   Designers   Patricia Belyea & Christian Salas

5. Client   Veenendaal Cave
   Designers   Patricia Belyea
               & Anne Daugherty

6. Client   Disabilities Awareness Issues
               Leaders Inc.
   Designers   Norbert C. Saez & James Barry

7. Client   Meredith & Crew
   Designers   Patricia Belyea & Naomi Murphy

8. Client   UtilX
   Designers   Patricia Belyea
               & Ron Lars Hansen

9. Client   Cruise West
   Designers   Patricia Belyea
               & Ron Lars Hansen

10. Client   International Dining Adventures
    Designers Patricia Belyea & Christian Salas

11. Client   Holland America
    Designers Patricia Belyea
               & Ron Lars Hansen

12. Client   Cruise West
    Designers Patricia Belyea
               & Ron Lars Hansen

13. Client   Weyerhaeuser
    Designers Patricia Belyea
               & Ron Lars Hansen

14. Client   Maison de France
    Designers Patricia Belyea & Christian Salas

15. Client   GeoTrust
    Designers Patricia Belyea
               & Ron Lars Hansen

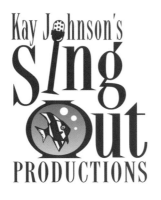

1.

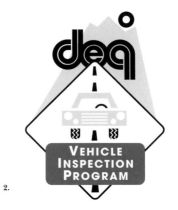

2.

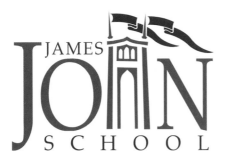

3.

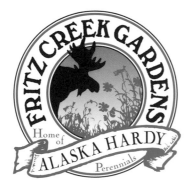

4.

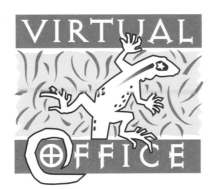

5.

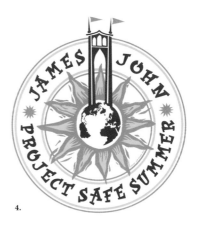

6.

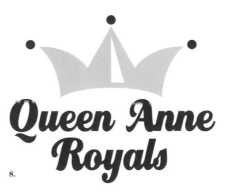

7.

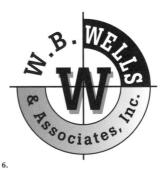

8.

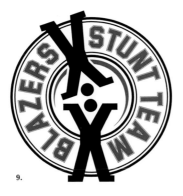

9.

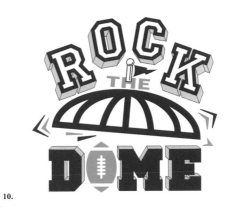

10.

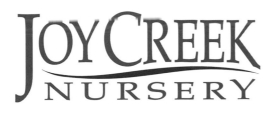

11.

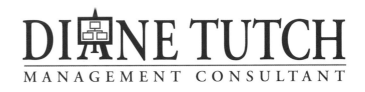

12.

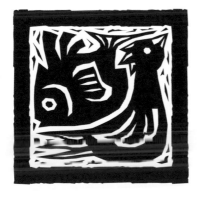

13.

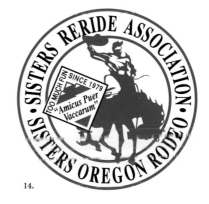

14.

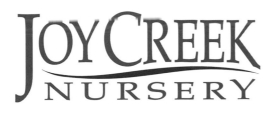

15.

(all)
Design Firm Jeff Fisher LogoMotives

1. Client	Kay Johnson's Sing Out Productions	
Designer	Jeff Fisher	
2. Client	Oregon Dept. of Environmental Quality	
Designers	Jeff Fisher & Marcia Danah	
3, 4 Client	James John School	
Designer	Jeff Fisher	
5. Client	Frit Creek Gardens	
Designer	Jeff Fisher	
6. Client	W.B. Wells & Associates	
Designers	Jeff Fisher & Esther Lorance	
7. Client	Virtual Office	
Designer	Jeff Fisher	

8. Client	Queen Anne Royals
Designer	Jeff Fisher
9. Client	Portland Trail Blazers
Designers	Jeff Fisher & Sara Perrin
10. Client	Seattle Seahawks
Designers	Jeff Fisher & Sara Perrin
11. Client	Joy Creek Nursery
Designer	Jeff Fisher
12. Client	Diane Tutch
Designer	Jeff Fisher
13. Client	Kristin & Tim Kelly
Designer	Jeff Fisher
14. Client	Sisters Reride Association
Designer	Jeff Fisher
15. Client	Website Today
Designer	Jeff Fisher

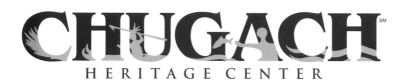

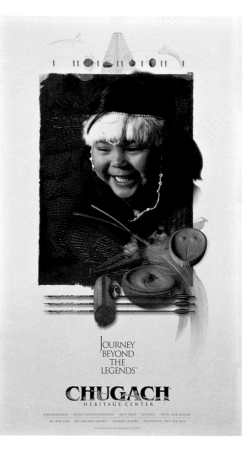

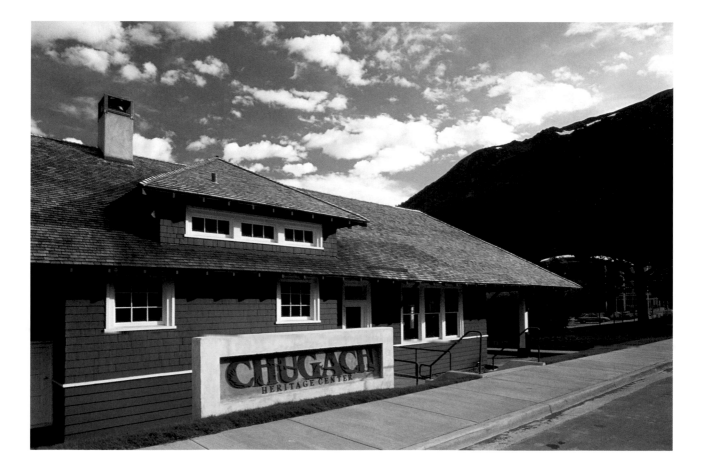

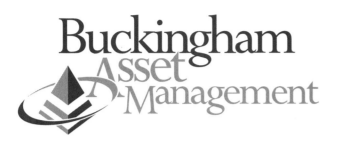

1.

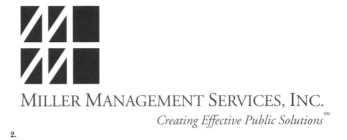

2.

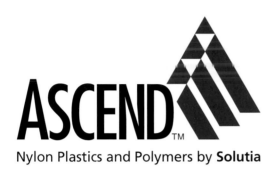

3.

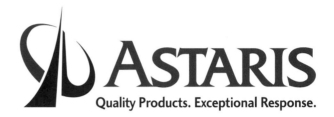

4.

NGA '99
ST. LOUIS
91st ANNUAL MEETING

5.

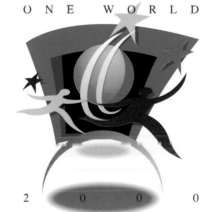

6.

gb**i**net

www.goinet.com

7.

(opposite)
Design Firm Walsh & Associates, Inc.

Client   Chugach Heritage
             Center/Alaska
Designer Miriam Lisco

1 - 7
**Design Firm Stan Gellman
Graphic Design Inc.**

1. Client   Buckingham Asset Management
    Designers Chris Reifschneider
            & Barry Tilson

2. Client   Miller Management
    Designers Barry Tilson & Erin Goter

3. Client   Solutia
    Designers Barry Tilson & Jill Lampen

4. Client   Astaris
    Designers Mike Donovan & Barry Tilson

5. Client   1999 National
             Governor's Association
    Designers Mike Donovan & Barry Tilson

6. Client   Promotional Consultants/
             The Peernet Group
    Designers Barry Tilson & Mike Donovan

7. Client   Goinet
    Designers Erin Goter & Barry Tilson

1.

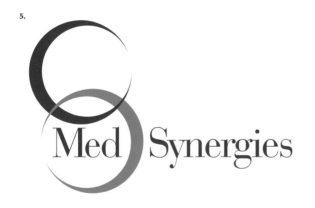

2.

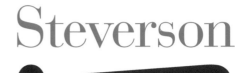

Steverson

3.

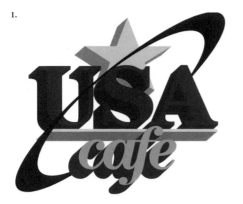

SECOND
BAPTIST
CHURCH

4.

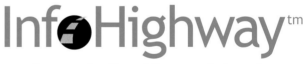

SHARPS COMPLIANCE INC.

5.

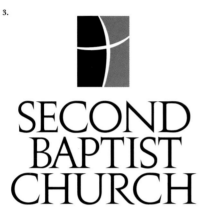

Med Synergies

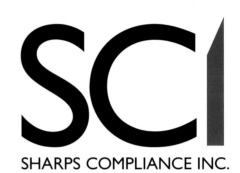

Communicating at the speed of now!

6.

7.

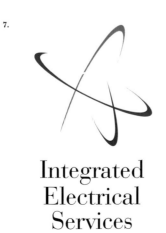

Integrated
Electrical
Services

8.

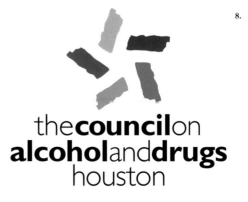

the**council**on
alcoholand**drugs**
houston

9.

Cornerstone Solutions

10.

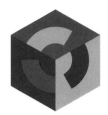

c e n t e g r a™

11.

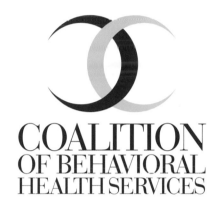

COALITION
OF BEHAVIORAL
HEALTH SERVICES

12.

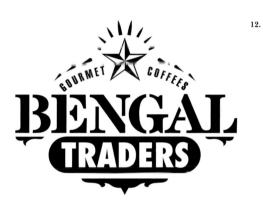

13.

ASSOCIATED COUNSEL of AMERICA ℠

14.

Oiltanking

15.

RESOURCENTER

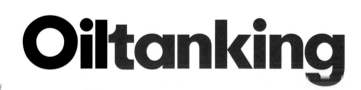

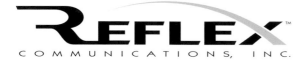

1.

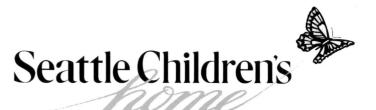

2.

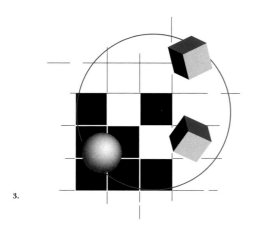

3.

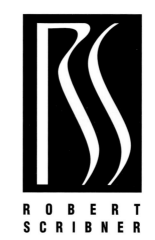

R O B E R T
S C R I B N E R

4.

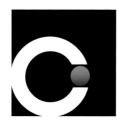

**GageTalker
CimWorks**

5.

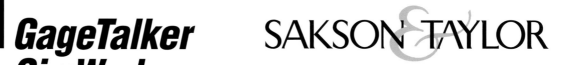

6.

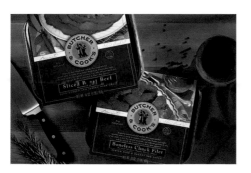

7.

1 - 6
Design Firm Walsh & Associates
7
Design Firm SBG Enterprise

1. Client   Reflex Communications
    Designers   Mark Ely & Miriam Lisco

2. Client   Seattle Children's Home
    Designer   Miriam Lisco

3. Client   Parker Le Pla,
                  Brand Development
    Designer   Miriam Lisco

4. Client   Robert Scribner Salon
    Designers   Miriam Lisco & Glen Yoshiyama

5. Client   GageTalker CimWorks
    Designer   Miriam Lisco

6. Client   Sakson & Taylor
    Designer   Miriam Lisco

7. Client   Excel Corp.
    Designer   Mark Bergman

(opposite)
Design Firm Walsh & Associates, Inc.

    Client   PC Fixx
    Designer   Miriam Lisco

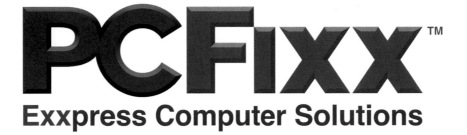

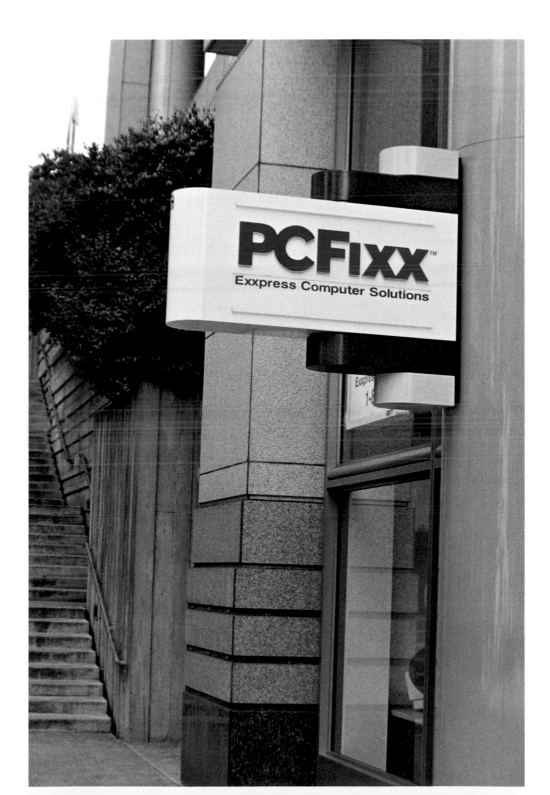

1.

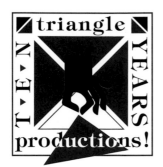

triangle productions!
T·E·N YEARS

2.

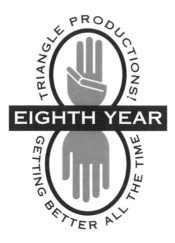

TRIANGLE PRODUCTIONS!
EIGHTH YEAR
GETTING BETTER ALL THE TIME

3.

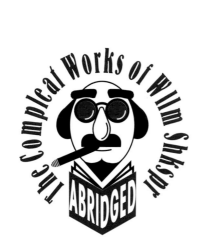

The Compleat Works of Wllm Shkspr
ABRIDGED

4.

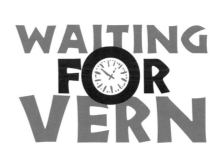

WAITING FOR VERN

5.

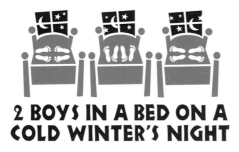

2 BOYS IN A BED ON A COLD WINTER'S NIGHT

6.

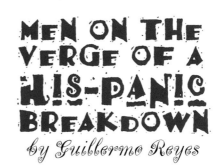

MEN ON THE VERGE OF A HIS-PANIC BREAKDOWN
by Guillermo Reyes

7.

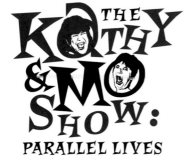

THE KATHY & MO SHOW: PARALLEL LIVES

8.

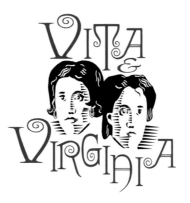

VITA & VIRGINIA

9.

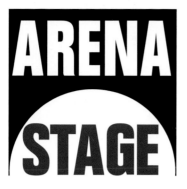

10.

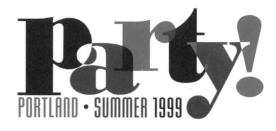

11.

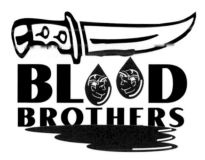

12.

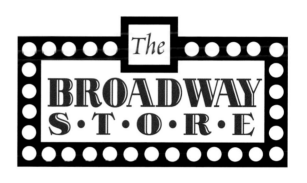

13.

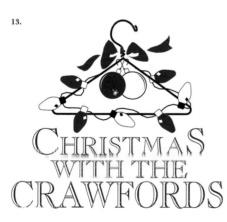

14.

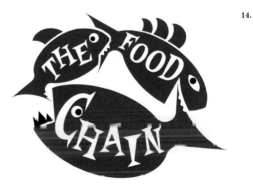

15.

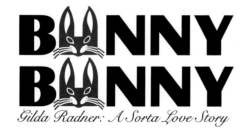

(all)
Design Firm Jeff FisherLogoMotives

1 - 15
  Client   triangle productions!
  Designer   Jeff Fisher

175

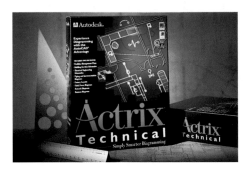

1.

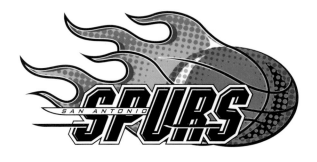

2.

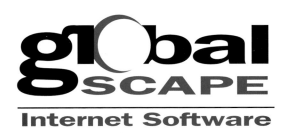

3.

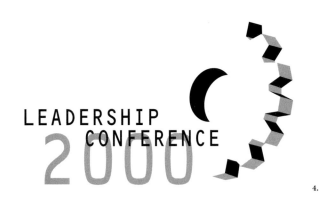

4.

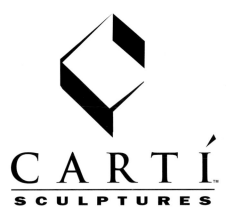

5.

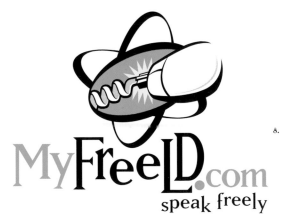

6.

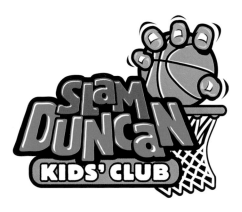

7.

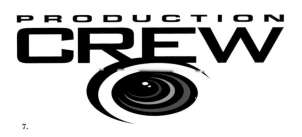

8.

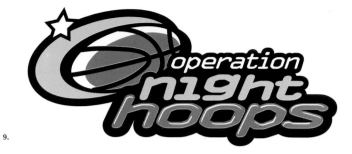

9.

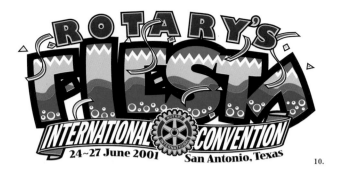

10.

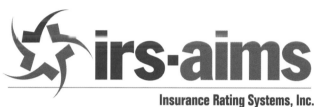

11.

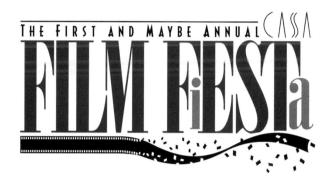

12.

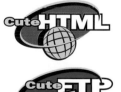

13.

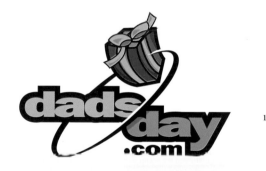

14.

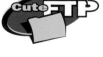

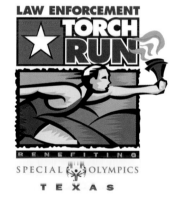

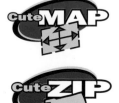

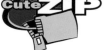

15.

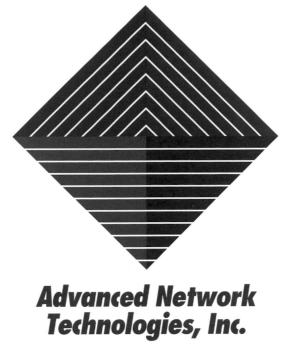

**Advanced Network
Technologies, Inc.**

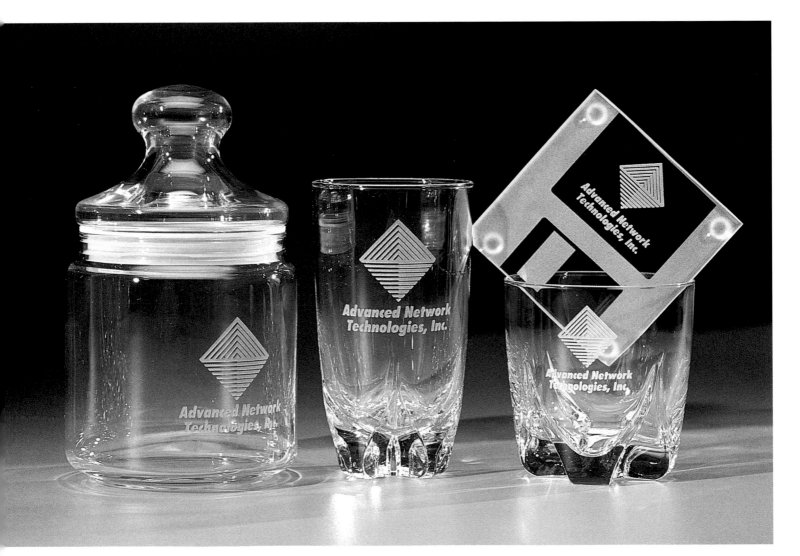

1.

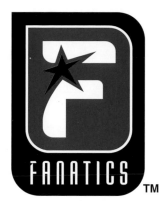

2.

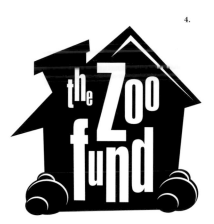

3.

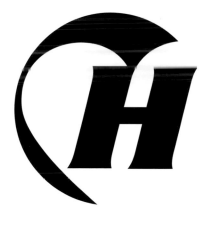

4.

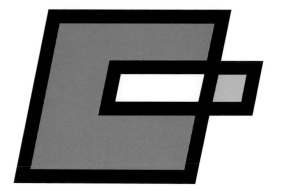

5.

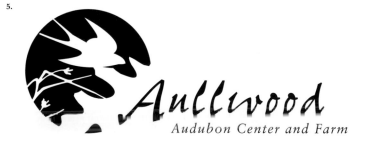

6.

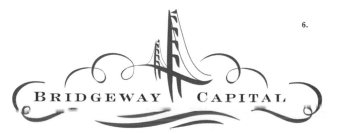

7.

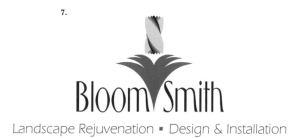

(opposite)
Design Firm Cathey Associates, Inc.

Client   Advanced Network
                Technologies, Inc.
Designer   Gordon Cathey

1 - 5
**Design Firm Visual Marketing
              Associates, Inc.**

6
Design Firm Lori Powell Design Exploration

7
Design Firm Cathey Associates, Inc.

1. Client   Telestar Interactive Corporation
   Designer   Tom Davie

2. Client   CYND Snowboard Apparel
   Designer   Jason Selke

3. Client   Heartland Airlines
   Designer   Lynn Sampson

4. Client   Columbus Zoo
   Designer   Tom Davie

5. Client   Aullwood Audubon Center
                and Farm
   Designer   Michael Butts

6. Client   Bridgeway Capital
   Designer   Lori Powell

7. Client   BloomSmith
   Designer   Matt Westapher

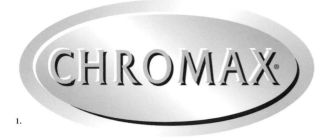

CHROMAX®

1.

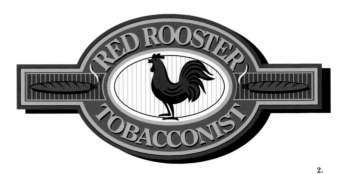

RED ROOSTER TOBACCONIST

2.

Squeezr®

3.

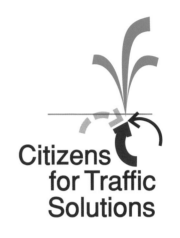

Citizens
for Traffic
Solutions

4.

e**Student**
Loan

5.

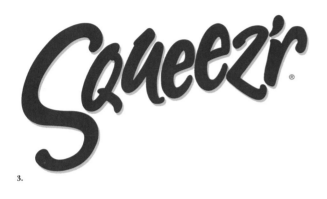

red**hat**

6.

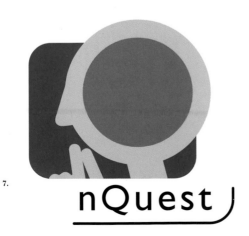

nQuest

7.

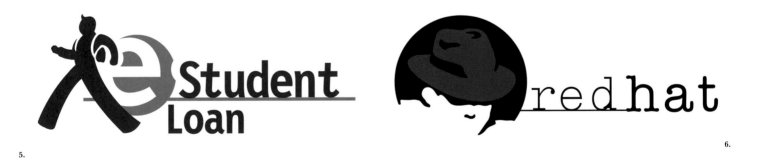

Foundation Labs

8.

180

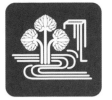

REGION

9.

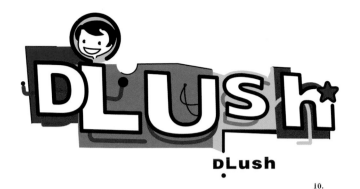

DLush

10.

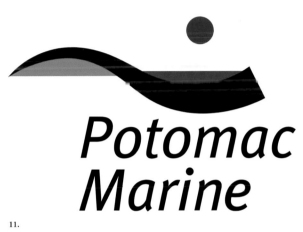

Potomac Marine

11.

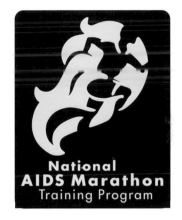

National **AIDS Marathon** Training Program

12.

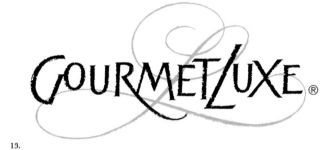

13.

11.

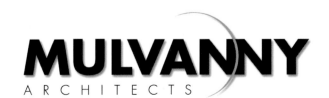

MULVANNY
ARCHITECTS

15.

1 - 3
Design Firm Kollberg/Johnson
4 - 12
Design Firm Blank
13 - 15
Design Firm Walsh & Associates, Inc.

1. Client   Ambi Inc.
   Designers   Kollberg/Johnson

2. Client   Red Rooster Tobacconist
   Designer   Gary Kollberg

3. Client   Brooklyn Bottling
   Designer   Eileen Strauss

4. Client   end gridlock.com
   Designers   Robert Kent Wilson
                & Susan Burch Ahlers

5. Client   e student loan
   Designers   Robert Kent Wilson
                & Suzanne Ultman

6. Client   Red Hat Software
   Designers   Robert Kent Wilson, Suzanne
                Ultman & Adam Cohn

7. Client   Natural Question Technology
   Designer   Robert Kent Wilson

8. Client   Foundation Labs
   Designer   Robert Kent Wilson

9. Client   Responsible Economic Growth
                In Our Nation
   Designer   Robert Kent Wilson

10. Client   Dlush
    Designers   Robert Kent Wilson
                & Suzanne Ultman

11. Client   Potomac Marine
    Designer   Robert Kent Wilson

12. Client   Walk the Talk Productions
    Designers   Robert Kent Wilson, Suzanne
                Ultman & Adam Cohn

13. Client   GourmetLuxe
    Designer   Miriam Lisco

14. Client   Encoding.com
    Designers   Mark Ely & Miriam Lisco

15. Client   Mulvanny Architects
    Designers   Lyn Blanchard &Miriam Lisco

1. **perry**design

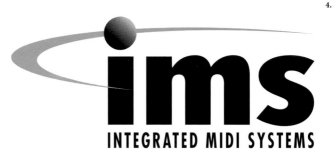

The Aurora Group
Manufacturers' Representatives

2.

3. 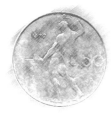 LiRA Enterprises

4.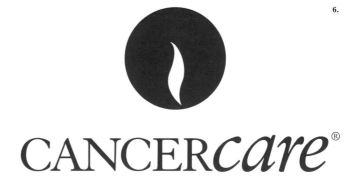

ims
INTEGRATED MIDI SYSTEMS

5.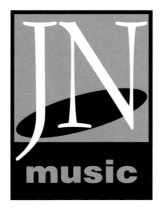

JN music

6.

CANCER*care*®

7.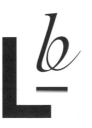

Lieber Brewster Design, Inc.

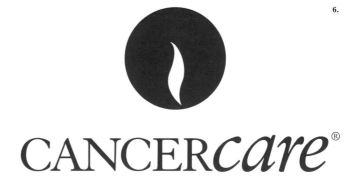

1 - 5
Design Firm Perry Design
6 -7
Design Firm Lieber Brewster Design, Inc.

1. Client   Perry Design
    Designer   Kim Perry

2. Client   The Aurora Group
    Designer   Kim Perry

3. Client   Lira Enterprises
    Designers   Kim Perry & Kenneth DiPaola

4. Client   Integrated Midi Systems
    Designer   Kim Perry

5. Client   JN Music
    Designer   Kim Perry

6. Client   Cancer Care
    Designers   Elisa Carson & Anna Lieber

7. Client   Lieber Brewster Design, Inc.
    Designer   Anna Lieber

(opposite)
Design Firm Zunda Design Group

    Client   Newman's Own Inc.
    Designers   Jon Voss & Charles Zunda

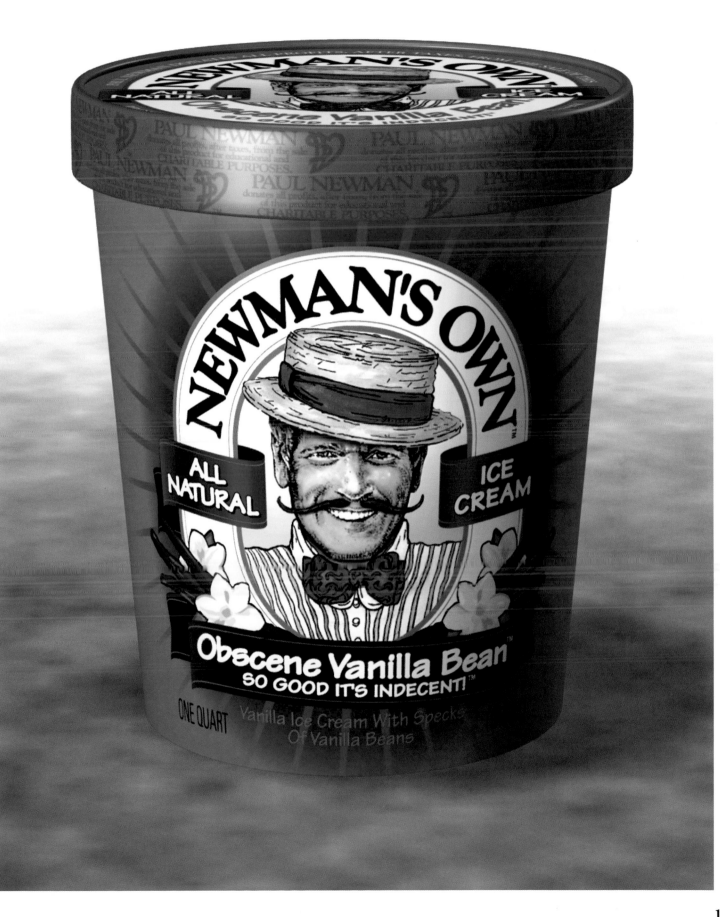

1.

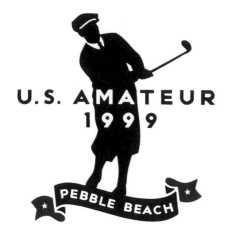

U.S. AMATEUR
1999

PEBBLE BEACH

2.

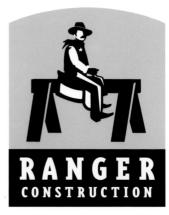

RANGER
CONSTRUCTION

3.

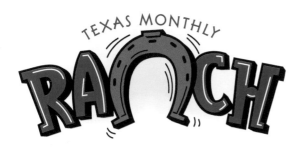

TEXAS MONTHLY
RANCH

4.

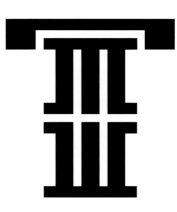

5.

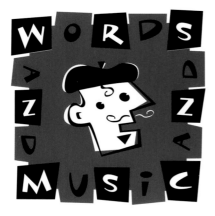

WORDS JAZZ MUSIC

6.

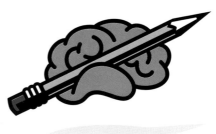

WRITE BRAIN
WORKS

7.

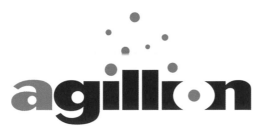

agillion

8.

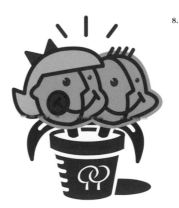

9.

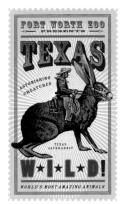

10.

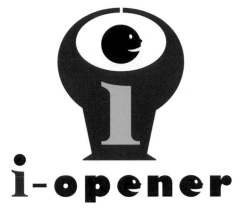

11.

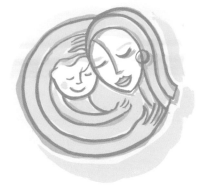

12.

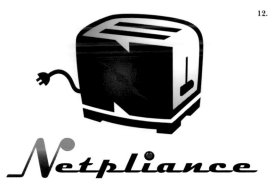

13.

SHRED DOC®

14.

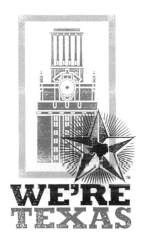

15.

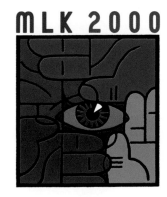

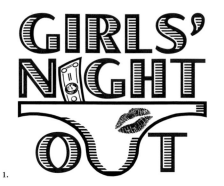

1.

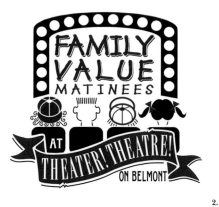

2.

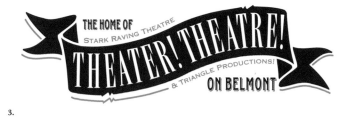

3.

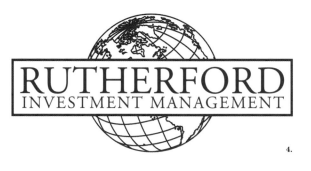

4.

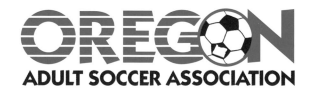

5.

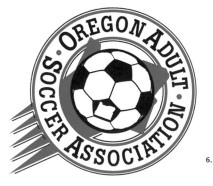

6.

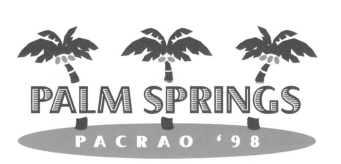

7.

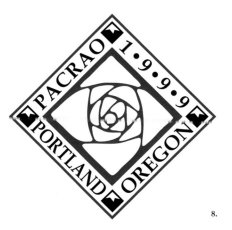

8.

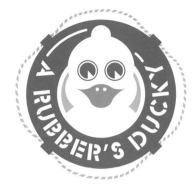

9.

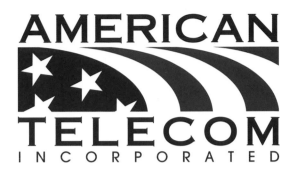

10.

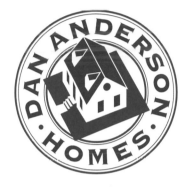

11.

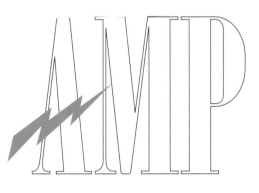

12.

archinetix
Architecture for Computing Infrastructures and Networks

13.

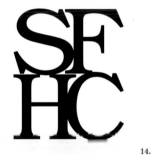

14.

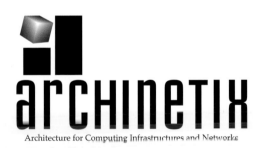

15.

(all)

Design Firm Jeff Fisher LogoMotives

1. Client   triangle productions!
   Designer   Jeff Fisher

2, 3
   Client   triangle productions!/
              Stark Raving Theatre
   Designer   Jeff Fisher

4. Client   Shleifer Marketing
              Communications (Rutherford
              Investment Management)
   Designer   Jeff Fisher

5. Client   Oregon Adult
              Soccer Association
   Designer   Jeff Fisher

6. Client   Oregon Adult
              Soccer Association
   Designer   Jeff Fisher

7. Client   Pacific Association of College
              Registrars and Admissions
              Officers
   Designer   Jeff Fisher

8. Client   Pacific Association of
              College Registrars and
              Admissions Officers
   Designer   Jeff Fisher

9. Client   A Rubber's Ducky
   Designer   Jeff Fisher

10. Client   Shleifer Marketing
              Communications
              (American Telecom)
   Designer   Jeff Fisher

11. Client   Dan Anderson Homes
   Designer   Jeff Fisher

12. Client   AMP/Anne-Marie Petrie
   Designer   Jeff Fisher

13. Client   Archinetix
   Designer   Jeff Fisher

14. Client   Smith Freed Heald & Chock
   Designer   Jeff Fisher

15. Client   Spirit Expressing
   Designer   Jeff Fisher

187

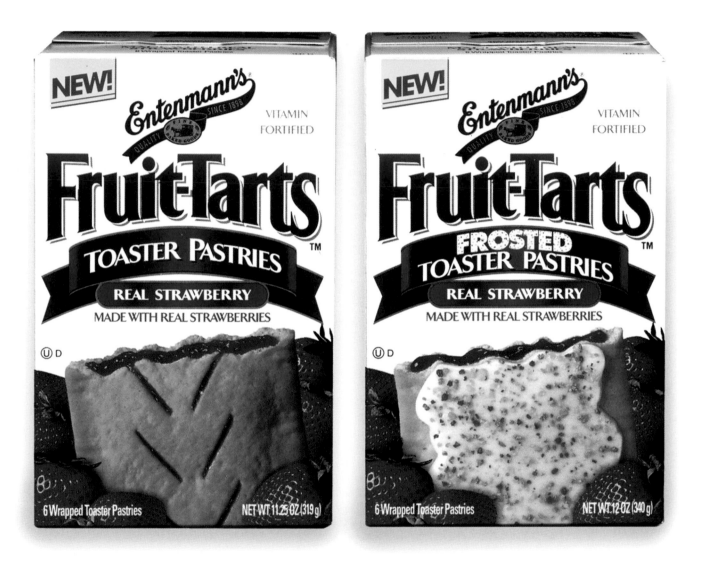

1. HEIDI GILMORE

2.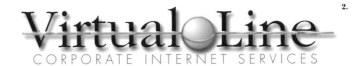
Virtual Line
CORPORATE INTERNET SERVICES

3.
AN EVENT FOR EVERY AGE
DINOSAUR
DASH
FRIENDS OF MILWAUKEE PUBLIC MUSEUM

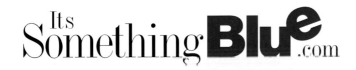
garbs
clothing   accessories   jewelry

4.

5.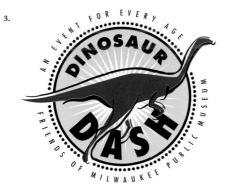
Its
SomethingBlue.com

6.
G
GRAPHICSOURCE
PRODUCTION/FULFILLMENT

7.
fA
FRAMING AMY

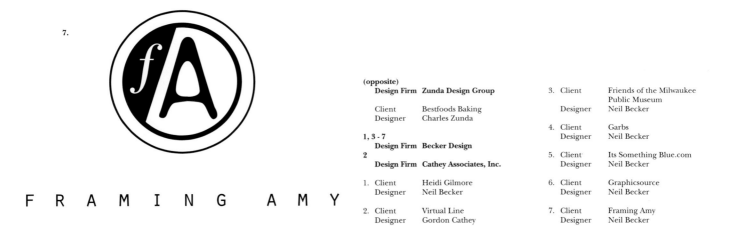

(opposite)
Design Firm Zunda Design Group

Client   Bestfoods Baking
Designer   Charles Zunda

1, 3 - 7
Design Firm Becker Design

2
Design Firm Cathey Associates, Inc.

1. Client   Heidi Gilmore
    Designer   Neil Becker

2. Client   Virtual Line
    Designer   Gordon Cathey

3. Client   Friends of the Milwaukee
               Public Museum
    Designer   Neil Becker

4. Client   Garbs
    Designer   Neil Becker

5. Client   Its Something Blue.com
    Designer   Neil Becker

6. Client   Graphicsource
    Designer   Neil Becker

7. Client   Framing Amy
    Designer   Neil Becker

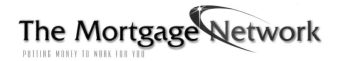

The Mortgage Network

PUTTING MONEY TO WORK FOR YOU

1.

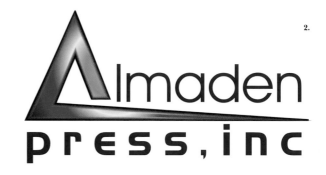

almaden
press, inc

2.

3.

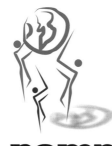
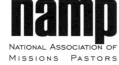

namp

NATIONAL ASSOCIATION OF
MISSIONS PASTORS

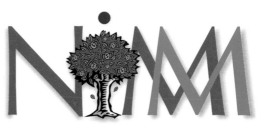

Nevada Institute for
Money Management

4.

5.

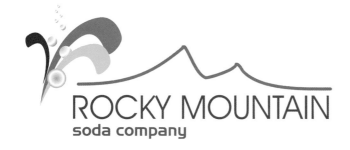

ROCKY MOUNTAIN
soda company

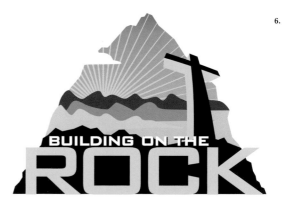

BUILDING ON THE
ROCK

6.

7.

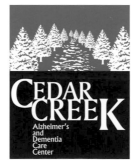

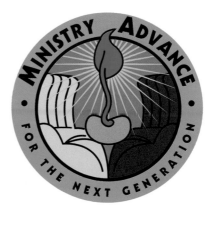

8.

9.

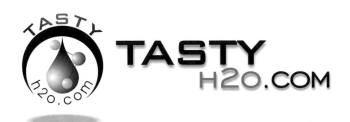

10.

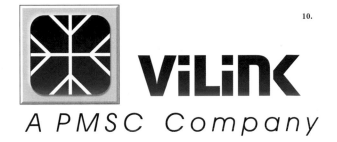

11.

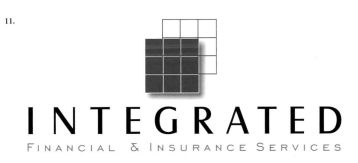

12.

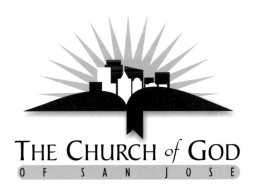

13.

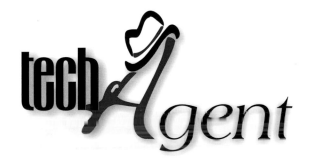

14.

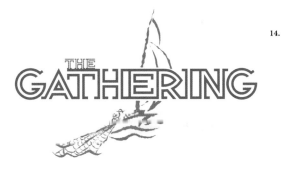

15.

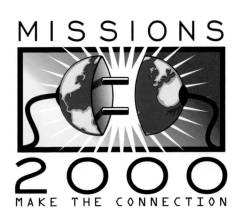

(all)

Design Firm Imagine Graphics

1. Client   The Mortgage Network
   Designer Steve Guy

2. Client   Almaden Press
   Designer Steve Guy

3. Client   Nat'l Assoc. of Missions Pastors
   Designer Steve Guy

4. Client   Nevada Institute for
           Money Management
   Designer Steve Guy

5. Client   Rocky Mountain Soda Company
   Designer Steve Guy

6. Client   South Valley Christian Church
   Designer Kyle Maxwell

7. Client   The Creeks Alzheimer's
           & Dementia Care Ctrs.
   Designer Kyle Maxwell

8. Client   First Baptist Church of Los Altos
   Designer Kyle Maxwell

9. Client   TastyH$_2$O.com
   Designer Steve Guy

10. Client   ViLink
    Designer Steve Guy

11. Client   Integrated Financial
    Designers Steve Guy & Kyle Maxwell

12. Client   Church of God of San Jose
    Designer Kyle Maxwell

13. Client   Tech-Agent, Inc.
    Designer Steve Guy

14 - 15
   Client   South Valley Christian Church
   Designer Kyle Maxwell

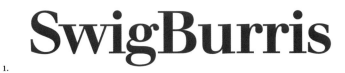

1.

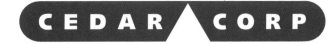

2.

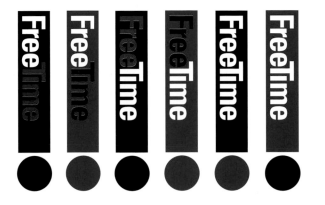

3.

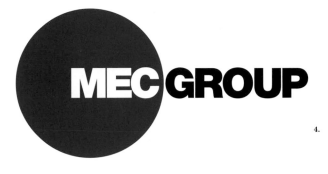

4.

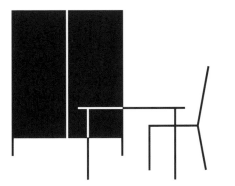

5.

6.

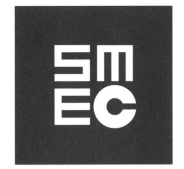

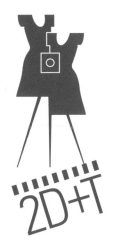

7.

1 - 7
Design Firm   Red Square Design

1. Client   Swig Burris
    Designer   Nadine Hajjar

2. Client   Cedar Corp.
    Designers   Lev Zeitlin & Nadine Hajjar

3. Client   Free Time
    Designer   Lev Zeitlin

4. Client   Middle East Capital Group
    Designers   Lev Zeitlin & Nadine Hajjar

5. Client   Borja Veciana
    Designer   Lev Zeitlin

6. Client   Société Moderne D'Enterprise
                  et de commerce (SMEC)
    Designer   Lev Zeitlin

7. Client   Two Dresses and a Tripod
    Designer   Lev Zeitlin

(opposite)
Design Firm   Walsh & Associates

    Designers   Miriam Lisco, Iskra Johnson
                  & Mark Ely

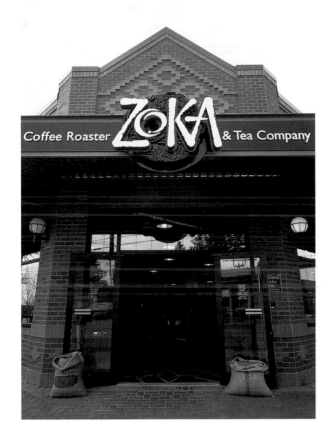

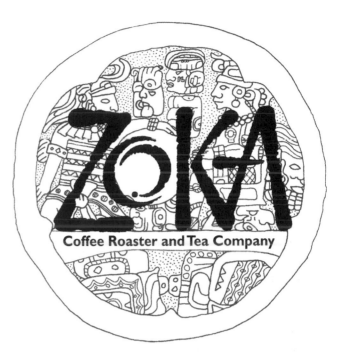

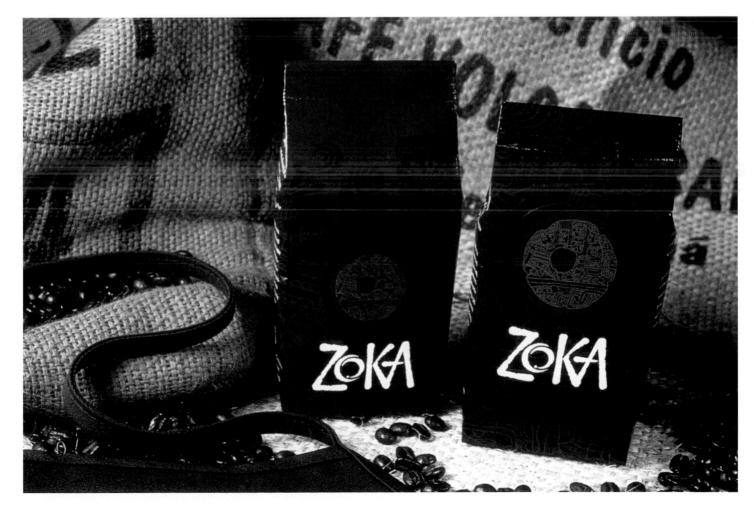

1.

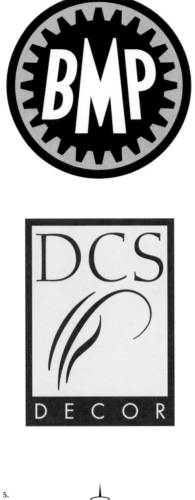

2.

GroupWyse

Working Together Wisely

3.

DCS

DECOR

4.

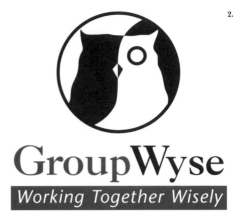

5.

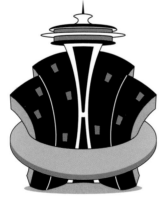

6.

MERRY HAVEN

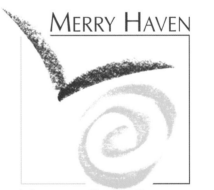

HEALTH CARE CENTER

7.

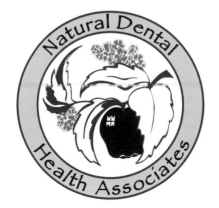

8.

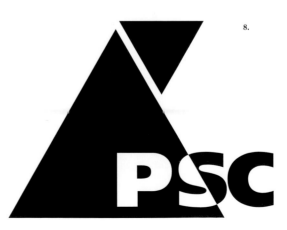

9.

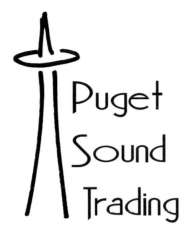

Puget Sound Trading

10.

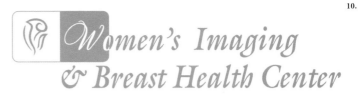

Women's Imaging & Breast Health Center

11.

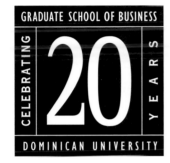

GRADUATE SCHOOL OF BUSINESS
CELEBRATING **20** YEARS
DOMINICAN UNIVERSITY

12.

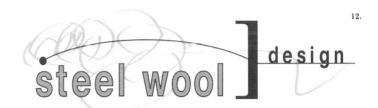

steel wool] design

13.

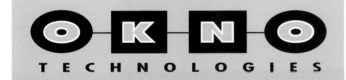

OKNO TECHNOLOGIES

14.

OIL CAPITAL ELECTRIC

15.

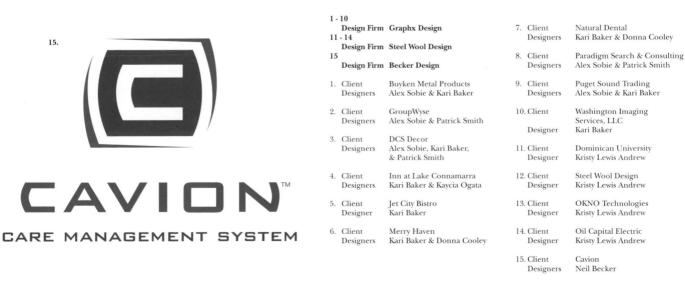

CAVION™
CARE MANAGEMENT SYSTEM

1 - 10
Design Firm Graphx Design
11 - 14
Design Firm Steel Wool Design
15
Design Firm Becker Design

1. Client   Buyken Metal Products
   Designers   Alex Sobie & Kari Baker

2. Client   GroupWyse
   Designers   Alex Sobie & Patrick Smith

3. Client   DCS Decor
   Designers   Alex Sobie, Kari Baker,
               & Patrick Smith

4. Client   Inn at Lake Connamarra
   Designers   Kari Baker & Kaycia Ogata

5. Client   Jet City Bistro
   Designer   Kari Baker

6. Client   Merry Haven
   Designers   Kari Baker & Donna Cooley

7. Client   Natural Dental
   Designers   Kari Baker & Donna Cooley

8. Client   Paradigm Search & Consulting
   Designers   Alex Sobie & Patrick Smith

9. Client   Puget Sound Trading
   Designers   Alex Sobie & Kari Baker

10. Client   Washington Imaging
               Services, LLC
    Designer   Kari Baker

11. Client   Dominican University
    Designer   Kristy Lewis Andrew

12. Client   Steel Wool Design
    Designer   Kristy Lewis Andrew

13. Client   OKNO Technologies
    Designer   Kristy Lewis Andrew

14. Client   Oil Capital Electric
    Designer   Kristy Lewis Andrew

15. Client   Cavion
    Designers Neil Becker

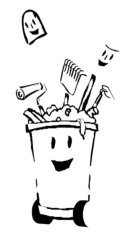

1.

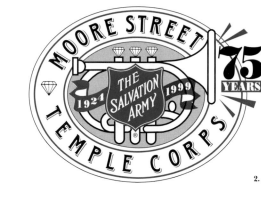

2.

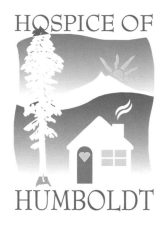

3.

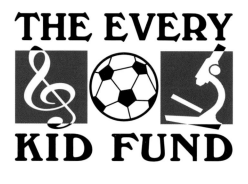

4.

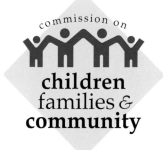

5.

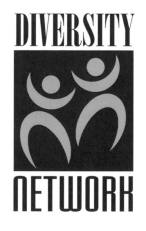

6.

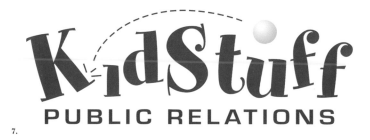

7.

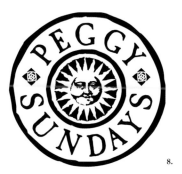

8.

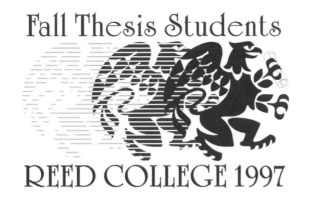

Fall Thesis Students

REED COLLEGE 1997

9.

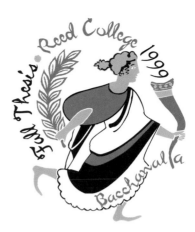

10.

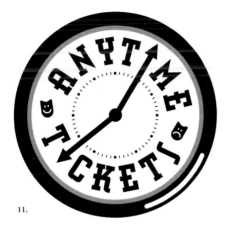

11.

BLACK BOX

12.

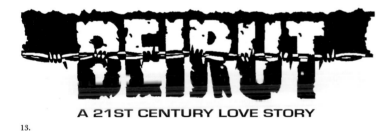

BEIRUT

A 21ST CENTURY LOVE STORY

13.

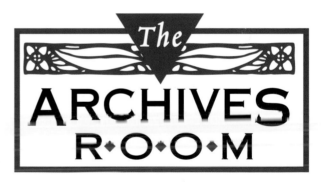

The
ARCHIVES
R·O·O·M

14.

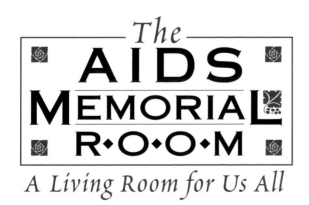

The
AIDS
MEMORIAL
R·O·O·M
A Living Room for Us All

15.

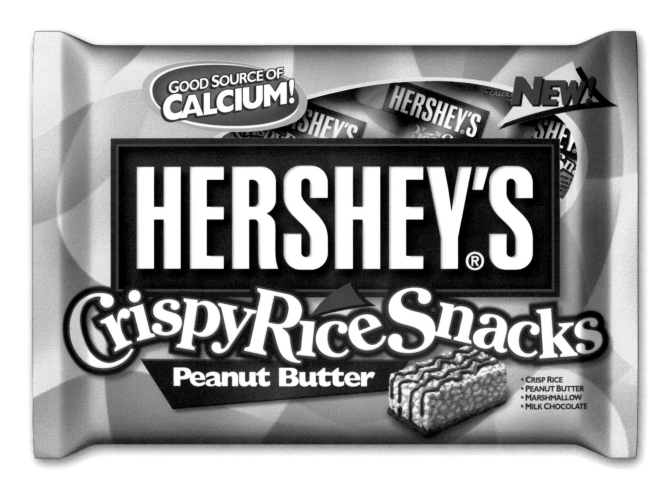

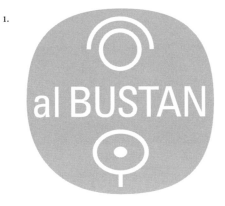

1.

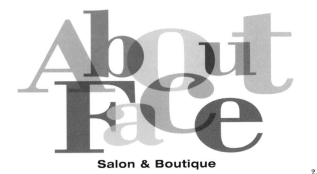

2.

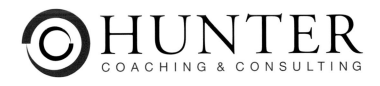

3.

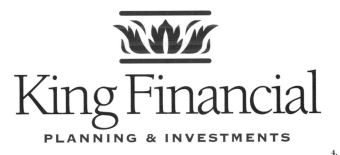

4.

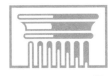

5.

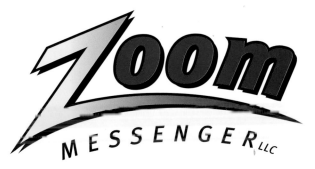

6.

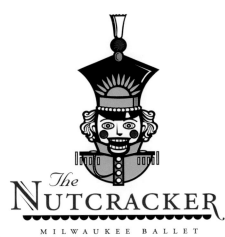

7.

(opposite)
Design Firm Zunda Design Group

Client   Hershey Chocolate U.S.A.
Designers   Jon Voss & Charles Zunda

1.
Design Firm Red Square Design
2 - 7
Design Firm Becker Design

1. Client   Al Bustan
   Designers   Lev Zeitlin & Nadine Hajjar

2. Client   About Face
   Designer   Neil Becker

3. Client   Hunter Coaching
              and Consulting
   Designers   Neil Becker, Lisa Gaertig

4. Client   King Financial
   Designer   Neil Becker

5. Client   CUNA Brokerage Services, Inc.
   Designer   Neil Becker

6. Client   Zoom Messenger, llc
   Designer   Neil Becker

7. Client   Milwaukee Ballet
   Designer   Neil Becker

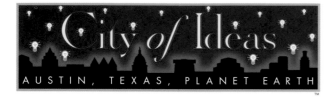

1.

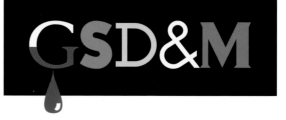

2.

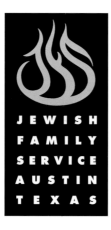

3.

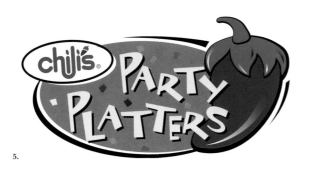

4.

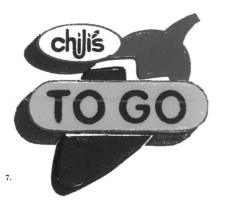

5.

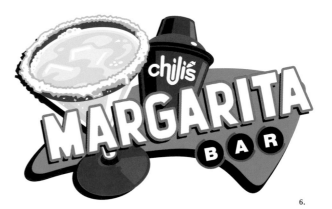

6.

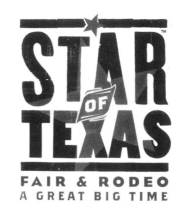

7.

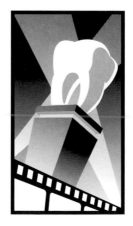

8.

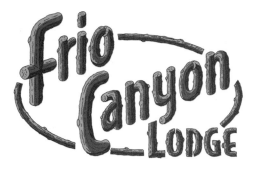

9.

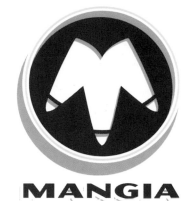

MANGIA

10.

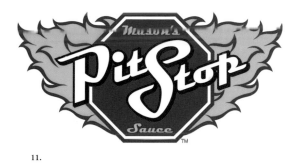

11.

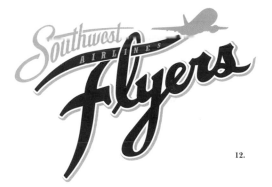

12.

14.

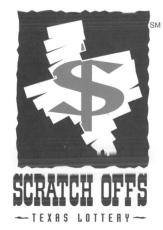

SCRATCH OFFS
- TEXAS LOTTERY -

13.

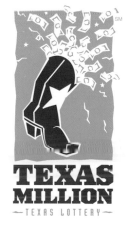

TEXAS
MILLION
- TEXAS LOTTERY -

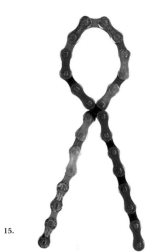

15.

(all)
Design Firm GSD&M

1. Client   City of Austin
    Designers   Marty Erhart & Tim McClure

2. Client   GSD&M
    Designers   Marty Erhart & Heather Segrest

3. Client   Jewish Family Service
    Designer   Marty Erhart

4. Client   Star of Texas Fair & Rodeo
    Designer   Patrick Nolan

5, 6
    Client   Chili's Grill & Bar
    Designer   Matt Mason

7. Client   Chili's Grill & Bar
    Designers   Matt Mason & Paul Rogers

8. Client   Dr. Larry "Hoppy" Lane, Dentist
    Designer   Matt Mason

9. Client   Frio Canyon Lodge
    Designer   Matt Mason

10. Client   Mangia Pizza
    Designer   Matt Mason

11. Client   Mason's Pit Stop Sauce
    Designer   Matt Mason

12. Client   Southwest Airlines
    Designer   Matt Mason

13, 14
    Client   Texas Lottery Commission
    Designer   Matt Mason

15. Client   Hill Country Ride for AIDS
    Designer   Marty Erhart

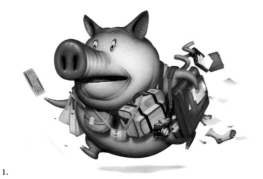

1.

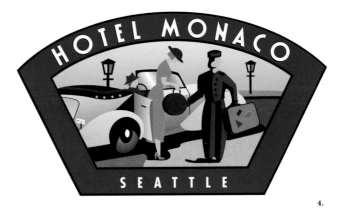

2.

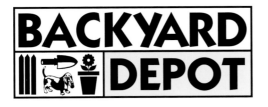

3.

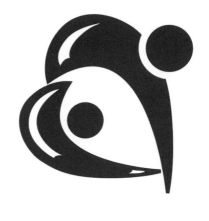

4.

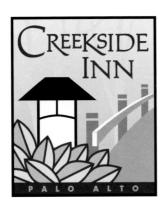

5.

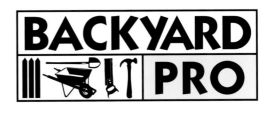

6.

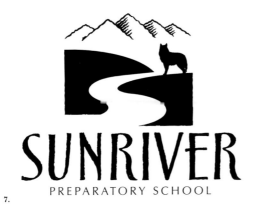

7.

1 - 2
Design Firm GSD&M
3 - 4
Design Firm Lori Powell Design Exploration
5 - 7
Design Firm Jeff Fisher LogoMotives

1. Client   Southwest Airlines
   Designers   Marty Erhart & Dale Minor

2. Client   Pennzoil/Avance
                 Educational Program
   Designer   Neyssan Moshref

3. Client   Greystone Hospitality
   Designer   Lori Powell

4. Client   Kimpton Group
   Designer   Lori Powell

5, 6 Client   Backyard Depot
    Designers   Jeff Fisher

7. Client   TriAd
                 (Sunriver Preparatory School)
   Designers   Jeff Fisher & Sue Fisher

(opposite)
Design Firm Kollberg/Johnson

   Client   Ambi Inc.
   Designers   Kollberg/Johnson

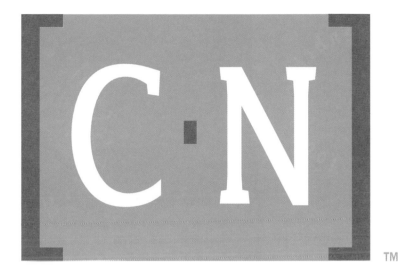

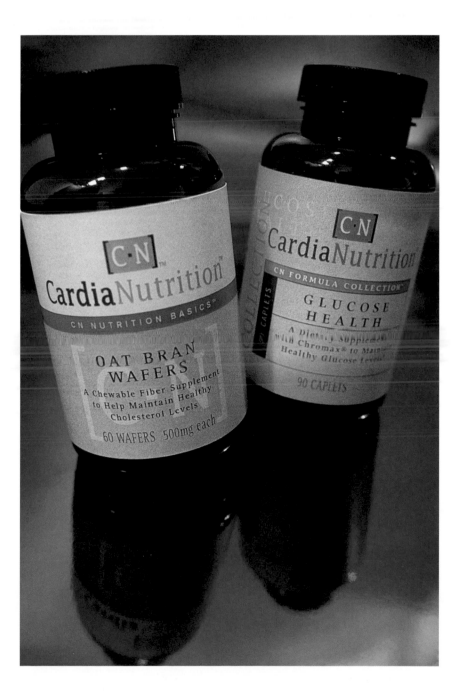

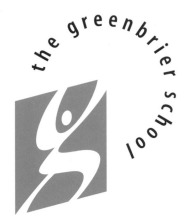

1.

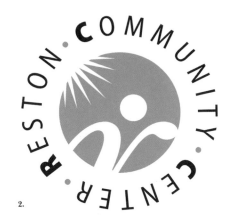

2.

SYNTONICS

3.

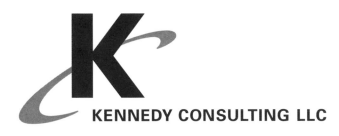

KENNEDY CONSULTING LLC

4.

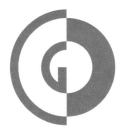

Cox Design Group llc

5.

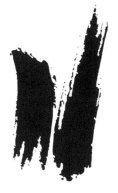

namasté

6.

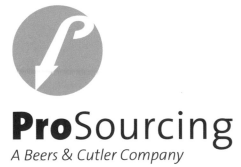

ProSourcing

A Beers & Cutler Company

7.

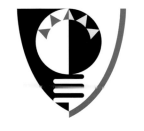

Jagtiani+Associates

Protecting your ideas

8.

204

9.

10.

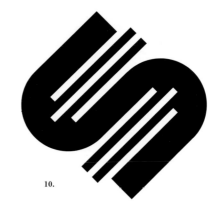

12.

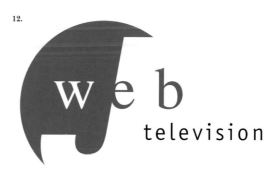

11.

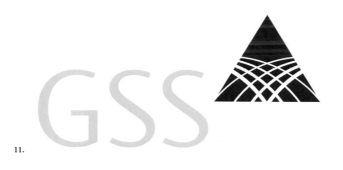

GSS

w e b
television

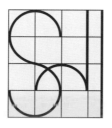

SAYLORS
Dental Laboratory, Inc.

13.

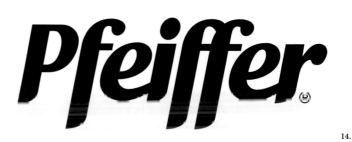

Pfeiffer

14.

15.

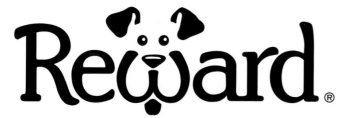

Reward®

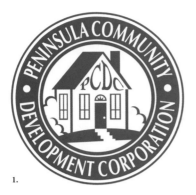

1.

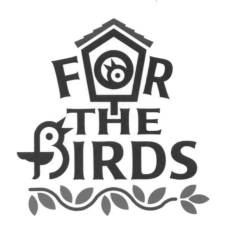

2.

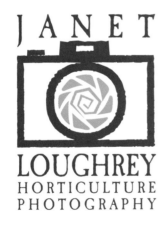

3.

Oregon Emerald

4.

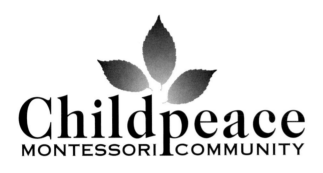

5.

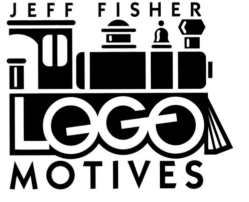

6.

7.

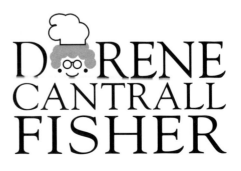

8.

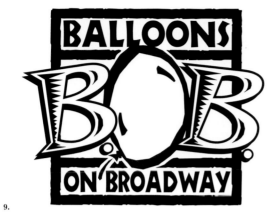

9.

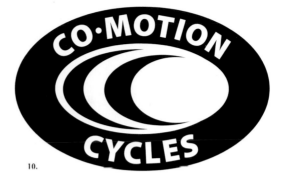

10.

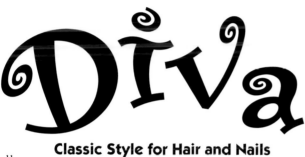

Classic Style for Hair and Nails

11.

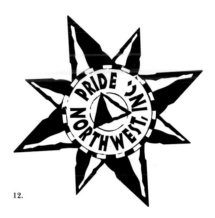

12.

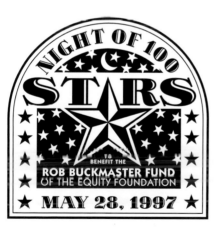

13.

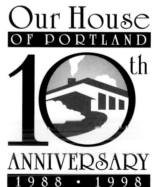

14.

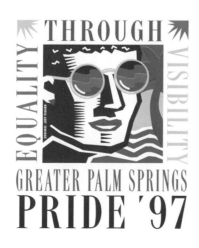

15.

1 - 15

Design Firm Jeff Fisher LogoMotives

1. Client   Portsmouth Community
            Development Corporation
   Designer   Jeff Fisher

2. Client   Junior League of Portland
   Designer   Jeff Fisher

3. Client   Childpeace Montessori
            Community
   Designer   Jeff Fisher

4. Client   Oregon Daily Emerald
   Designer   Jeff Fisher

5. Client   Janet Loughrey
            Horticulture Photography
   Designer   Jeff Fisher

6. Client   Jeff Fisher LogoMotives
   Designer   Jeff Fisher

7. Client   Kimberly Webster
   Designer   Jeff Fisher

8. Client   Dorene Cantrall Fisher
   Designer   Jeff Fisher

9. Client   Balloons on Broadway
   Designer   Jeff Fisher

10. Client   Co•Motion Cycles
    Designers   Jeff Fisher & Jerril Nilson

11. Client   Diva
    Designer   Jeff Fisher

12. Client   Pride Northwest, Inc.
    Designer   Jeff Fisher

13. Client   Rob Buckmaster Fund
    Designer   Jeff Fisher

14. Client   Our House of Portland
    Designer   Jeff Fisher

15. Client   Greater Palm Springs Pride, Inc.
    Designer   Jeff Fisher

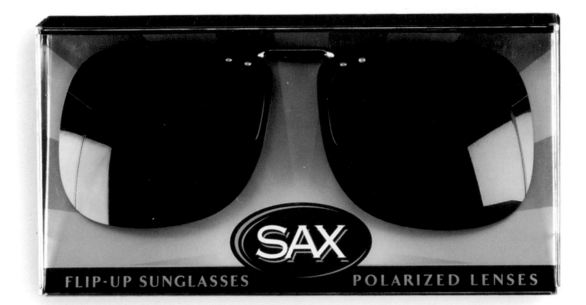

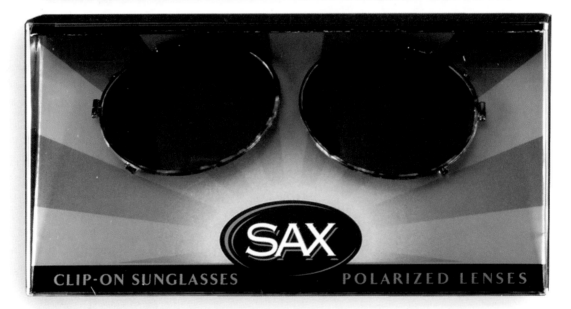

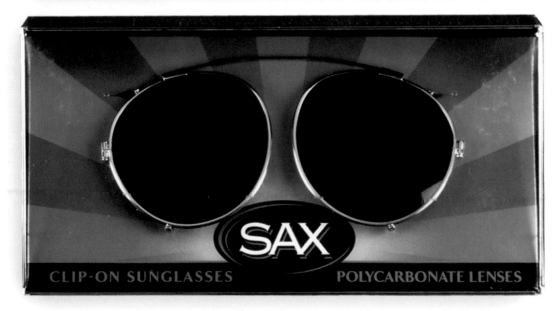

1.

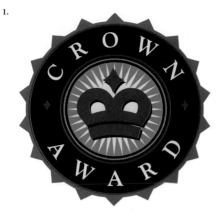

2.

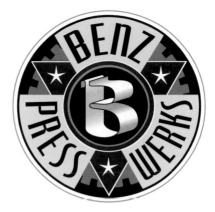

3.

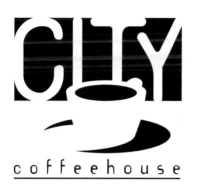

4.

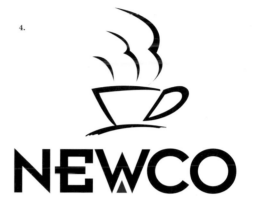

5.

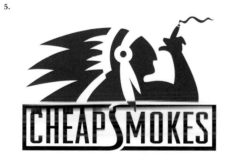

6.

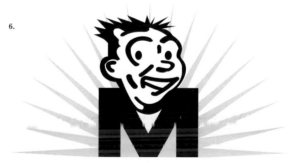

7.

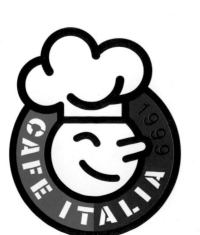

(opposite)
Design Firm Zunda Design Group

Client   Sax
Designers   Charles Zunda & Todd Nickel

1 - 7
Design Firm Bartels & Company, Inc.

1. Client   The Crown Awards
    Designers   Ron Rodemacher
                & David Bartels

2. Client   Benz Press Werks
    Designers   Bob Thomas & David Bartels

3. Client   City Coffee House
    Designer   John Postlewait

4. Client   Newco, Inc.
    Designers   David Bartels &
                Ron Rodemacher

5. Client   Cheap Smokes
    Designers   John Postlewait & David Bartels

6. Client   Cybermill
    Designers   David Bartels &
                Ron Rodemacher

7. Client   Holy Redeemer Church
    Designers   Ron Rodemacher &
                David Bartels

J J Gumberg Co.

2. VICTORIA + CO

1.

3.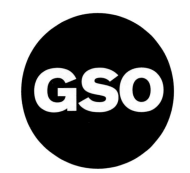

4.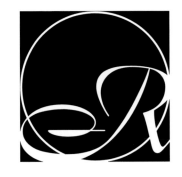

5.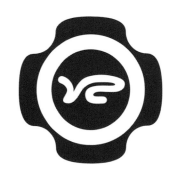

6.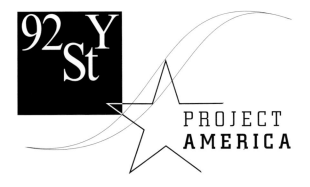

7.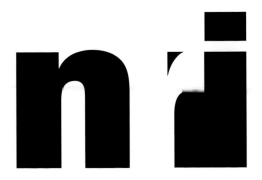

8.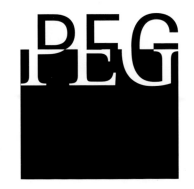

9.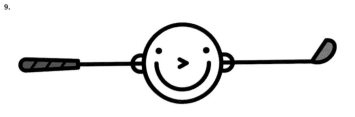

10.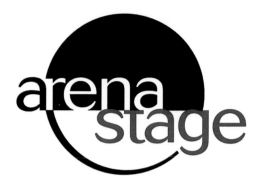

11.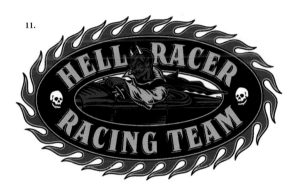

12.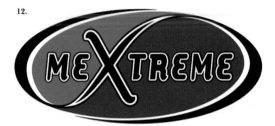

14.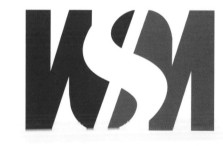

13.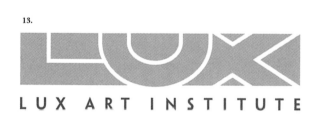

15.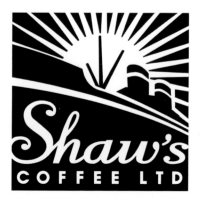

1 - 4, 6 - 8
Design Firm Poulin + Morris
5
Design Firm Swieter Design
9 - 13
Design Firm Mires Design
14 - 15
Design Firm Bartels & Co., Inc.

1. Client   J. J. Gumberg Co
   Designers   L. Richard Poulin
   & Jonathan Posnett

2. Client   Victoria + Co
   Designers   Douglas Morris &
   L. Richard Poulin

3. Client   GSO Graphics Inc.
   Designers   Douglas Morris &
   Robert Patrick Festino

4. Client   Ridgeway Center
   Designer   Douglas Morris

5. Client   The Dr. Benjamin Remedy

6. Client   Bratskeir + Company
   Designers   Douglas Morris &
   L. Richard Poulin

7. Client   National Reprographics, Inc.
   Designers   Douglas Morris &
   L. Richard Poulin

8. Client   Planned Expansion Group Inc.
   Designer   Douglas Morris

9. Client   G.ball.com
   Designers   Scott Mires, Miguel Perez,
   & Tracy Sabin

10. Client   Arena Stage
    Designers   Scott Mires & Miguel Perez

11. Client   Hell Racer
    Designers   José Serrano, Miguel Perez,
    & Dan Thoner

12. Client   Schiedermayer & Assoc.
    Designers   José Serrano, Jeff Samaripa,
    & Miguel Perez

13. Client   Lux Art Institute
    Designers   John Ball & Miguel Perez

14. Client   Magna Bank
    Designers   Ron Rodemacher
    & David Bartels

15. Client   Shaw's Coffee Ltd.
    Designer   Brian Barclay

1.

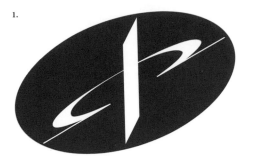

2.

Lightship

3.

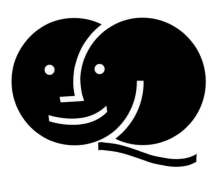

4.

CM
OG

5.

Holiday
Open
house

6.

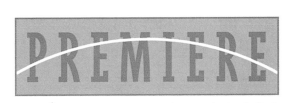

PREMIERE
WE'RE GOING PLACES

7.

Luau on the Lagoon
Sea Breeze School

1 - 5
Design Firm Q. Cassetti
6 - 7
Design Firm Look

1. Client   Omega One Communications
    Designer   Q. Cassetti

2. Client   Lightship Telecom LLC
    Designer   Q. Cassetti

3. Client   Quest Diagnostics Incorporated
    Designer   Q. Cassetti

4. Client   Corning Museum of Glass
    Designers   Q. Cassetti & Rob Cassetti

5. Client   Corning Museum of Glass
    Designers   Q. Cassetti & Rob Cassetti

6. Client   Premiere, Limousine Company
    Designer   Betsy Todd

7. Client   Sea Breeze Preschool
    Designer   Betsy Todd

(opposite)
Design Firm DYNAPAC DesignGroup

    Client   Advance Plastics
    Designer   Lee A. Aellig

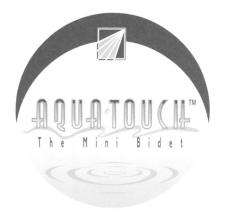

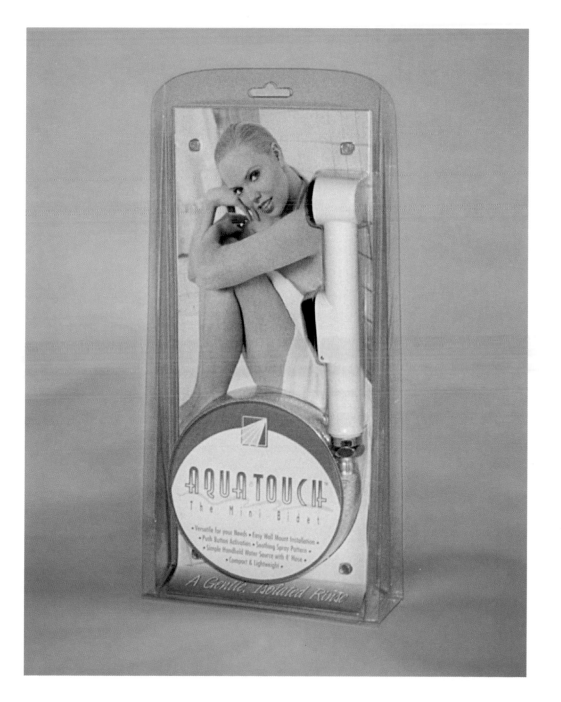

1.

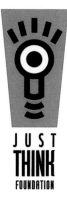

JUST
THINK
FOUNDATION

2.

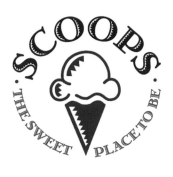

3.

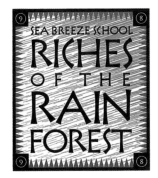

SEA BREEZE SCHOOL
RICHES
OF THE
RAIN
FOREST

4.

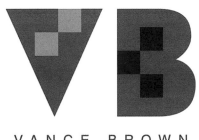

VANCE BROWN
BUILDERS

5.

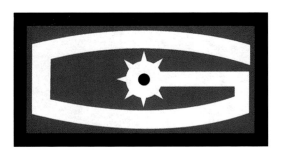

6.

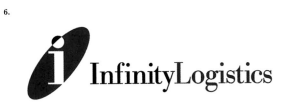

InfinityLogistics

7.

TexasExecs
EXECUTIVES OF TEXAS
HOMES FOR CHILDREN

8.

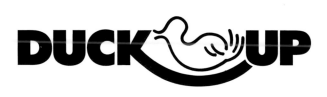

214

9.

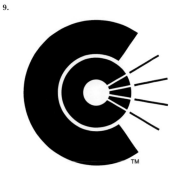

10.

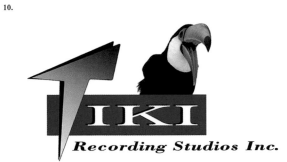

11.

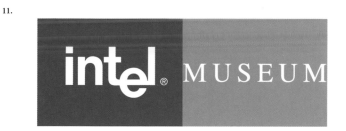

12.

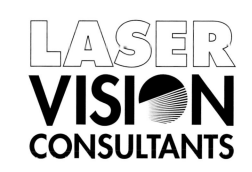

13.

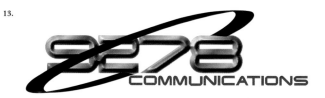

14.

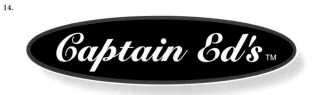

15.

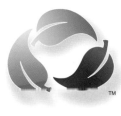

ZOELLNER
ARTS
CENTER

LEHIGH University

1.

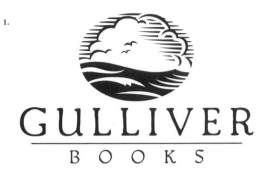

GULLIVER
B O O K S

2.

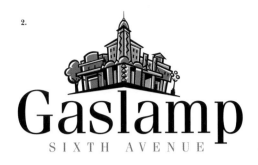

Gaslamp
SIXTH AVENUE

3.

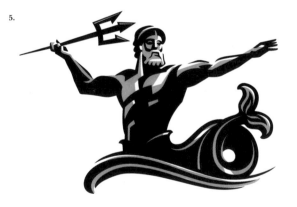

4.

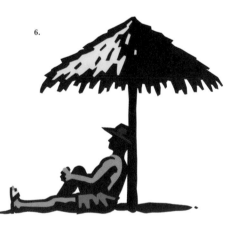

5.

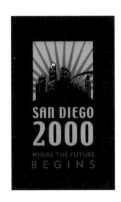

6.

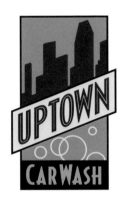

7.

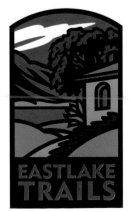

8.

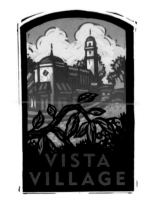

9.

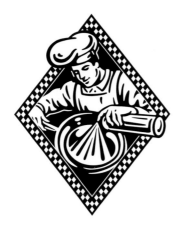

10.

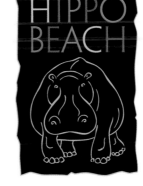

11.

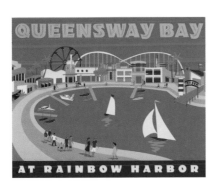

HIPPO BEACH

12.

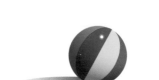

14.

the **W**ordsmith

OCEANPLACE

13.

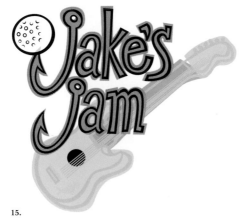

15.

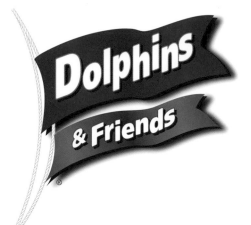

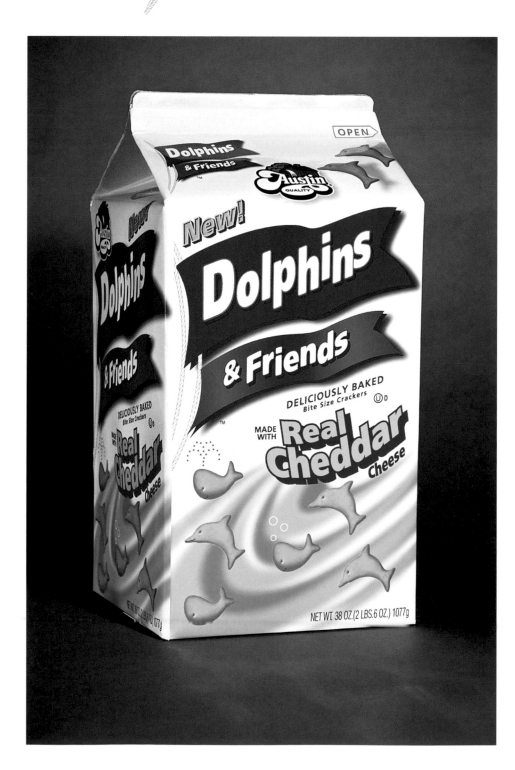

1.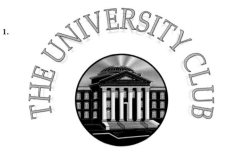

2.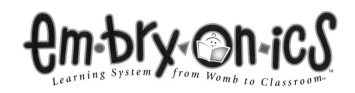

3.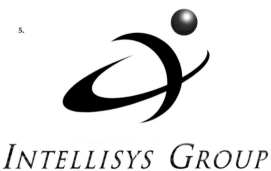

4.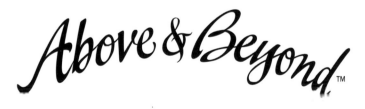

5.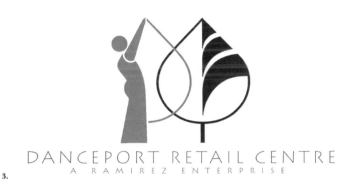

6.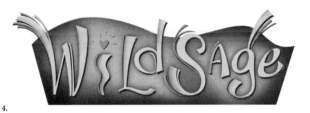

7.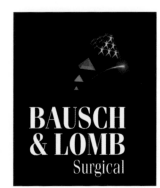

(opposite)
Design Firm   Dixon & Parcels Associates, Inc.

Client	Austin Quality Foods

1

Design Firm   Cathey Associates, Inc.
2 - 4, 6 - 7
Design Firm   The Dupuis Group
5

Design Firm   Callery & Company

1. Client   The University Club
   Designers   Matt Westapher
                & Gordon Cathey

2. Client   Munchkin
   Designers   Bill Corridori, Jack Halpern,
                & Nobuko Komine

3. Client   Firehouse Subs
   Designer   John Silva

4. Client   Local Squeeze
   Designers   Steven DuPuis &
                Nobuko Komine

5. Client   Danceport
   Designer   Kelley Callery

6. Client   Van Kind Foods
   Designers   Bill Corridori, Nobuko Komine,
                & Jack Halpern

7. Client   Bausch & Lomb Surgical
   Designers   Bill Corridori & Jack Halpern

1.

MARINA
ACCESSORIES

2.

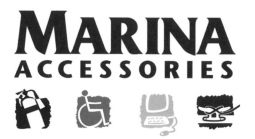

MONAGHAN
&COMPANY

BUILDING DOMINANT BRANDS

3.

BioMetrics
SUPPLEMENT SYSTEMS ™

4.

Botanical
LABORATORIES

5.

PACIFIC CREST

6.

DCI·ENGINEERS
D'AMATO CONVERSANO INC.

7.

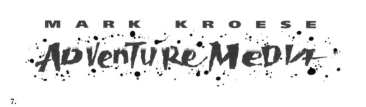

MARK KROESE
AdVenture MeDia

8.

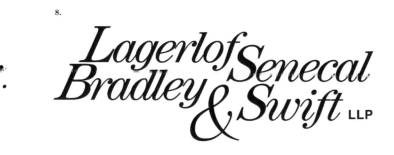

Lagerlof Senecal
Bradley & Swift LLP

220

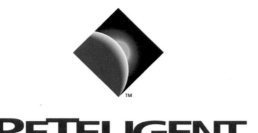

RETELIGENT
C O R P O R A T I O N

9.

10.

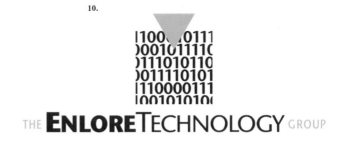

THE **ENLORE**TECHNOLOGY GROUP

11.

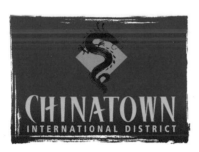

12.

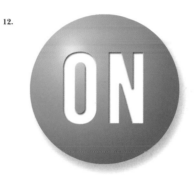

14.

13.

15.

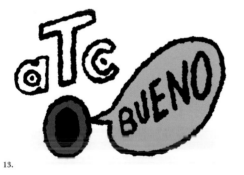

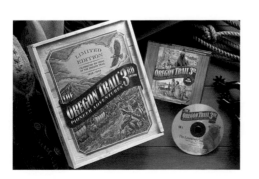

ALLCAR MOTORSPORTS
BOBBY ALLISON / DAVE CARROLL MOTORSPORTS

1.

2.

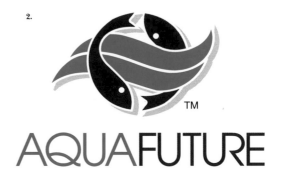

AQUAFUTURE

3.

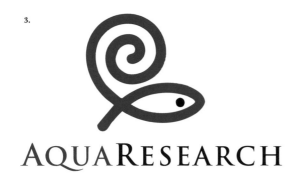

AQUARESEARCH

4.

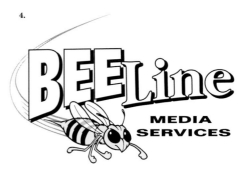

6.

BLUE FIN CAFE & BILLIARDS

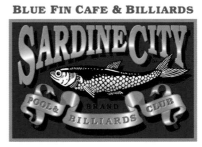

CANNERY ROW - MONTEREY, CA

5.

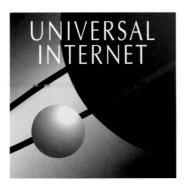

7.

UNIVERSAL INTERNET

1 - 7
Design Firm The Wecker Group

1   Client   Allcar Motor Sports
    Designer   Robert Wecker

2. Client   Aqua Future, Inc.
    Designers   Robert Wecker & Matt Gnibus

3. Client   Aqua Future, Inc.
    Designers   Robert Wecker & Matt Gnibus

4. Client   Beeline Media Services
    Designer   Robert Wecker

5. Client   Blue Fin Billiards
    Designer   Robert Wecker

6. Client   Blue Fin Billiards
    Designer   Robert Wecker

7. Client   Universal Internet
    Designer   Robert Wecker

(opposite)
Design Firm Lister Butler Consulting

    Client   Horizon Blue Cross Blue Shield
                  of New Jersey
    Designer   William Davis

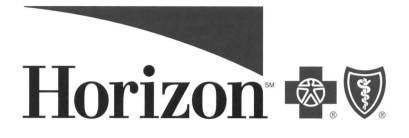

Horizon Blue Cross Blue Shield
of New Jersey

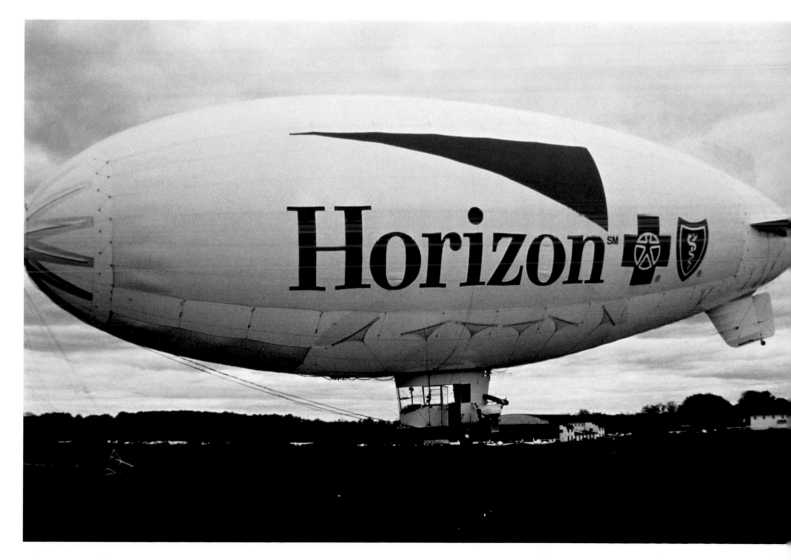

223

1.

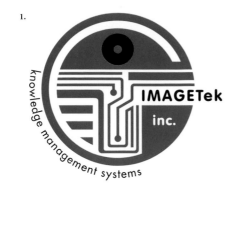

2.

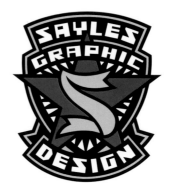

3.

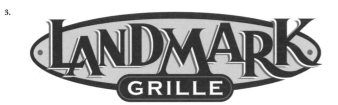

4.

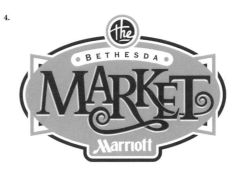

5.

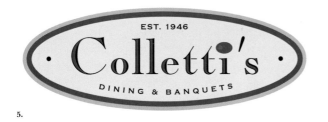

6.

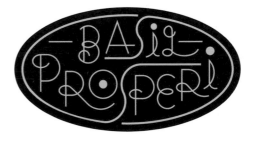

7.

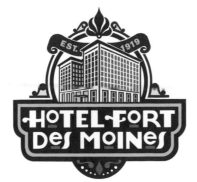

8.

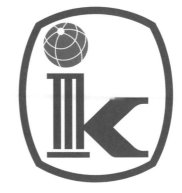

224

9.

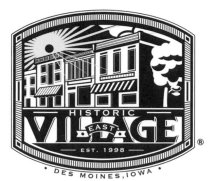

10.

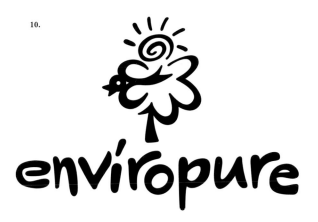

11.

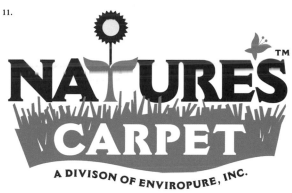

12.

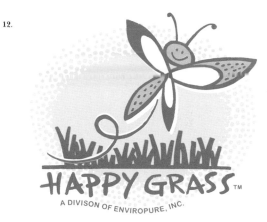

13.

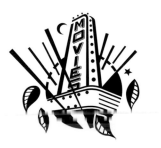

14.

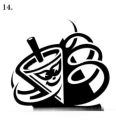  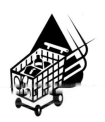 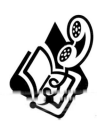

"Ariel"

"Hawk"

15.

1.

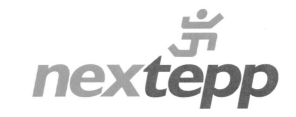

2.

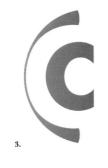

nextepp

3.

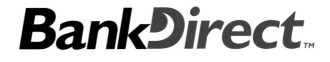

4.

5.

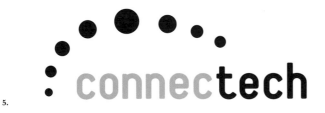

6.

BankDirect™

7.

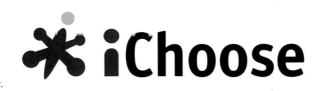

iChoose

8.

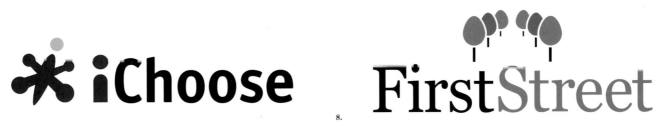

FirstStreet

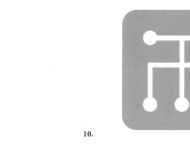

9.

10.

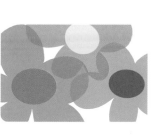

11.

12.

13.

Mary McMinn

14.

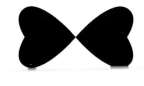

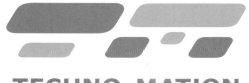

TECHNO-MATION

15.

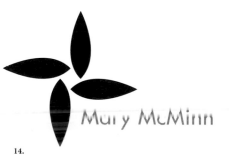

1
Design Firm Cathey Associates, Inc.
2 - 15
Design Firm Swieter Design

1. Client   Media Research Corporation
             of America
   Designers   Isabel Campos
             & Gordon Cathey

2. Client   Nextepp
   Designer   Mark Ford

3. Client   Supre Inc.
   Designers   Mark Waggoner
             & Carlos A. Perez

4. Client   Supre - Skin System
   Designer   Erica Brinker

5. Client   Connectech
   Designer   Mark Waggoner

6. Client   Bank Direct
   Designer   Carlos A. Perez

7. Client   iChoose
   Designers   Mark Waggoner, John Swieter,
             & Carlos A. Perez

8. Client   First Street
   Designers   Ray Gallegos & Carlos A. Perez

9. Client   Techtonic
   Designer   Carlos A. Perez

10. Client   T-Mech
    Designer   Ray Gallegos

11. Client   Melissa Ronan
    Designer   Mark Waggoner

12. Client   Inertia
    Designer   Carlos A. Perez

13. Client   Dallas Heart Ball
    Designer   Ray Gallegos

14. Client   Mary McMinn
    Designer   Mark Waggoner

15. Client   Techno-Mation
    Designer   Carlos A Perez

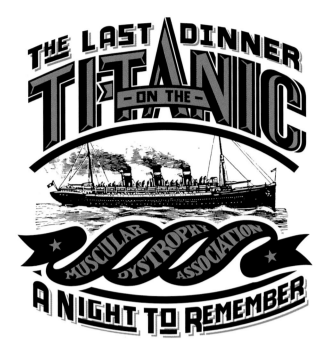

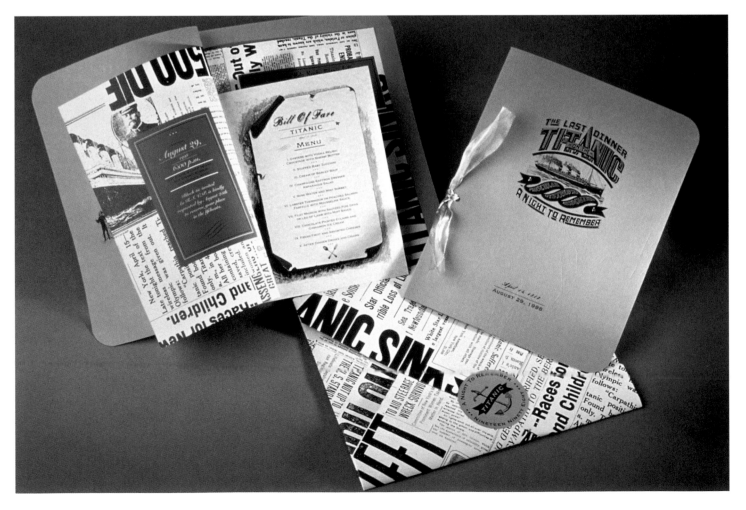

1.

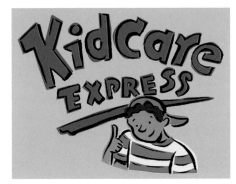

2.

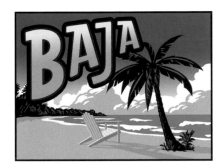

3.

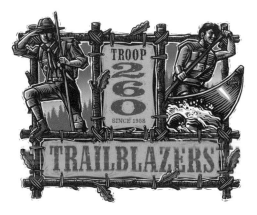

4.

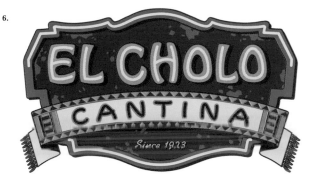

5.

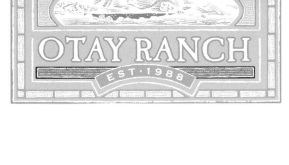

6.

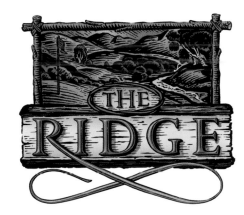

7.

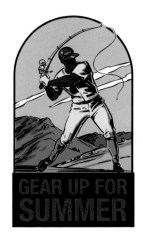

(opposite)

Design Firm	**Sayles Graphic Design**	1.	Client	Kidcare Express
			Designers	June Lewis & Tracy Sabin
Client	Muscular Dystrophy Association "Last Dinner on the Titanic"	2.	Client	Rubio's Baja Grill
Designer	John Sayles		Designers	Jeff Payne & Tracy Sabin
1		3.	Client	Otay Ranch
Design Firm	**Lewis Design**		Designers	Ron Fleming & Tray Sabin
2, 7				
Design Firm	**Vitro Robertson**	4.	Client	The Ridge
3			Designers	Cory Sheehan & Tracy Sabin
Design Firm	**Tyler Blik Design**	5.	Client	Boy Scout Troop 260
4			Designers	José Serrano & Tracy Sabin
Design Firm	**The Flowers Group**			
5		6.	Client	El Cholo
Design Firm	**Mires Design**		Designers	Clare Sebenius & Tracy Sabin
6				
Design Firm	**Maddocks & Co.**	7.	Client	Shimano Resort
			Designers	John Bade & Tracy Sabin

1.

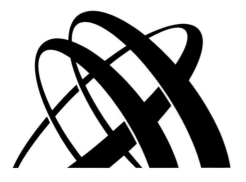

3.

2.

4.

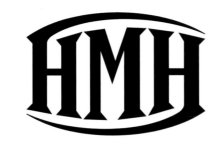

5.

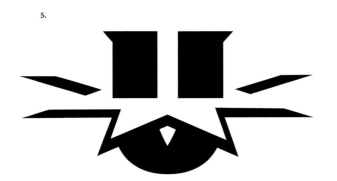

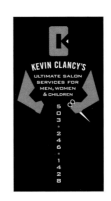

6.

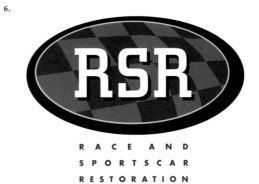

7.

8.

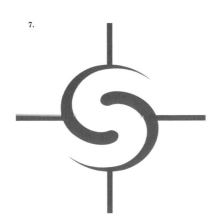

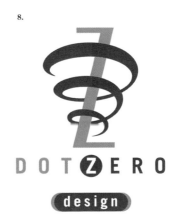

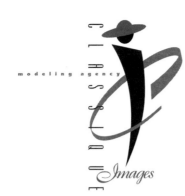

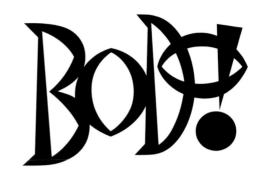

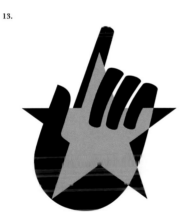

14

TechShield

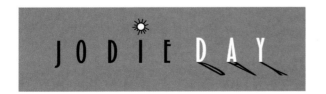

JODIE DAY

(all)

Design Firm	**Dotzero Design**	
1. Client	Miller-Norris	
Designers	Jon Wippich & Karen Wippich	
2. Client	Literacy Volunteers	
Designers	Jon Wippich & Karen Wippich	
3. Client	HMH Advertising & Public Relatons	
Designer	Jon Wippich	
4. Client	Kevin Clancy's	
Designers	Jon Wippich & Karen Wippich	
5. Client	Underground Storage	
Designers	Karen Wippich & Jon Wippich	
6. Client	RSR	
7. Client	Standard Printing	
Designers	Jon Wippich & Karen Wippich	

8. Client	Dotzero Design	
Designers	Karen Wippich & Jon Wippich	
9. Client	Classique Images	
Designers	Karen Wippich & Jon Wippich	
10. Client	The Bodo Ensemble	
Designers	Karen Wippich & Jon Wippich	
11. Client	Mostella Records	
Designers	Jon Wippich & Karen Wippich	
12. Client	Planet Salon	
Designers	Karen Wippich & Jon Wippich	
13. Client	Star Advisors	
Designers	Jon Wippich & Karen Wippich	
14. Client	HMH Adv./Louisiana-Pacific	
Designer	Jon Wippich	
15. Client	Jodie Day	
Designers	Karen Wippich & Jon Wippich	

1.

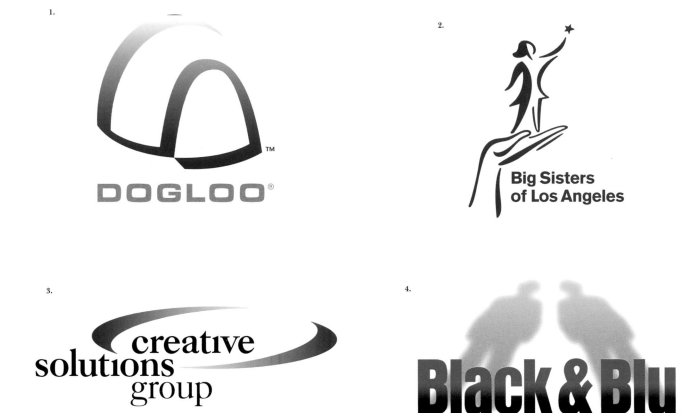

DOGLOO ®

2.

Big Sisters
of Los Angeles

3.

creative
solutions
group

4.

Black & Blu
ENTERTAINMENT

5.

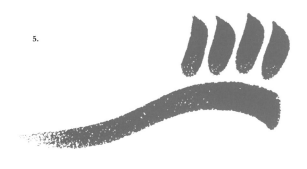

6.

C\\\C

7.

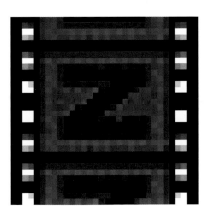

1 - 7

Design Firm Zamboo

1. Client   Dogloo
    Designer   Dave Zambotti

2. Client   Big Sisters of LA
    Designer   Dave Zambotti

3. Client   Creative Solutions Group
    Designer   Becca Bootes

4. Client   Black & Blu
    Designers   Dave Zambotti & Jeff Allison

5. Client   Premiere Dental
    Designers   Dave Zambotti & Becca Bootes

6. Client   CMC
    Designers   Becca Bootes & Dave Zambotti

7. Client   Zfilmmaker
    Designer   Dave Zambotti

(opposite)
Design Firm Sabingrafik, Inc.

    Client   Odyssey
    Designers   Lisa Peters & Tracy Sabin

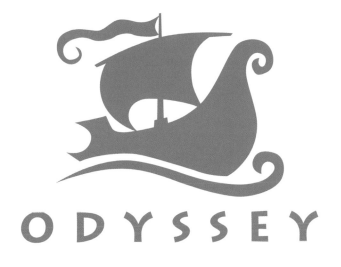

ODYSSEY

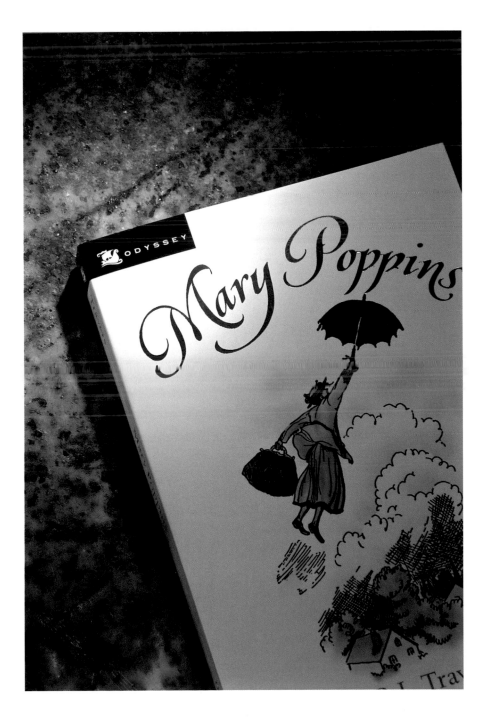

1.

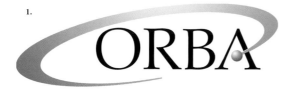

2.

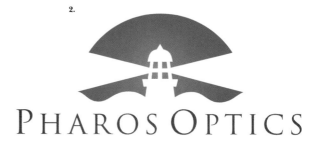

3.

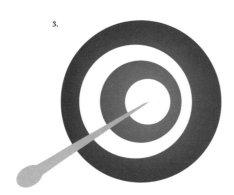

4.

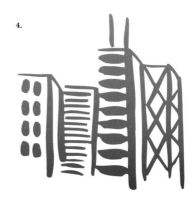

5.

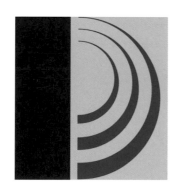

6.

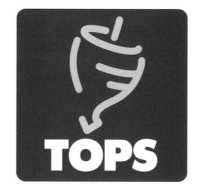

7.

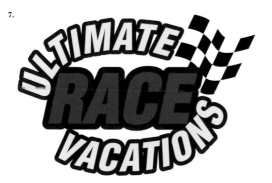

8.

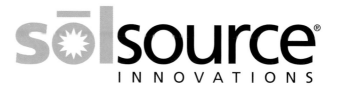

9.

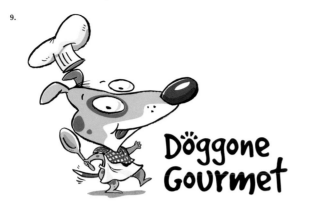

10.

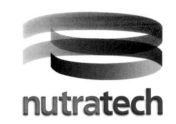

11.

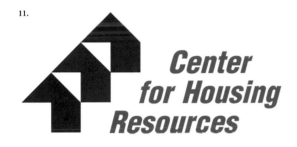

12.

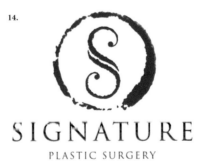

13.

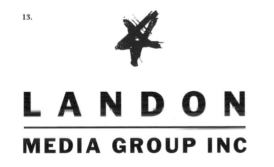

14.

SIGNATURE
PLASTIC SURGERY

15.

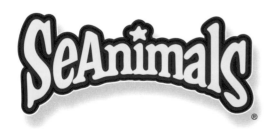

1.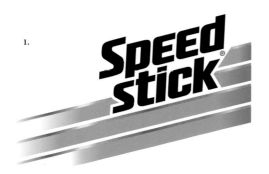

2.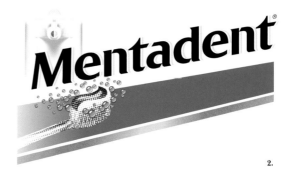

3.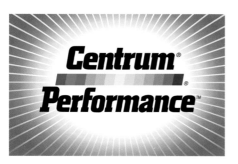

4.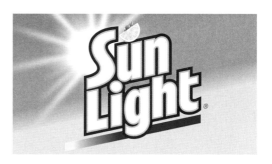

5.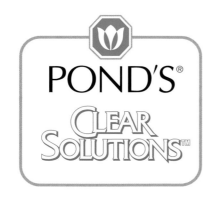

6.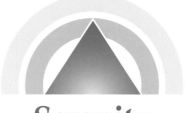

7.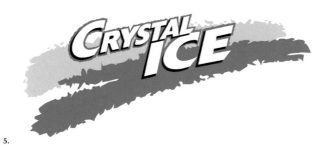

8.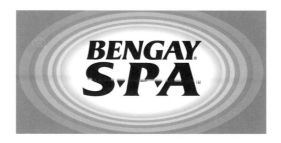

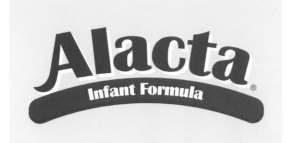

9.

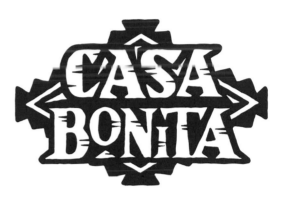

10.

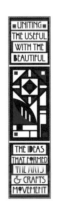

11.

12.

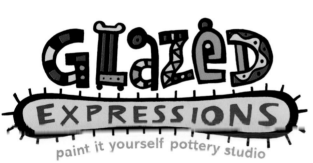

13.

14.

15.

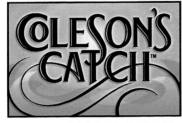

1 - 9
Design Firm Hans Flink Design Inc.
10 - 14
Design Firm Sayles Graphic Design
15
Design Firm Faine-Oller Productions, Inc.

1. Client   Colgate-Palmolive (Speed Stick)
   Designers   Mark Krukonis
        & Susan Kunschaft

2. Client   Unilever HPC, USA
        (Mentadent)
   Designer   Chang-Mei Lin

3. Client   Whitehall-Robins
        (Centrum Performance)
   Designers   Chang-Mei Lin
        & Susan Kunschaft

4. Client   Unilever HPC, USA (Sunlight)
   Designers   Michael Troian
        & Harry Bertschmann

5. Client   Unilever HPC, USA
        (Crystal Ice)
   Designers   Susan Kunschaft
        & Chang-Mi Lin

6. Client   Serenity Garden & Home
   Designers   Loi Van Name & Hans D. Flink

7. Client   Unilever HPC, USA
        (Pond's Clear Solutions)
   Designers   Chang Mei-Lin, Susan
        Kunschaft, & Michael Troian

8. Client   Pfizer Inc. (Bengay SPA)
   Designer   Chang-Mei Lin

9. Client   Mead Johnson (Alacta)
   Designer   Susan Kunschaft

10. Client   Starr Litigation Services, Inc.
    Designer   John Sayles

11. Client   Barrick Roofing
    Designer   John Sayles

12. Client   Casa Bonita
    Designer   John Sayles

13. Client   Glazed Expressions
    Designer   John Sayles

14. Client   Pattee Enterprises
    Designer   John Sayles

15. Client   Coleson Foods, Inc.
    Designers   Catherine Oller, Barbara Faine,
         Bruce Hale, & Steve Coppin

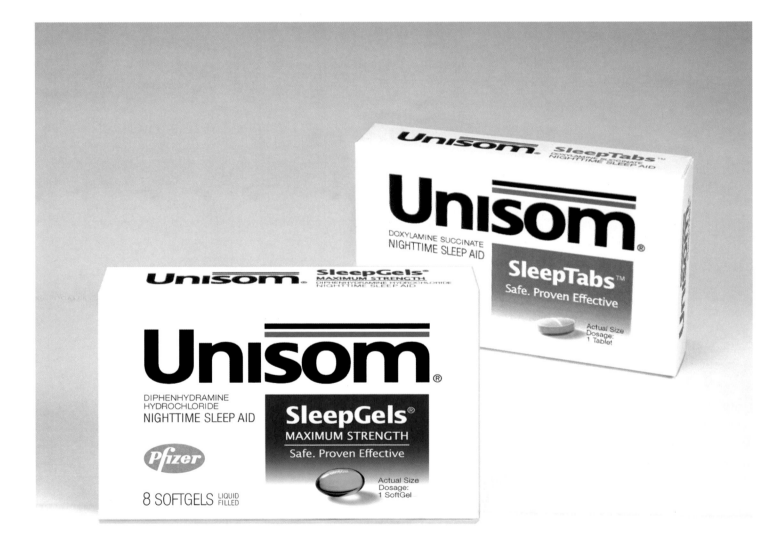

1.

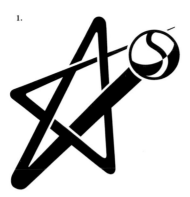

2.

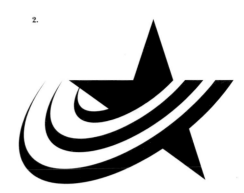

3.

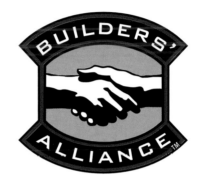

4.

5.

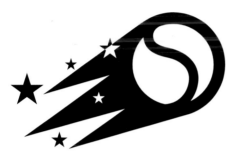

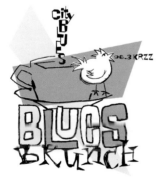

6.

7.

(opposite)
Design Firm Hans Flink Design Inc.

Client   Pfizer Inc. (Unisom)
Designers   Michael Troian
                  & Harry Berschmann

1 - 7
Design Firm Dotzero Design

1. Client   Star Advisors Softball Team
    Designers   Jon Wippich & Karen Wippich

2. Client   Star Advisors Program Logo
    Designers   Karen Wippich & Jon Wippich

3. Client   Star Advisors Night Flight Event
    Designers   Jon Wippich & Karen Wippich

4. Client   HMH Advertising/
                  Louisiana-Pacific
    Designer   Jon Wippich

5. Client   The Wichita Blues Society,
                  Blues Brunch
    Designers   Karen Wippich & Jon Wippich

6. Client   Wichita Blues Society
    Designers   Karen Wippich & Jon Wippich

7. Client   Andrew Tamerius Photography
    Designers   Karen Wippich & Jon Wippich

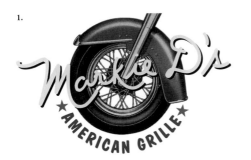

1.

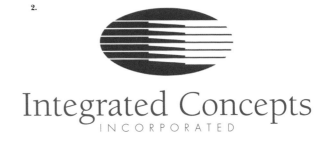

2.

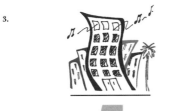

3.

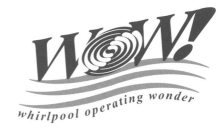

4.

Adamm's

5.

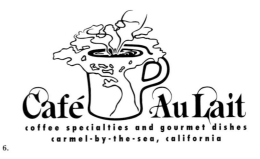

6.

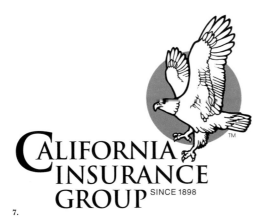

7.

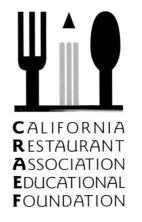

8.

9.

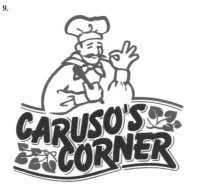

10.

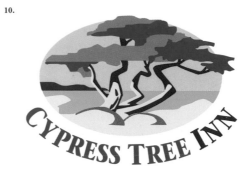

11.

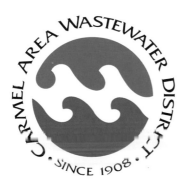

12.

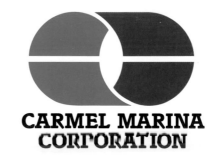

13.

14.

CARMEL MARINA
CORPORATION

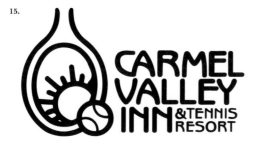

15.

CARMEL
VALLEY
INN &TENNIS
RESORT

1 - 5
Design Firm Innovative Design & Advertising
6 - 11, 13 - 15
Design Firm The Wecker Group
12
Design Firm Maxi Harper Graphics

1. Client   Markie D's Restaurant
   Designers   Kim Crossett-Neumann
                    & Susan Nickey-Newton

2. Client   ITM
   Designers   Kim Crossett-Neumann
                    & Susan Nickey-Newton

3. Client   ABC-5th Floor Production
                    Music Library
   Designers   Kim Crossett-Neumann
                    & Susan Nickey-Newton

4. Client   vico
   Designers   Kim Crossett-Neumann
                    & Susan Nickey-Newton

5. Client   Adamm's Stained Glass
   Designers   Kim Crossett-Neumann, Susan
                    Nickey-Newton, & Dan Cotton

6. Client   Café au Lait Restaurant
   Designers   Robert Wecker

7. Client   California Insurance Group
   Designer   Robert Wecker

8. Client   California
                    Restaurant Association
   Designer   Robert Wecker

9. Client   Caruso's Corner
   Designer   Robert Wecker

10. Client   Cypress Tree Inn
    Designer   Robert Wecker

11. Client   Cannery Row Inn
    Designer   Robert Wecker
    Illustrator   Mark Savee

12. Client   Terlingua
    Designer   Maxi Harper

13. Client   Carmel Area Waste
                    Management District
    Designer   Robert Wecker

14. Client   Carmel Marina Corporation
    Designer   Robert Wecker

15. Client   Carmel Valley Inn &
                    Tennis Resort
    Designer   Robert Wecker

1.

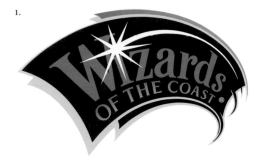

2.

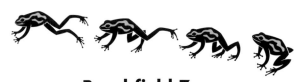

Brookfield Zoo

3.

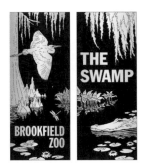

4.

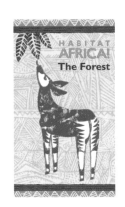

5.

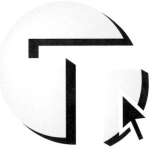

6.

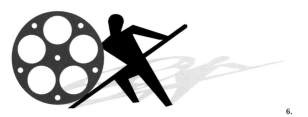

7.

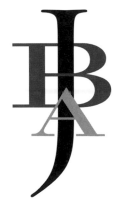

1
Design Firm Wizards/Spire Design
2 - 4
Design Firm Brookfield Zoo
5, 7
Design Firm Squires & Company
6
Designer   Brandon Murphy

1. Client   Wizards of the Coast

2, 3
    Client   Brookfield Zoo
    Designer   Hannah Jennings
    Illustrator   Edith Emmengger

4. Client   Brookfield Zoo
    Designers   Andrew Murashige &
                  Peter Skach
    Illustrator   Jeff O'Connor

5. Client   Techware Information Systems
    Designer   Anna Magruder

6. Client   Motion Projects
    Designer   Brandon Murphy

7. Client   Bill Jackson Associates
    Designer   Christie Grotheim

(opposite)
    Design Firm Sayles Graphic Design

8. Client   1999 Iowa State Fair
                  "Knock Yourself Out"
    Designer   John Sayles

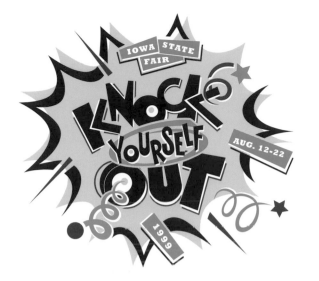

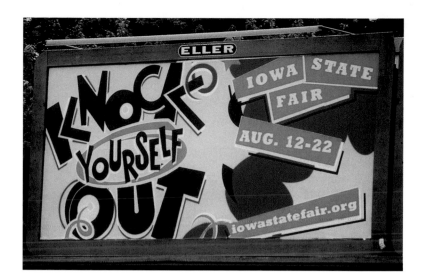

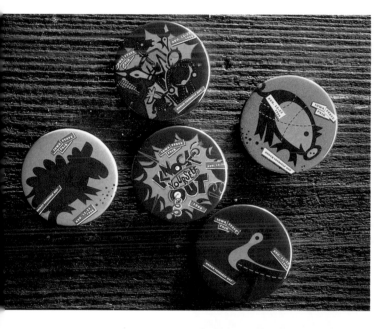

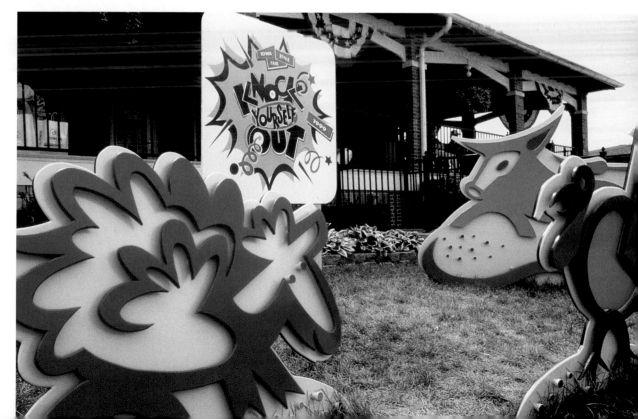

1.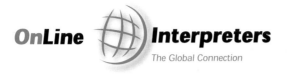

2.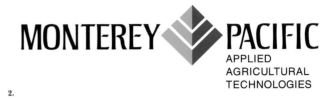

3.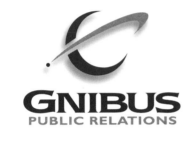

4.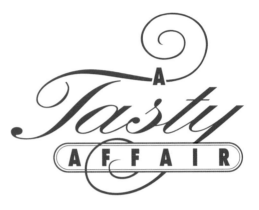

5.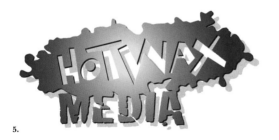

6.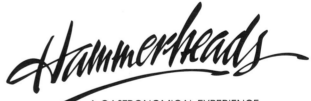

7.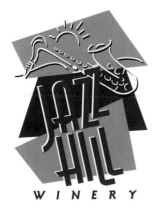

8.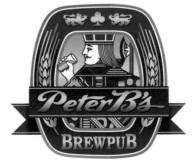

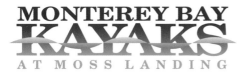

MONTEREY BAY
KAYAKS
AT MOSS LANDING

9.

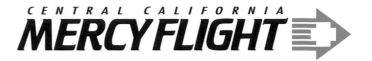

CENTRAL CALIFORNIA
MERCY FLIGHT

10.

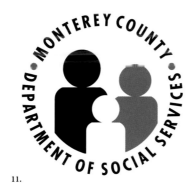

MONTEREY COUNTY · DEPARTMENT OF SOCIAL SERVICES ·

11.

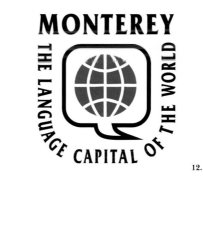

MONTEREY
THE LANGUAGE CAPITAL OF THE WORLD

12.

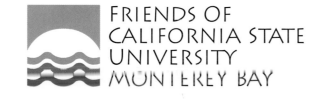

FRIENDS OF
CALIFORNIA STATE
UNIVERSITY
MONTEREY BAY

13.

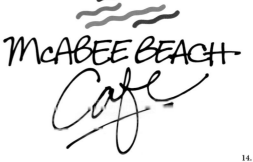

McABEE BEACH
Cafe

14.

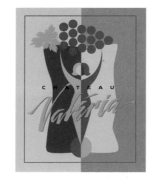

15.

(all)					
Design Firm	The Wecker Group		8. Client	Doubletree Monterey	
			Designers	Robert Wecker & Matt Gnibus	
1. Client	OnLine Interpreters, Inc.				
Designer	Robert Wecker		9. Client	Monterey Bay Kayaks	
			Designers	Robert Wecker & Matt Gnibus	
2. Client	Monterey Pacific, Inc.				
Designer	Robert Wecker		10. Client	Mercy Flight/Central California	
			Designer	Robert Wecker	
3. Client	Gnibus Public Relations				
Designer	Matt Gnibus		11. Client	Monterey County Department	
				of Social Services	
4. Client	KAZU Public Radio		Designer	Robert Wecker	
Designer	Robert Wecker				
			12. Client	City of Monterey	
5. Client	Hot Wax Media		Designer	Robet Wecker	
Designer	Robert Wecker				
			13. Client	CSU Monterey Bay	
6. Client	Hammerheads Restaurant		Designer	Robert Wecker	
Designers	Robert Wecker & Mark Savee				
			14. Client	McAbee Beach Cafe	
7. Client	CaskOne Vineyards		Designers	Robert Wecker & James Kyllo	
Designer	Robert Wecker				
			15. Client	Mink Vineyards	
			Designer	Robet Wecker	

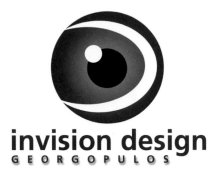

invision design
GEORGOPULOS

1.

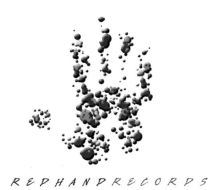

2. REDHANDRECORDS

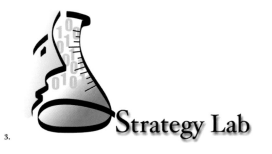
Strategy Lab

3.

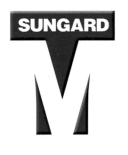

4.

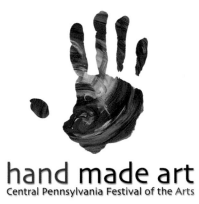

hand made art
Central Pennsylvania Festival of the Arts

5.

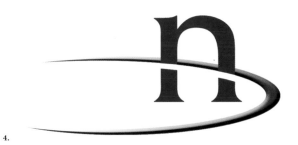

MARKETING TEAM

6.

neon

7.

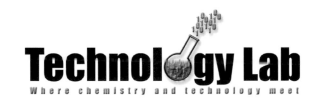

Technology Lab
Where chemistry and technology meet

8.

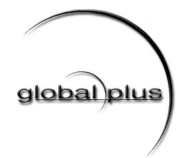

9.

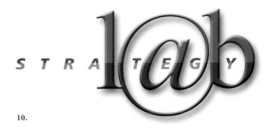

10.

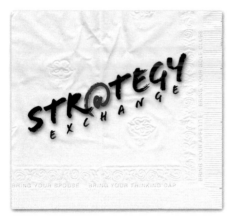

11.

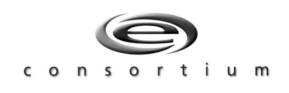

12.

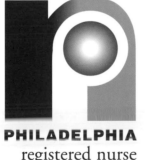

PHILADELPHIA
registered nurse
practitioner

13.

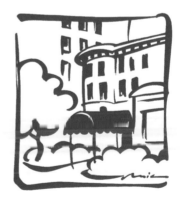

14.

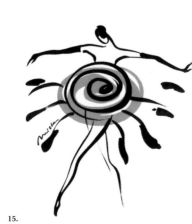

15.

1 - 13
Design Firm Georgopulos Design
14, 15
Design Firm Misha Design Studio

1. Client   Georgopulos Design
    Designer   Jonathan Georgopulos

2. Client   Red Hand Records
    Designer   Jonathan Georgopulos

3. Client   SunGard
    Designer   Jonathan Georgopulos

4. Client   N
    Designer   Jonathan Georgopulos

5. Client   Arts Fest 2000
    Designer   Jonathan Georgopulos

6. Client   SunGard
    Designer   Jonathan Georgopulos

7. Client   Neon
    Designer   Jonathan Georgopulos

8. Client   SunGard
    Designer   Jonathan Georgopulos

9. Client   Global Plus
    Designer   Jonathan Georgopulos

10, 11
    Client   SunGard
    Designer   Jonathan Georgopulos

12. Client   econsortium
    Designer   Jonathan Georgopulos

13. Client   PHL Nurse Association
    Designer   Jonathan Georgopulos

14. Client   Brookline Dental Studio
    Designer   Misha Lenn

15. Client   Boston Ballet
    Designer   Misha Lenn

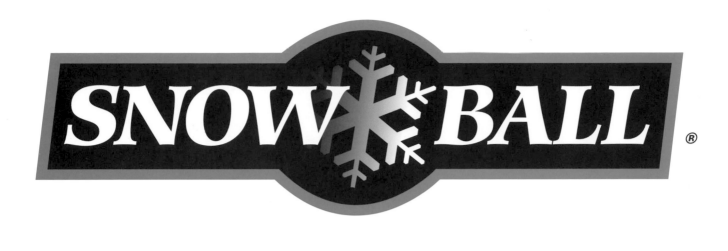

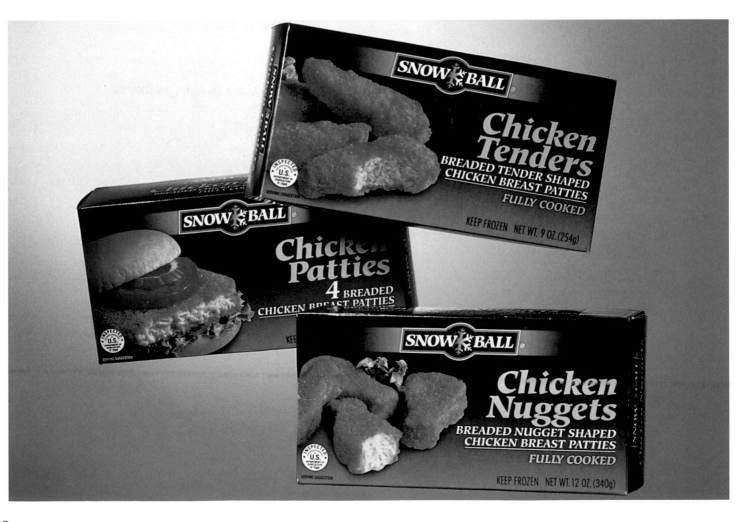

1.

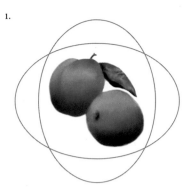

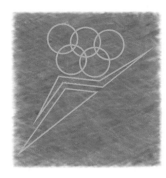

2.

3.

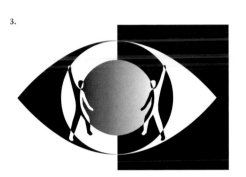

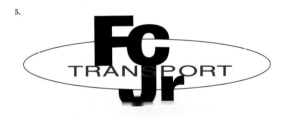

4.

5.

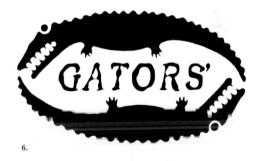

6.

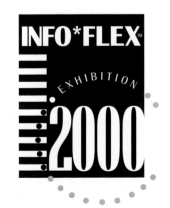

7.

(opposite)
Design Firm Kollberg/Johnson

Client   Snowball Foods
Designers   Kollberg/Johnson

1 - 6
Design Firm Rockmorris Design
7
Design Firm Callery & Company

1. Client   Peach²
    Designer   Rock Morris

2. Client   Olympic Sea & Sky
    Designer   Rock Morris

3. Client   Vis•Tech
    Designer   Rock Morris

4. Client   Inhaus Strategies
    Designer   Rock Morris

5. Client   F.C. Jr. Transport
    Designer   Rock Morris

6. Client   Gators'
    Designer   Rock Morris

7. Client   Flexographic Tech Assoc.
    Designer   Kelley Callery

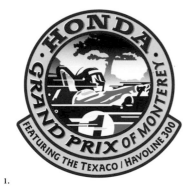

1.

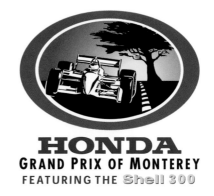

2.

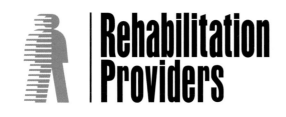

3.

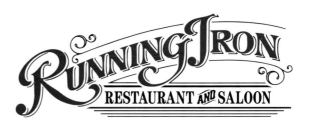

4.

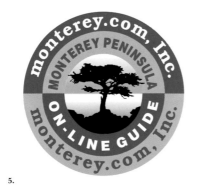

5.

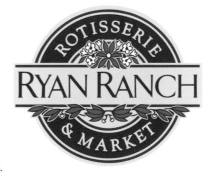

6.

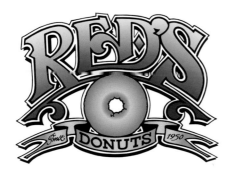

7.

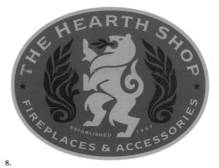

8.

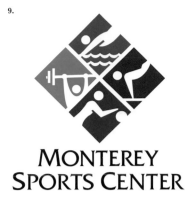

9.

MONTEREY
SPORTS CENTER

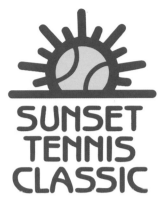

SUNSET
TENNIS
CLASSIC

10.

MONTEREY
PENINSULA
CHAMBER OF
COMMERCE

11.

LIST
ENGINEERING
COMPANY

Mechanical
Consultants

12.

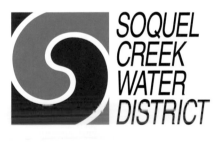

SOQUEL
CREEK
WATER
DISTRICT

13.

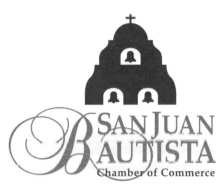

SAN JUAN
BAUTISTA
Chamber of Commerce

14.

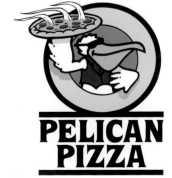

PELICAN
PIZZA

15.

1 - 15
Design Firm The Wecker Group

1, 2
Client   Laguna Seca Raceway
Designer   Robert Wecker

3. Client   Rehabilitation Providers
    Designer   Robert Wecker

4. Client   Running Iron Restaurant
    Designer   Robert Wecker
    Illustrator Mark Savee

5. Client   Monterey.com, Inc.
    Designer   Robert Wecker

6. Client   Ryan Ranch Rotisserie
    Designer   Robert Wecker

7. Client   Red's Donuts
    Designer   Robert Wecker
    Illustrator Mark Savee

8. Client   The Hearth Shop
    Designer   Robert Wecker

9. Client   Monterey Sports Center
    Designer   Robert Wecker

10. Client   Pacific Grove Rotary Club
    Designer   Robert Wecker

11. Client   Monterey Peninsula
                Chamber of Commerce
    Designer   Robert Wecker

12. Client   List Engineering Company
    Designer   Robert Wecker

13. Client   Soquel Creek Water District
    Designer   Robert Wecker

14. Client   San Juan Bautista
                Chamber of Commerce
    Designer   Robert Wecker

15. Client   Pelican Pizza
    Designer   Robert Wecker

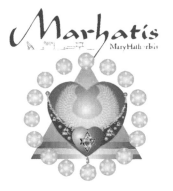

1.

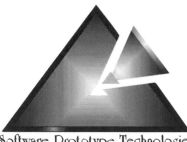

Software Prototype Technologies

2.

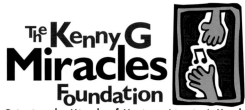

Bringing the Miracle of Music to America's Youth

3.

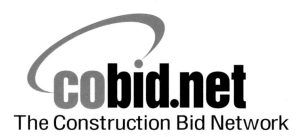

4.

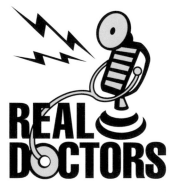

REAL DOCTORS

5.

Art Turock & Associates

6.

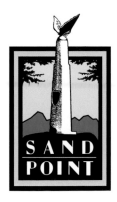

7.

1 - 2
Design Firm Maxi Harper Graphics
3 - 7
Design Firm Gable Design Group

1. Client   Marhatis: Spiritual-Healer
               of Three Goddesses
   Designer   Maxi Harper

2. Client   SPT
   Designer   Maxi Harper

3. Client   Kenny G
   Designer   Damon Nakagawa

4. Client   cobid.net
   Designer   Damon Nakagawa

5. Client   Glenn Sound
   Designers   Damon Nakagawa
               & Ayumi Inoue

6. Client   Art Turock & Associates
   Designers   Tony Gable & Damon Nakagawa

7. Client   City of Seattle
   Designers   Tony Gable & Damon Nakagawa

(opposite)
Design Firm DYNAPAC Design Group

   Client   Harbor Lights Candle Shop
   Designer   Lee A. Aellig

252

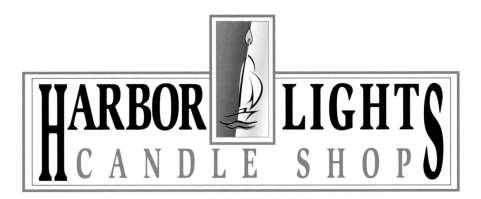

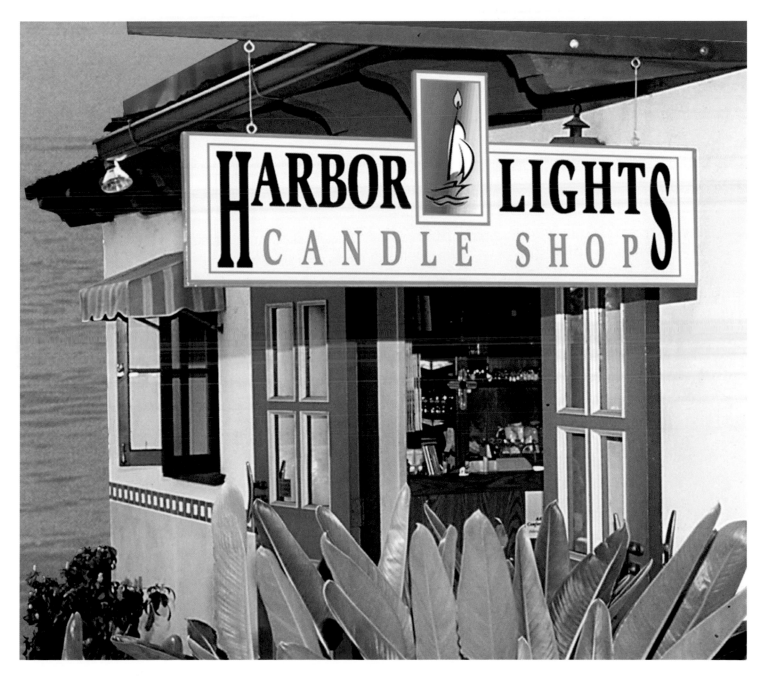

Rubbish

1.

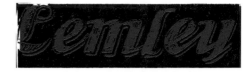

2.

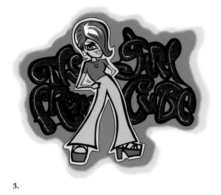

3.

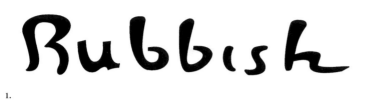

4.

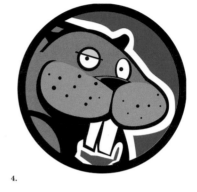

5.

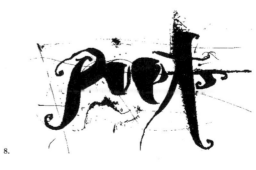

jacknabbit.com

6.

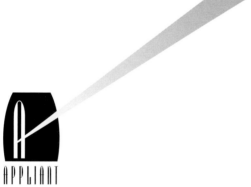

7.

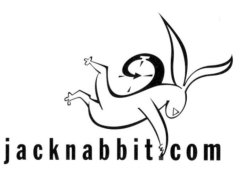

8.

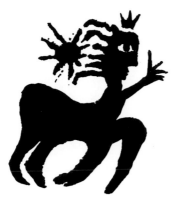

9.

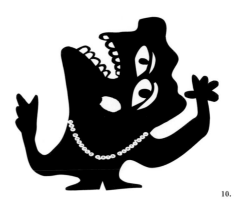

10.

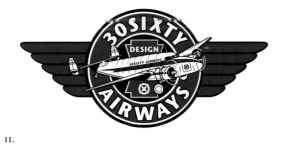

11.

CLUB 30|0|

12.

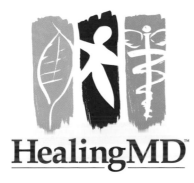

HealingMD™

13.

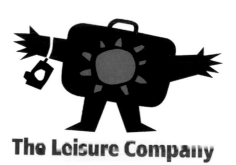

The Leisure Company

11.

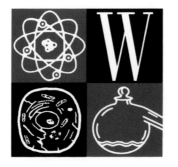

15.

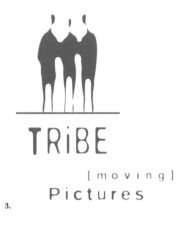

distilled images

a picture's worth

1.

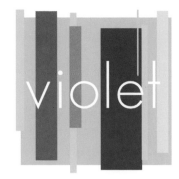

2.

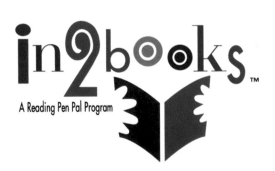

TRIBE

[moving]

Pictures

3.

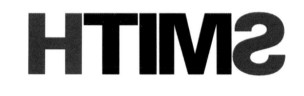

4.

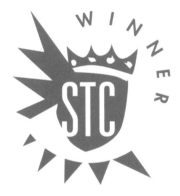

in2books™

A Reading Pen Pal Program

5.

WINNER

STC

6.

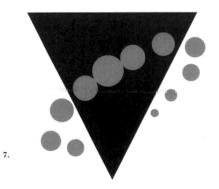

7.

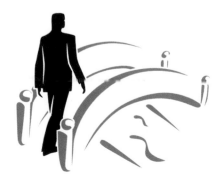

8.

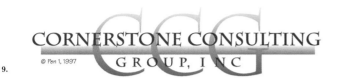

9.

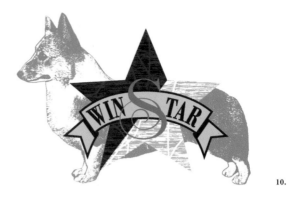

10.

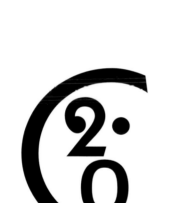

11.

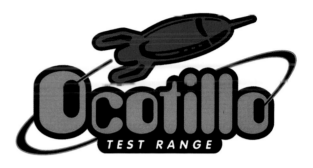

12.

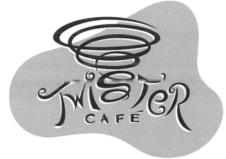

13.

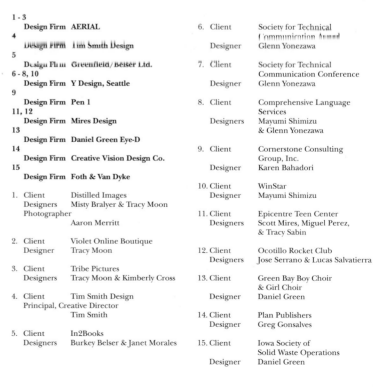

PLAN PUBLISHERS INC.

RESIDENTIAL DESIGN SOFTWARE

14.

15.

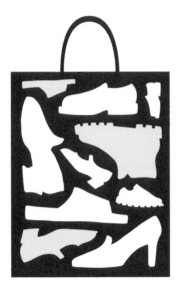

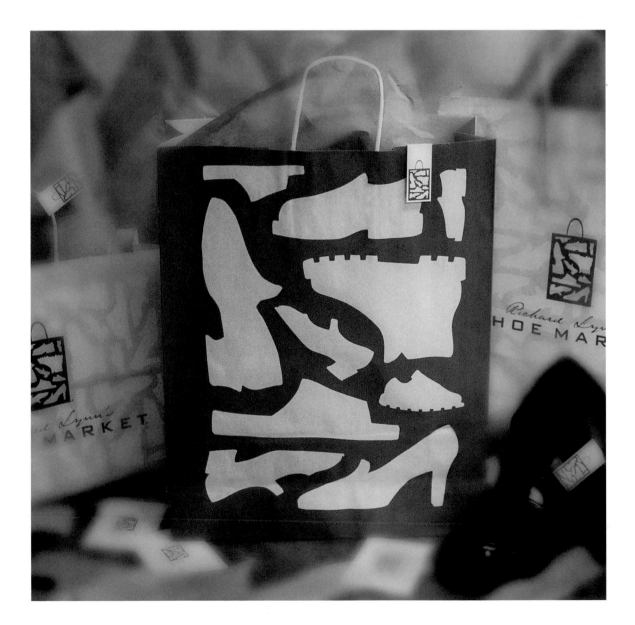

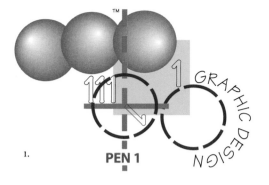

1.

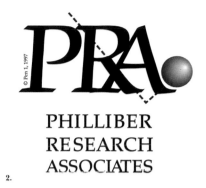

2.

PHILLIBER
RESEARCH
ASSOCIATES

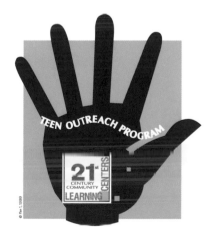

3.

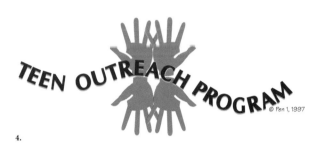

4.

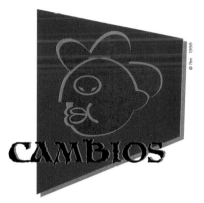

5.

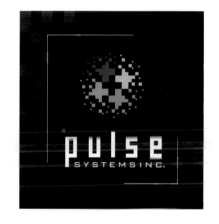

6.

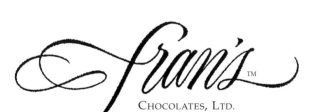

7.

(opposite)
Design Firm Insight Design Communications

Client   Richard Lynn's Shoe Market
Designers   Sherrie & Tracy Holdeman

1 - 5
Design Firm Pen 1
6
Design Firm Insight Design Communications
7
Design Firm Walsh & Associates, Inc.

1. Client   Pen 1
   Designer   Karen Bahadori

2. Client   Philliber Research Associates
   Designer   Karen Bahadori

3. Client   Teen Outreach Program/
              Cambios
   Designers Karen Bahadori &
              Alicia Colina-Ashby

4, 5
   Client   Teen Outreach Program
   Designer   Karen Bahadori

6. Client   Pulse System Inc.
   Designers Sherrie & Tracy Holdeman

7. Client   Fran's Chocolates Ltd.
   Designer   Miriam Lisco

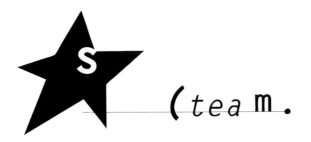

1.

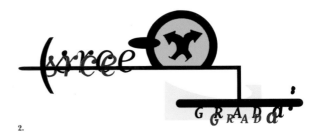

2.

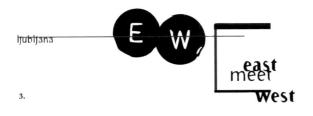

3.

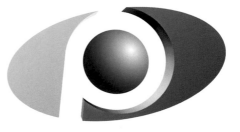

4.

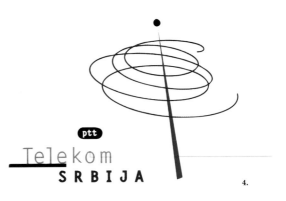

5.

PPI Entertainment

6.

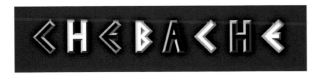

7.

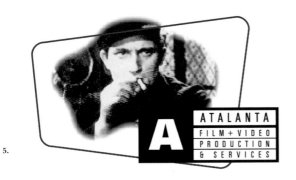

AKADÉMOS.COM

8.

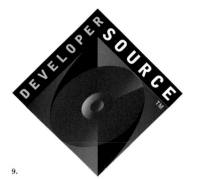

9.

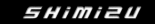 SHIMIZU DESIGN STUDIO INC.

10.

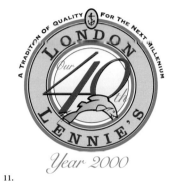

11.

Harvest Moon™

The best meals under the moon.

12.

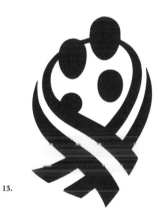

13.

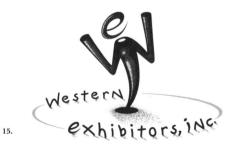

15.

ASSASSINS

14.

1 - 5
Design Firm A+B (In Exile)
6 - 9
Design Firm Iron Design
10
Design Firm Shimizu Design Studio, Inc.
11 - 12
Design Firm Adkins/Balchunas
13
Design Firm Dever Designs
14
Design Firm Rickabaugh Graphics
15
Design Firm Fine Design Group

1. Client   "S"-Team, Ljubljana

2. Client   "Heart of the City"
   Designer   Eduard Cehovin

3. Client   National Examination Center
               (Slovenia)/East Meet West
   Designer   Eduard Cehovin

4. Client   Telekom-Srbija

5. Client   "A Atalanta"
   Designer   Eduard Cehovin

6. Client   Peter Pan Industries
   Designer   Ted Skibinski

7. Client   Pandee Games
   Designer   Todd Edmonds

8. Client   Akademos.com
   Designer   Ted Skibinski

9. Client   Imode Retrieval Systems
   Designer   Todd Edmonds

10. Client   Shimizu Design Studio, Inc.
    Designers Ichiro Shimizu &
               Hiroto Takahashi

11. Client   London Lennies
    Designers Jerry Balchunas
               & Susan DeAngelis

12. Client   Harvest Moon
    Designers Jerry Balchunas
               & Susan DeAngelis

13. Client   Center for Population
               Health and Nutrition
    Designer   Jeffrey L. Dever

14. Client   Players Theatre
    Designer   Eric Rickabaugh

15. Client   Western Exhibitors, Inc.
    Designers Jake Barlow, John Taylor,
               & Kenn Fine

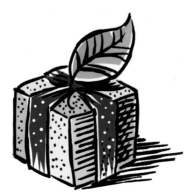

1.

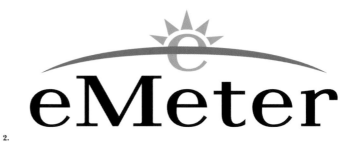

2.

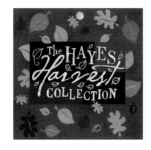

3.

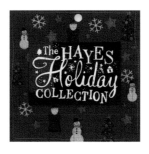

4.

5.

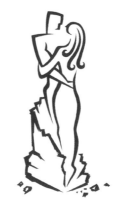

6.

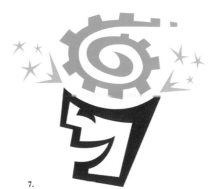

7.

(all)

Design Firm Insight Design Communications

1. Client   gardenandholiday.com
     Designers   Sherrie and Tracy Holdeman

2. Client   eMeter
     Designers   Sherrie and Tracy Holdeman

3, 4
     Client   The Hayes Co.
     Designers   Sherrie and Tracy Holdeman

5. Client   Howard's Optique
     Designers   Sherrie and Tracy Holdeman

6. Client   Physique Enhancement
     Designers   Sherrie and Tracy Holdeman

7. Client   Gear Up
     Designers   Sherrie and Tracy Holdeman

(opposite)
Design Firm Whitney Stinger, Inc.

     Client   Bone Daddy +
                 The Blues Shakers
     Designers   Mike Whitney & Karl Stinger

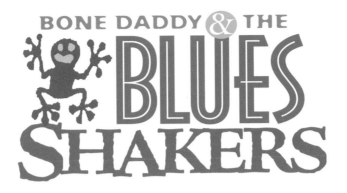

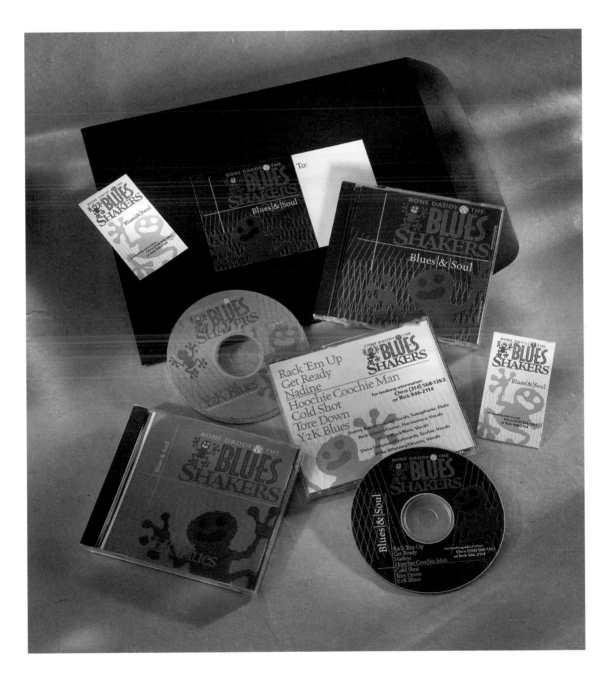

1. d'MUIR

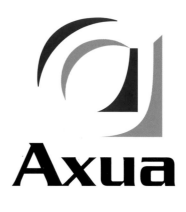

2. Axua

3.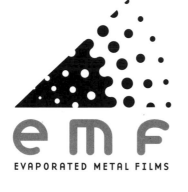

emf
EVAPORATED METAL FILMS

4.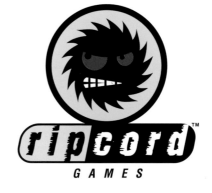

G★ball

5. im○de

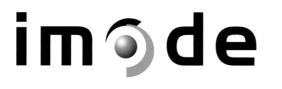
retrieval systems

6.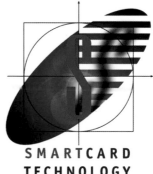

ripcord™
GAMES

7.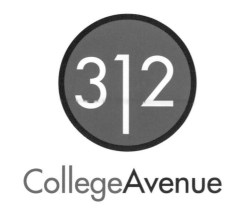

312

CollegeAvenue

8.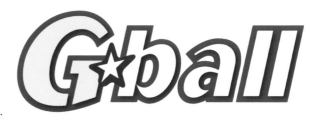

SMARTCARD
TECHNOLOGY
CENTER

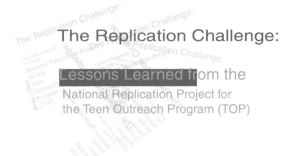

The Replication Challenge:

Lessons Learned from the

National Replication Project for
the Teen Outreach Program (TOP)

9.

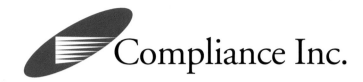

Compliance Inc.

10.

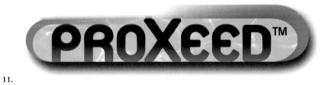

11.

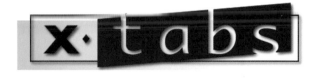

12.

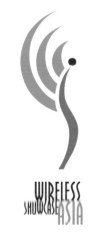

13.

14.

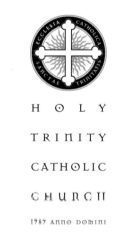

H O L Y

T R I N I T Y

C A T H O L I C

C H U R C H

1987 Anno Domini

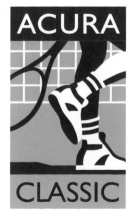

15.

LAMSON, DUGAN & MURRAY

1.

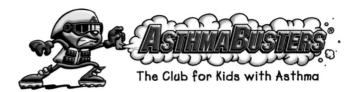

2.

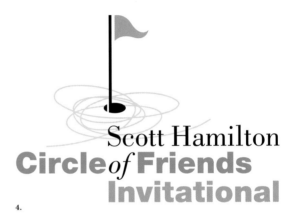

3.

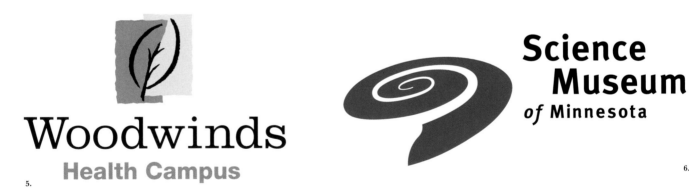

4.

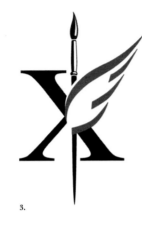

Woodwinds
Health Campus

5.

Science Museum *of* **Minnesota**

6.

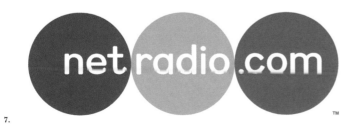

7.

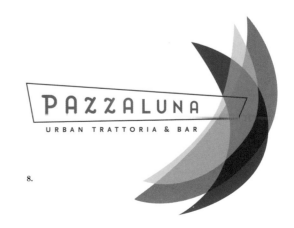

8.

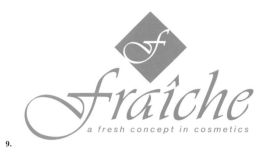

9.

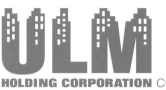

ULM

HOLDING CORPORATION COMMERCIAL REAL ESTATE
1776 BROADWAY ▮ SUITE 2000 ▮ NEW YORK, NY 10019

10.

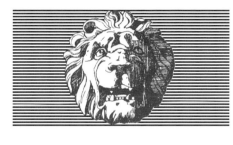

11.

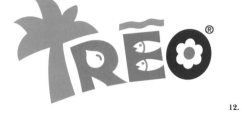

12.

BEST BUYER'S BROKER REALTY INC.

13.

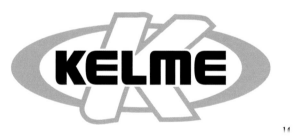

14

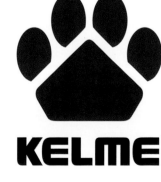

KELME

15.

1, 2			
Design Firm	**Dotzler Creative Arts**		
3			
Design Firm	**Curry Design Associates**		
4 - 8			
Design Firm	**Little & Company**		
9 - 13			
Design Firm	**Hirschhorn & Young Inc.**		
14, 15			
Design Firm	**Lawson Design**		

1. Client — Lamson, Dugan & Murray

2. Client — AsthmaBusters

3. Client — Muse X Editions
   Designer — Steve Curry

4. Client — Scott Hamilton Circle of Friends
   Designers — Monica Little, Jim Jackson, Mike Schacherer, & Viet Do

5. Client — Woodwinds Health Campus
   Designers — Monica Little, Jim Jackson, Scott Sorenson, & Viet Do

6. Client — Science Museum of Minnesota
   Designers — Monica Little, Jim Jackson, & Michael Lizama

7. Client — Netradio.com
   Designers — Monica Little, Stefan Hartung, & Scott Sorenson

8. Client — Morissey Hospitality— Pazzaluna Restaurant
   Designers — Monica Little, Jim Jackson, Michael Lizama, & Viet Do

9. Client — Urban Retreat Day Spa
   Designer — Barbara Reed

10. Client — ULM Holding Corporation
    Designer — Barbara Reed

11. Client — The Lion Construction Group Inc.
    Designer — Barbara Reed

12. Client — Primavera Laboratories, Inc.
    Designer — Barbara Reed

13. Client — Best Buyer's Broker Realty
    Designer — Barbara Reed

14, 15
    Client — Concept 21 (Kelme Shoes)
    Designers — Jeff Lawson &, Brent James

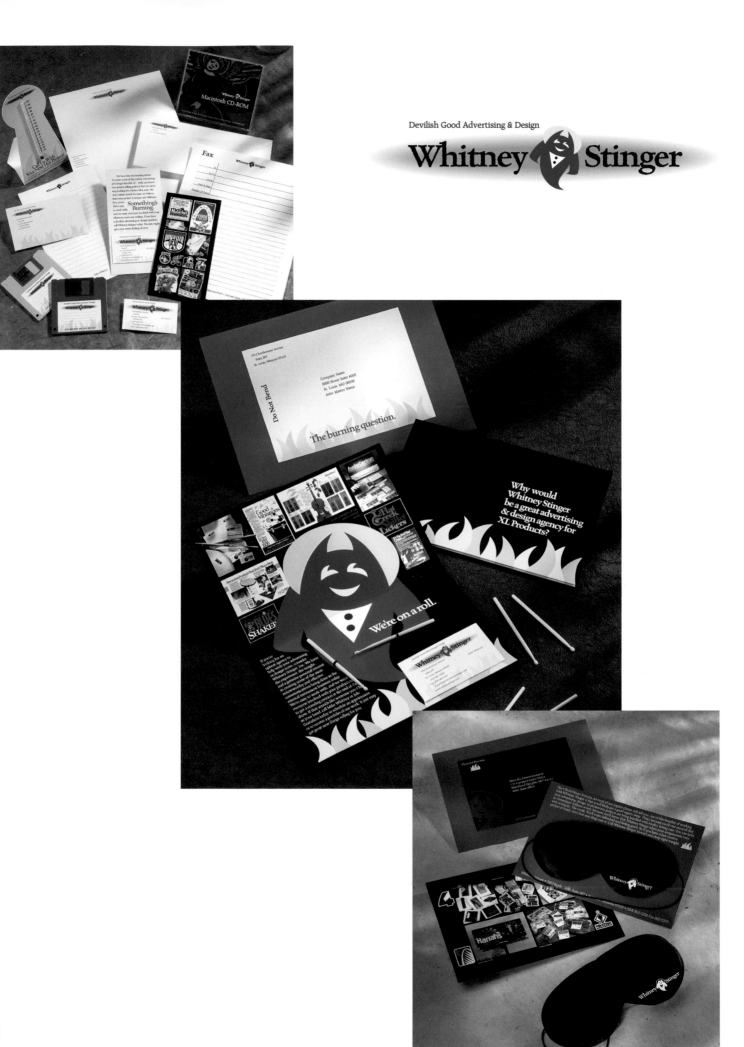

Devilish Good Advertising & Design

Whitney Stinger

1.

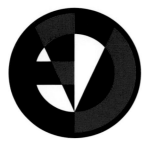

EVD Advertising

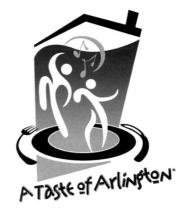

A Taste of Arlington

2.

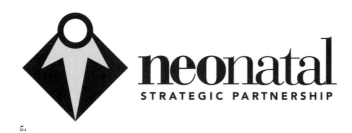

3.

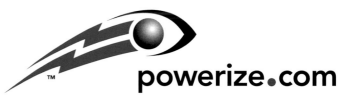

4.

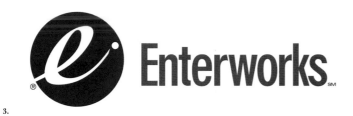

neonatal
STRATEGIC PARTNERSHIP

5.

6.

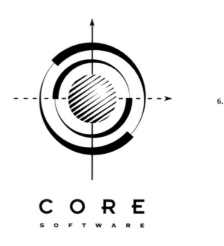

CORE
SOFTWARE

V A N S C O Y ∞

7.

(opposite)
Design Firm Whitney Stinger

Client   Whitney Stinger, Inc
Designers   Mike Whitney & Karl Stinger

1 - 5
Design Firm EVD Advertising
6, 7
Design Firm Curry Design Associates

1. Client   EVD Advertising
    Designers   Rachel Deutsch & David Street

2. Client   Taste of Arlington
    Designers   Rachel Deutsch & Marc Foelsch

3. Client   Enterworks
    Designers   Rachel Deutsch, Blake Stenning,
                      & Marc Foelsch

4. Client   Powerize
    Designers   Rachel Deutsch &
                      Tom Cosgrove

5. Client   Neonatal Strategic Partnership
    Designers   Rachel Deutsch & Marc Foelsch

6. Client   Core Software Technology
    Designer   Jason Scheideman

7. Client   VanScoy Photography
    Designer   Jason Scheideman

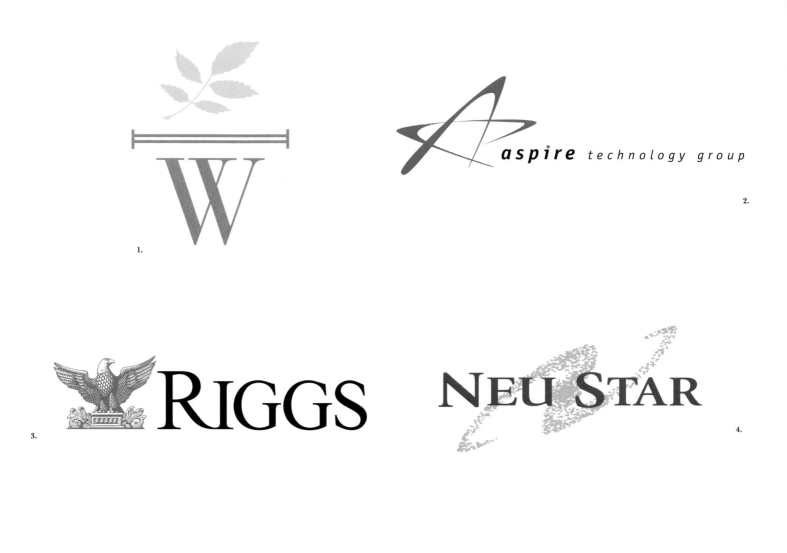

1.

aspire *technology group*

2.

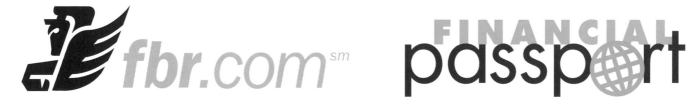

RIGGS

3.

NEU★STAR

4.

fbr.com^{sm}

5.

FINANCIAL
passport

6.

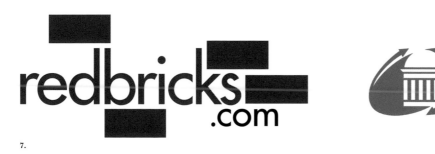

redbricks
.com

7.

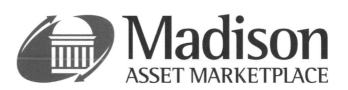

Madison
ASSET MARKETPLACE

8.

WINGATE
UNIVERSITY

9.

excel

10.

Mississippi Valley State University

11.

✝

✝

12.

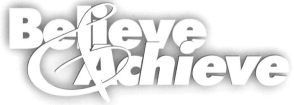

10.

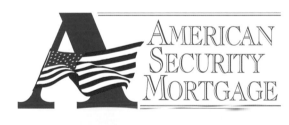
AMERICAN SECURITY MORTGAGE

14.

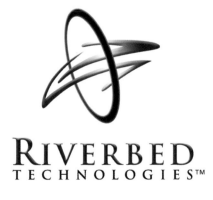
RIVERBED
TECHNOLOGIES™

15.

1 - 8
Design Firm Iconixx
(Iconixx Web Development)
9 - 14
Design Firm Steve Thomas
Marketing Communications
15
Design Firm EVD Advertising

1. Client   The Mark Winkler Company
    Designers   Gretchen Frederick &
                 Anjeanette Agro

2. Client   Aspire Technology Group
    Designers   John Cabot Lodge &
                 Robin Clay Diamond

3. Client   Riggs Bank NA
    Designers   John Cabot Lodge &
                 Andrew Johnson
    Illustrator Mark Summers

4. Client   Neu Star, Inc.
    Designers   John Cabot Lodge &
                 Lara Santos

5. Client   FBR.com
    Designer   Andrew Johnson

6. Client   Pace Financial Network, LLC
    Designers   John Cabot Lodge &
                 Lara Santos

7. Client   Redbricks.com
    Designers   John Cabot Lodge &
                 Lara Santos

8. Client   Madison Asset Marketplace
    Designers   John Cabot Lodge, Mary
                 Parsons, & Chuck Sundin

9. Client   Wingate University
    Designer   Steve Thomas

10. Client   UNC Charlotte
    Designer   Steve Thomas

11. Client   Mississippi Valley State
                 University
    Designer   Steve Thomas

12. Client   Church of the Beloved
    Designer   Steve Thomas

13. Client   Charlotte Country Day School
    Designers   Steve Thomas & Dan Wold

14. Client   American Security Mortgage
    Designer   Steve Thomas

15. Client   Riverbed Technologies
    Designers   Rachel Deutsch &
                 Marc Foelsch

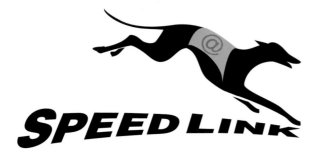

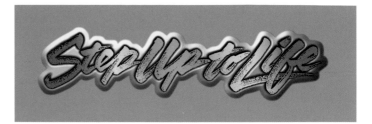

SPEED LINK

1.

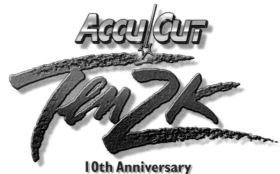

2.

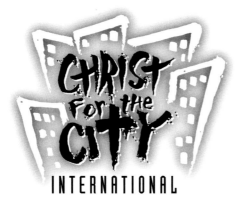

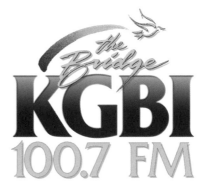

3.

**10th Anniversary
Year 2000 Celebration**

4.

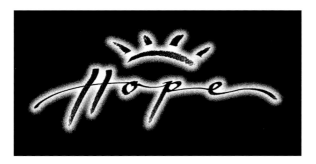

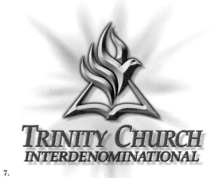

5.

6.

7.

1

**Design Firm California Design
International**

2 - 7

Design Firm Dotzler Creative Arts

1. Client   Diamond Lane
              Communication
   Designers   Linda Kelley & Dan Liew

2. Client   Step Up To Life

3. Client   Christ For The City

4. Client   Accu-Cut

5. Client   Hope Center

6. Client   KGBI

7. Client   Trinity Church

(opposite)

Design Firm Templin Brink Design

   Client   Classic Company
   Designer   Joel Templin

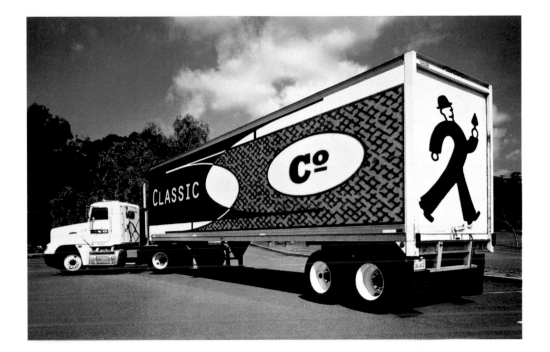

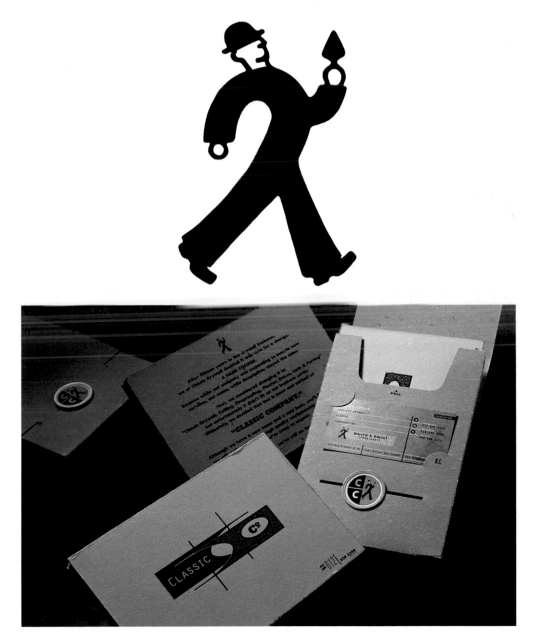

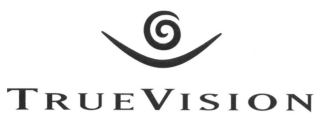

TRUEVISION

1.

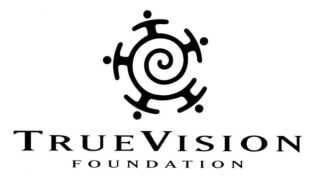

TRUEVISION
FOUNDATION

2.

formfunction

3.

4.

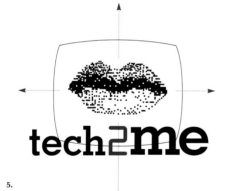

tech2me

5.

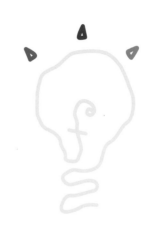

SOUTHWEST
TIRE & AUTO
GENERAL

6.

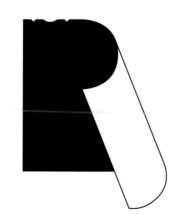

7.

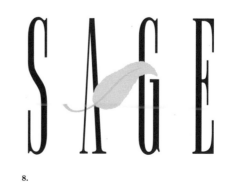

8.

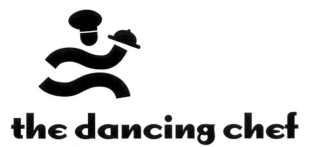

the dancing chef

9.

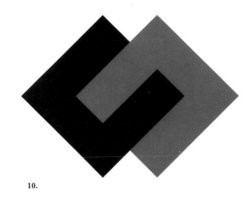

10.

T H E

A R T

I C H

O K E

C A F E

11.

RAA

12.

N A T I O N A L

ATOMIC

M U S E U M

13.

Portobello

14.

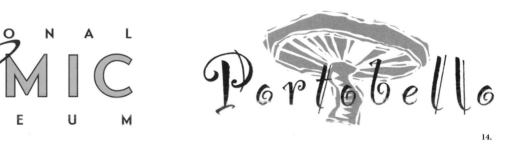

CLIF SHOT®

15.

1 - 14
Design Firm Studio Hill Design
15
Design Firm California Design International

1, 2
Client   TrueVision International
Designer   Sandy Hill

3, 4
Client   Form + Function
Designers   Sandy Hill & Emma Roberts

5. Client   Tech2Me
    Designers   Sandy Hill & Emma Roberts

6. Client   Southwest General Tire
    Designers   Sandy Hill & Emma Roberts

7. Client   Robert Reck Photography
    Designers   Sandy Hill & Emma Roberts

8. Client   Sage
    Designers   Sandy Hill & Emma Roberts

9. Client   Dancing Chef
    Designer   Sandy Hill

10. Client   Christy Construction
    Designer   Sandy Hill

11. Client   Artichoke Cafe
    Designers   Sandy Hill & Emma Roberts

12. Client   Radiology Associates
    Designers   Sandy Hill & Emma Roberts

13. Client   National Atomic Museum
    Designers   Sandy Hill, Alan Shimato,
                 & Mary Lambert

14. Client   Portobello Restaurant
    Designers   Sandy Hill & Emma Roberts

15. Client   Clif Shot
    Designers   Linda Kelley & Suzy Leung

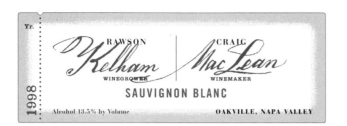

1.

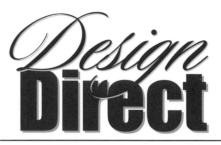

Vantis' Complete Programmable Logic Software Solution

2.

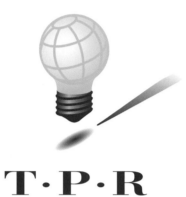

T·P·R

3.

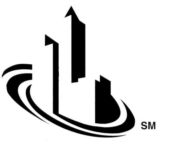

Real Estate Energy Solutions

4.

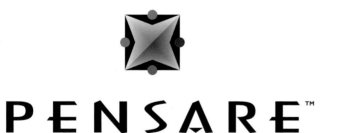

PENSARE™

5.

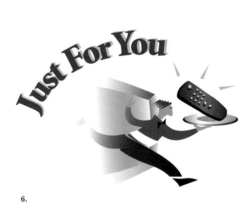

6.

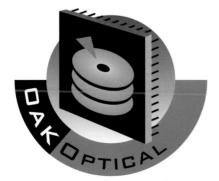

7.

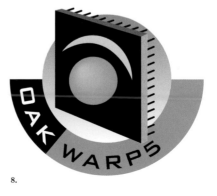

8.

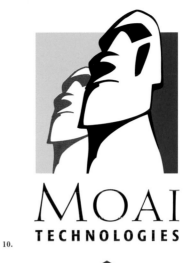

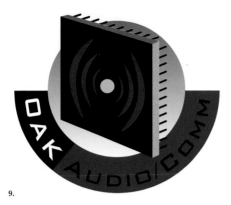

9.

MOAI
TECHNOLOGIES

10.

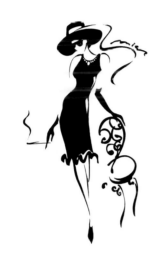

11.

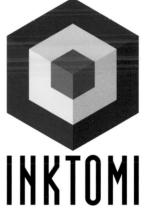

INKTOMI

12.

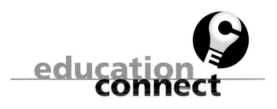

education
connect

13.

GALIL
WE MOVE THE WORLD

14.

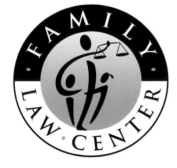

15.

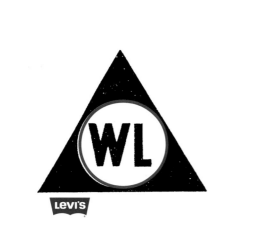

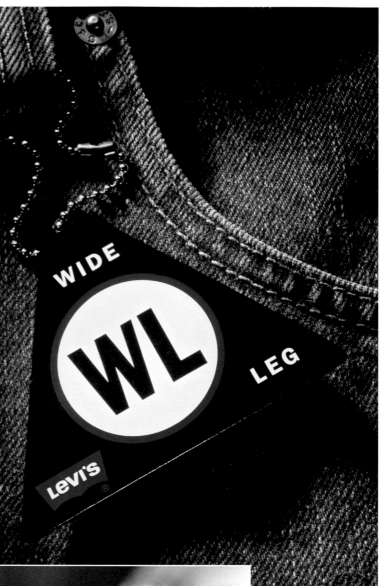

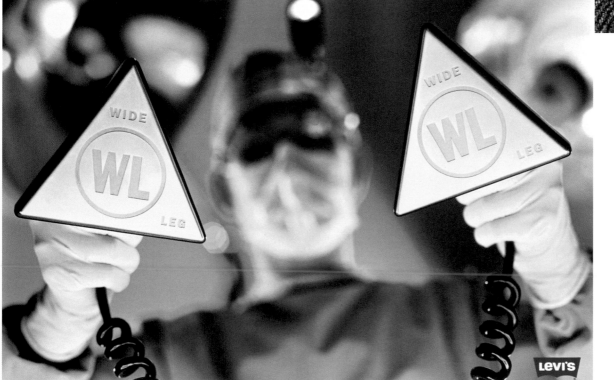

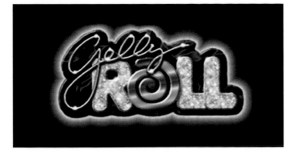

1.

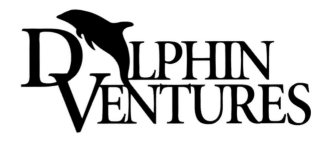

2.

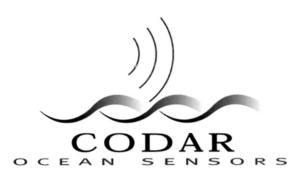

3.

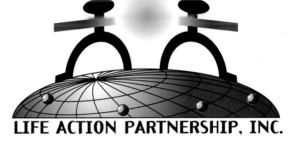

4.

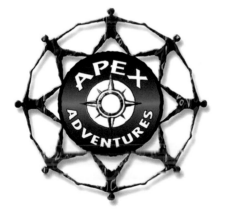

5.

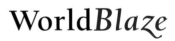

6.

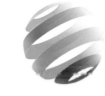

7.

(opposite)
Design Firm Foote, Cone, & Belding

Client   Levi Strauss & Co.
Designer   Joel Templin

1 - 5
Design Firm Gunion Design
6, 7
Design Firm California Design International

1. Client   Sakura of America
    Designer   Jefrey Gunion

2. Client   Dolphin Ventures
    Designer   Jefrey Gunion

3. Client   Codår Ocean Sensors
    Designer   Jefrey Gunion

4. Client   Life Action Partnership, Inc.
    Designer   Jefrey Gunion

5. Client   Apex Adventures
    Designer   Jefrey Gunion

6. Client   World Blaze
    Designers   Linda Kelley & Dan Liew

7. Client   Vivant!
    Designers   Linda Kelley & Brian Sasville

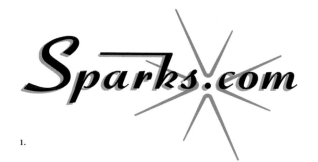

1.

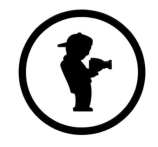

2.

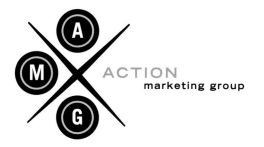

3.

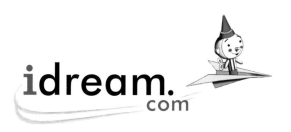

4.

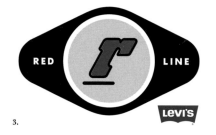

5.

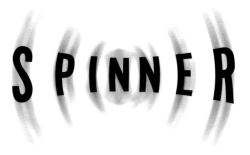

6.

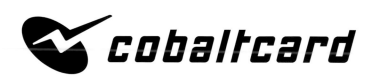

7.

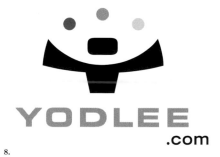

8.

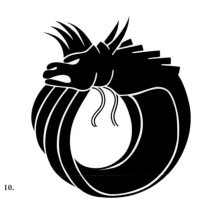

9.

10.

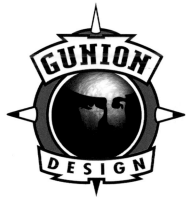

11.

12.

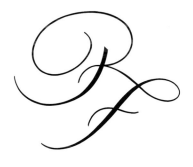

13.

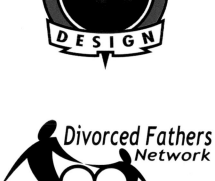

1 4.

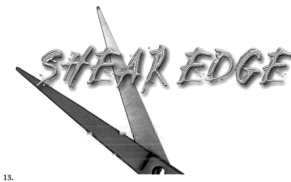

15.

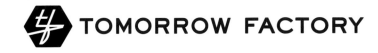 TOMORROW FACTORY

1.

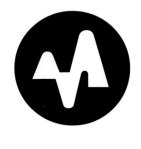

2.

phoenix pop

3.

AMAZ○N.COM

4.

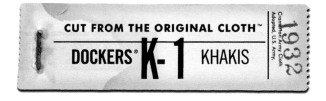

CUT FROM THE ORIGINAL CLOTH™

DOCKERS® **K-1** KHAKIS

1932 Cramerton Army Cloth, Adopted, U.S. Army.

5.

Designed by

SOUTHPARK FABRICATORS   San Francisco, CA

tel   415-897-6622

6.

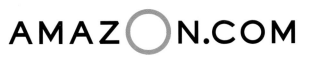

7.

1 - 7

Design Firm Templin Brink Design

1. Client   Tomorrow Factory
    Designer   Joel Templin

2. Client   Warren Miller
    Designers   Joel Templin, Paul Howalt,
                   & Gaby Brink

3. Client   Phoenix- Pop
    Designer   Joel Templin

4. Client   Amazon.com
    Designer   Joel Templin

5. Client   Dockers Khakis
    Designer   Gaby Brink

6. Client   Southpark Fabricators
    Designer   Gaby Brink

7. Client   WineShopper.com
    Designers   Gaby Brink & Joel Templin

(opposite)
**Design Firm Insight Design
             Communications**

Client   With A Twist
Designers   Sherrie Holdeman
               & Tracy Holdeman

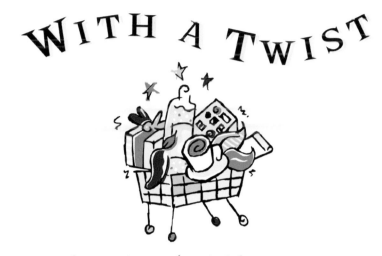

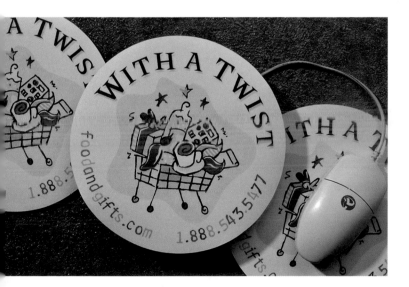

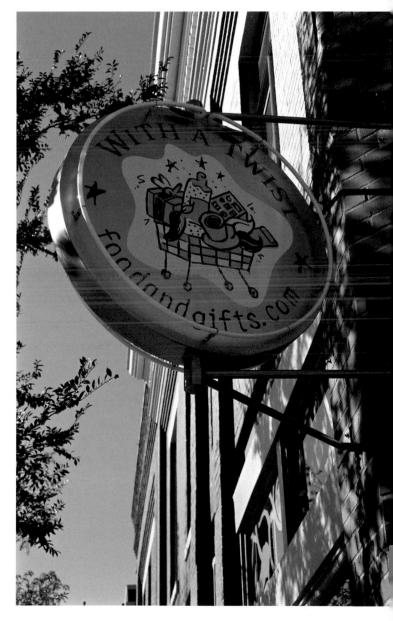

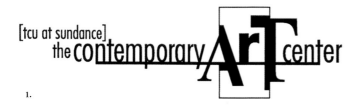

1.

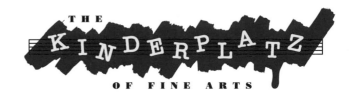

2.

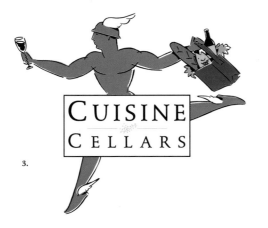

3.

AGRI AMERICA

4.

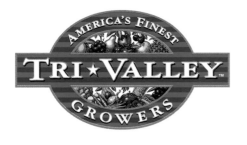

5.

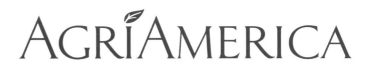

6.

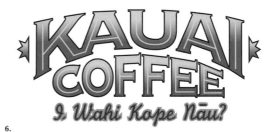

7.

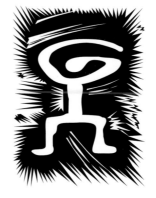

8.

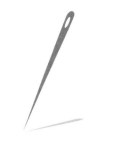

Lucille & Henry
Home Textiles

9.

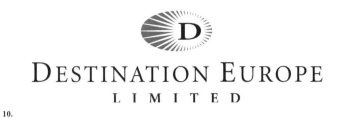

DESTINATION EUROPE
LIMITED

10.

SANTANA ROW

11.

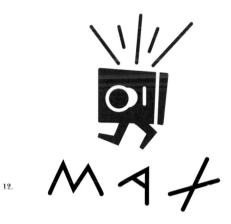

12.

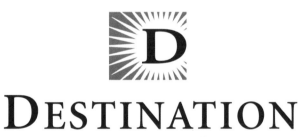

DESTINATION
HOTELS & RESORTS

13.

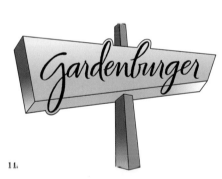

14.

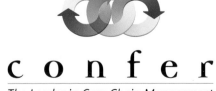

confer
The Leader in Care Chain Management ™

15.

BRIDGE FILM

2.

1.

BALLENTINE
D E S I G N S

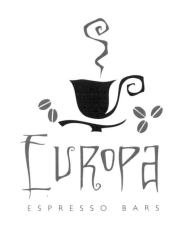

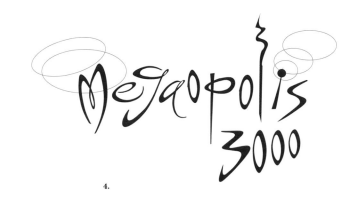

4.

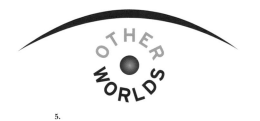

3.

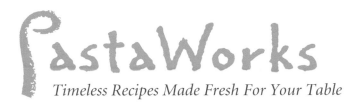

5.

Centurion
DEVELOPMENT PARTNERS

6.

FANTASTIC

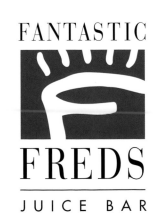

FREDS

7. JUICE BAR

PastaWorks
Timeless Recipes Made Fresh For Your Table

8.

MEADOWBANK ESTATES

9.

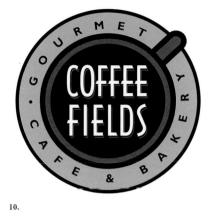

GOURMET · COFFEE FIELDS · CAFE & BAKERY

10.

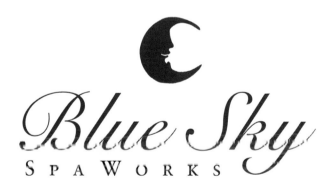

SJ Corio Company
AUCTIONS   APPRAISALS   LIQUIDATIONS

11.

BAYOU
CARDIOTHORACIC
SURGERY ASSOCIATES, LTD

12.

Blue Sky
SPAWORKS

13.

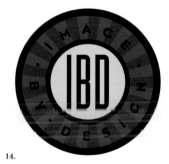

IBD
IMAGE · BY · DESIGN

14.

Pi✓ot   MARKETING DATA
SERVICES, LLC.

15.

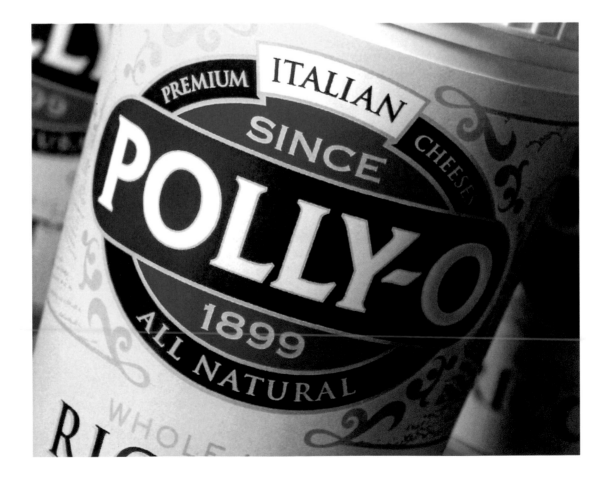

1.

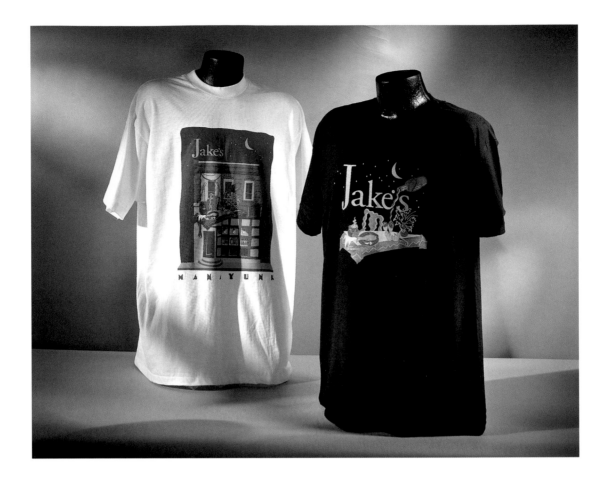

2.

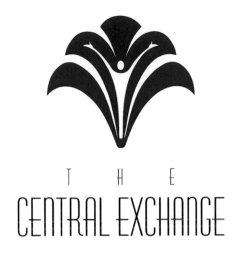

T H E
CENTRAL EXCHANGE

3.

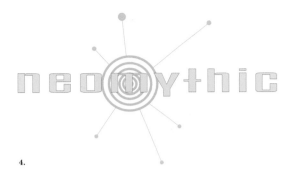

4.

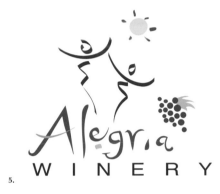

Alegria
W I N E R Y

5.

SCHELLING

6.

SCOTT'S
S E A F O O D

7.

Kristen Anacker
COSTUME DESIGN & PRODUCTION

8.

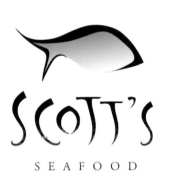

9.

1
Design Firm Hanson Associates, Inc.
2
Design Firm Wallace Church Ass., Inc.
3
Design Firm EAT Advertising & Design
4 - 6, 8, 9
Design Firm Monica Reskala
7
Design Firm O & Co.

1. Client   Jake's Restaurant
   Designer   Christy Beck

2. Client   Kraft Foods
   Designers   Stan Church, Nin Glaister, &
                 John Bruno

3. Client   The Central Exchange
   Designers   Patrice Jobe & John Storey

4. Client   Neomythic
   Designer   Monica Reskala

5. Client   Alegria Winery
   Designer   Monica Reskala

6. Client   Susan Schelling Photography
   Designer   Monica Reskala

7. Client   Scott's Restaurant
   Designer   Monica Reskala

8. Client   Kristen Anacker
   Designer   Monica Reskala

9. Client   Salon 265
   Designer   Monica Reskala

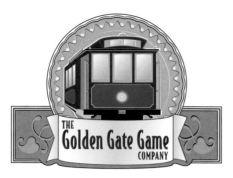

1.

Pacific
PET SERVICE℠

2.

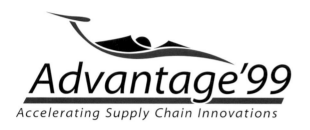

Accelerating Supply Chain Innovations

3.

the**centric**group

4.

BUSINESS
TO BUSINESS
DIALOGUES

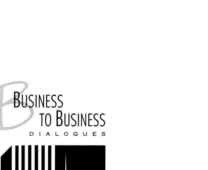

5.

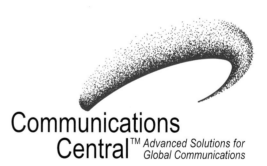

Communications
Central™ *Advanced Solutions for Global Communications*

6.

CSS
Complete Software Solutions

7.

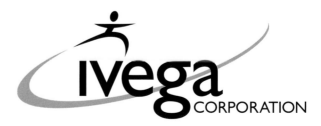

ivega CORPORATION

8.

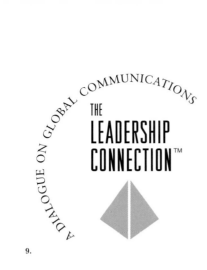

9.

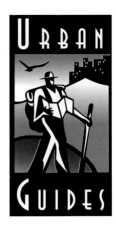

10.

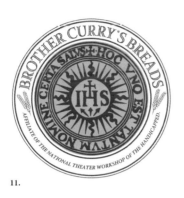

11.

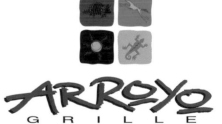

12.

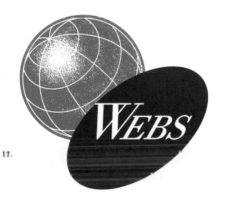

13.

ARROYO
G R I L L E

14.

CHASE FUNDS

15.

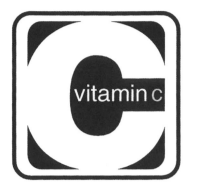

1.

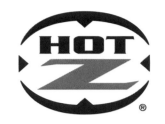

2.

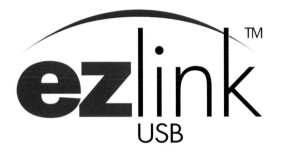

3.

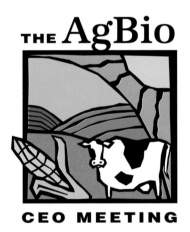

4.

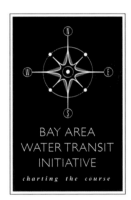

5.

6.

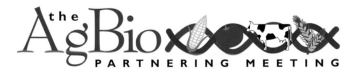

7.

1
  Design Firm **Elektra Entertainment**
2, 3
  Design Firm **Miriello Grafico Inc.**
4 - 7
  Design Firm **McKenzie & Associates, Inc.**

1. Client   Vitamin C
    Designer   Alli Truch

2. Client   Hot Z
    Designer   Chris Keeney

3. Client   ezlink
    Designer   Michelle Aranda

4. Client   PC Professional
    Designers   Jean McKenzie &
                Debbi Merzyn

5. Client   Bay Area Water Transit
                & Initiative
    Designers   Dan Wen & Debbi Merzyn

6. Client   Burrill & Company
    Designers   Jean McKenzie & Debbi Merzyn

7. Client   Burrill & Company
    Designers   Jean McKenzie & Debbi Merzyn

(opposite)
    Design Firm **Hanson Associates, Inc.**

    Client   The Eyeglass Works
    Designer   Mary Zook

ᵗʰᵉeyeglass works

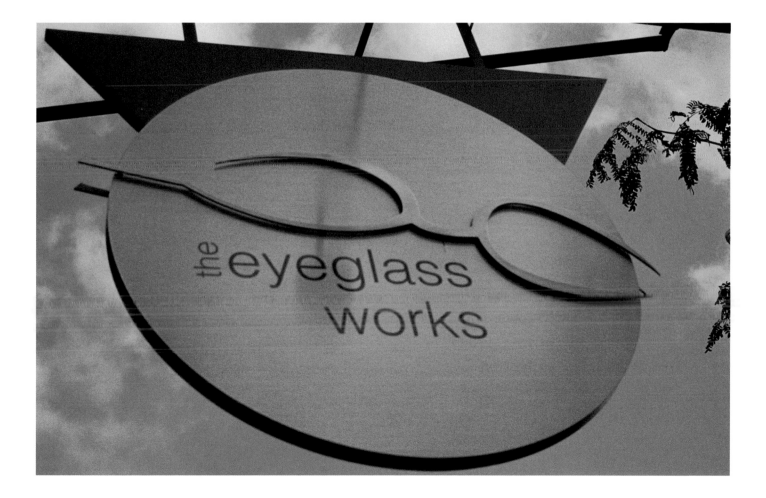

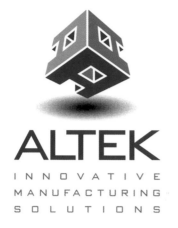

ALTEK
INNOVATIVE MANUFACTURING SOLUTIONS

1.

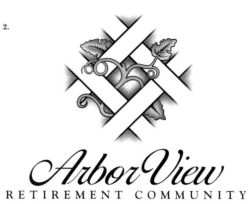

ArborView
RETIREMENT COMMUNITY

2.

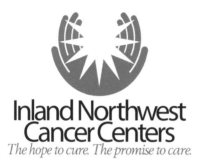

Inland Northwest Cancer Centers
The hope to cure. The promise to care.

3.

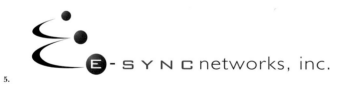

AISLE *of* VIEW
A WEDDING FROM YOUR POINT OF VIEW

4.

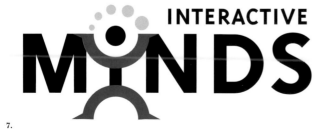

E-SYNC networks, inc.

5.

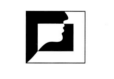

CHRIS L. CHAFFIN, DDS
GENERAL, COSMETIC & IMPLANT DENTISTRY

6.

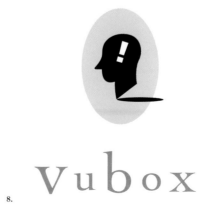

INTERACTIVE **MINDS**

7.

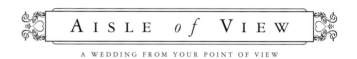

Vubox

8.

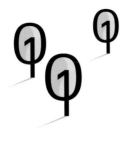

Application
Park™

9.

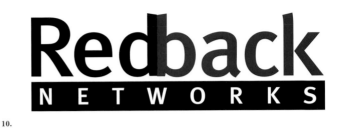

10.

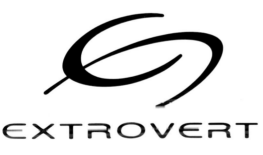

11.

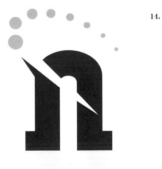

12.

14.

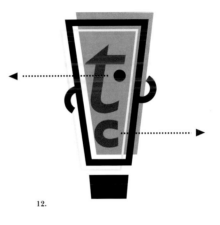

EXTROVERT

13.

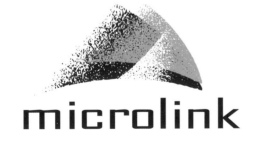

microlink

15.

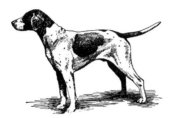

Dog Goods, Ltd.

1.

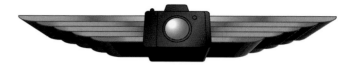

"CHEQUE-6"

2.

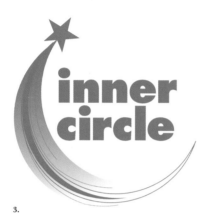

3.

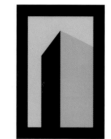

THE EQUITABLE BUILDING

4.

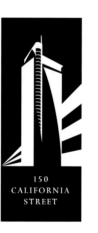

150
CALIFORNIA
STREET

5.

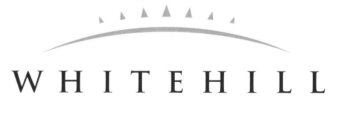

W H I T E H I L L

6.

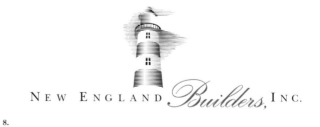

7.

NEW ENGLAND *Builders*, INC.

8.

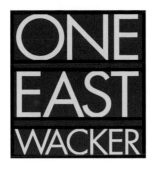

9.

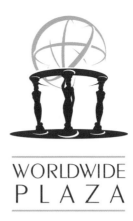

WORLDWIDE
PLAZA

10.

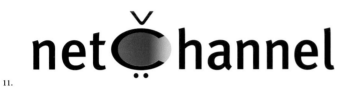

11.

12.

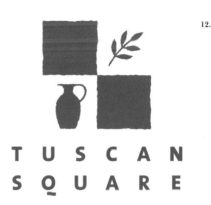

T U S C A N
S Q U A R E

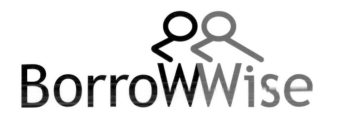

13.

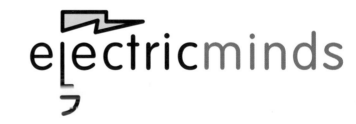

14.

arzoon

15.

1 - 10
Design Firm Pivot Design, Inc.
11, 13 - 15
Design Firm Long Design
12
Design Firm Studio Morris

1. Client   Dog Goods, Ltd.
    Designer   Elizabeth Johnson

2. Client   Cheque 6
                Aviation Photography
    Designer   Brock Haldeman

3. Client   Focal Communications Corp.
    Designer   Bonnie Cauble

4. Client   Jones Lang LaSalle
    Designer   Brock Haldeman

5. Client   Equity Office
    Designer   Brock Haldeman

6. Client   Whitehill Technologies
    Designer   Brock Haldeman

7. Client   Uppercase Books
    Designer   Elizabeth Johnson

8. Client   New England Builders, Inc.
    Designer   Tim Hogan

9. Client   Jones Lang LaSalle
    Designer   Brock Haldeman

10. Client   Jones Lang LaSalle
    Designer   Brock Haldeman

11. Client   NetChannel
    Designer   Jennifer Long

12. Client   Tuscan Square
    Designers   Patricia Kovic & Jeff Morris

13. Client   BorrowWise
    Designer   Jennifer Long

14. Client   Electric Minds
    Designer   Jennifer Long

15. Client   arzoon.com
    Designer   Jennifer Long

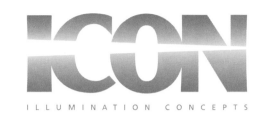

1.

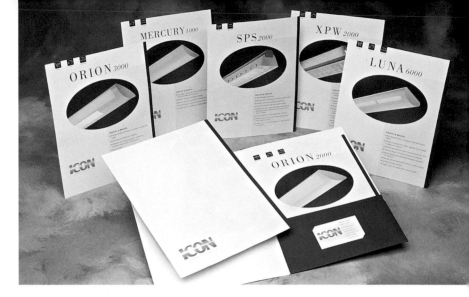

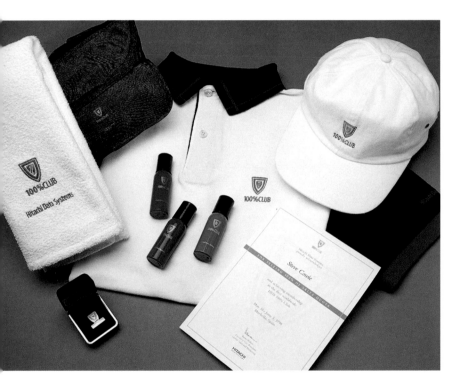

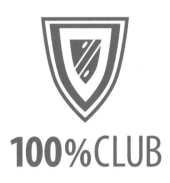

100%CLUB

2.

Navigator

INVESTMENTS

3.

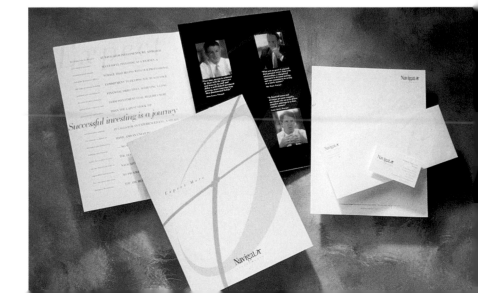

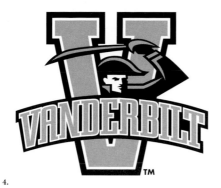

4.

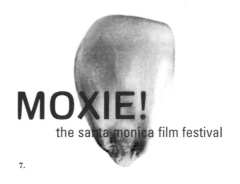

5.

stil life

NATURAL FURNITURE

6.

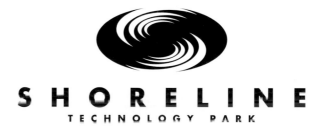

7.

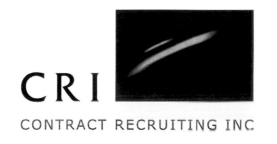

CONTRACT RECRUITING INC

8.

SHORELINE

TECHNOLOGY PARK

9.

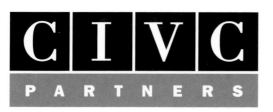

10.

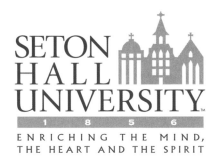

1.

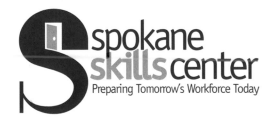

2.

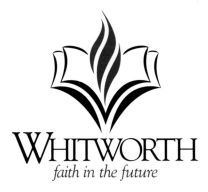

3.

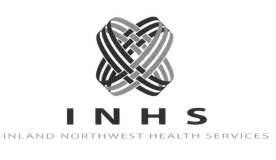

4.

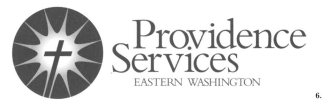

5.

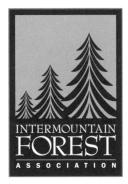

6.

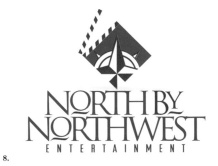

7.

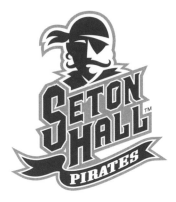

8.

PROGRESSIVE
LENDING LLC

9.

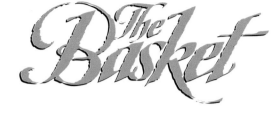

10.

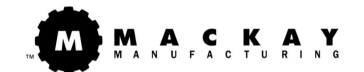

11.

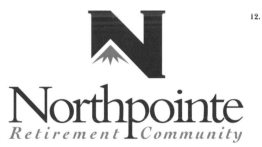

12.

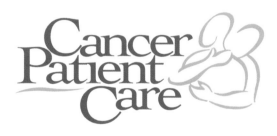

14.

AURORA
CONSULTING GROUP

15.

1, 2
Design Firm Rickabaugh Graphics
3 - 15
Design Firm Klundt Hosmer Design

1. Client   Seton Hall University
   Designer Eric Rickabaugh

2. Client   Seton Hall University
   Designers Eric Rickabaugh & Dave Cap

3. Client   Inland Northwest
             Health Services
   Designers Darin Klundt & Henry Ortega

4. Client   Intermountain Forest Assoc.
   Designers Darin Klundt & Amy Gunter

5. Client   Whitworth
   Designers Brian Gage & Darin Klundt

6. Client   Providence Services of E.W.
   Designers Darin Klundt & Henry Ortega

7. Client   Spokane Skills Center
   Designers Darin Klundt & Amy Gunter

8. Client   North by Northwest
             Entertainment
   Designers Darin Klundt & Brian Gage

9. Client   Progressive Lending
   Designers Darin Klundt &
             Judy Heggum-Davis

10. Client   The Basket
    Designer Brian Cage

11. Client   Mel
    Designers Brian Gage & Darin Klundt

12. Client   North Pointe
             Retirement Community
    Designers Darin Klundt & Brian Gage

13. Client   MacKay Manufacturing
    Designers Darin Klundt & Brian Gage

14. Client   Cancer Patient Care
    Designers Darin Klundt & Amy Gunter

15. Client   Aurora Consulting Group
    Designers Darin Klundt , Judy
             Heggum-Davis, & Brian Gage

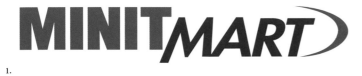

1.

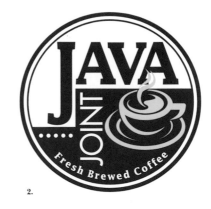

3.

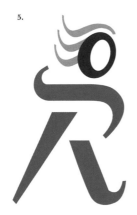

5.

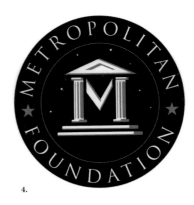

2.

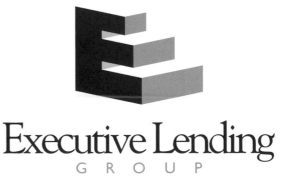

4.

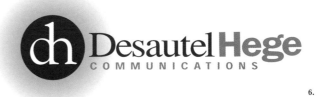

6.

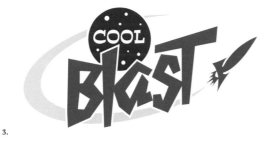

7.

1 - 3
Design Firm Babcock, Schmid, Louis, & Partners

4
Design Firm Iron Design

5
Design Firm Long Design

6, 7
Design Firm Klundt Hosmer Design

1. Client   Minit Mart
    Designers   Babcock, Schmid, Louis,
                    & Partners

2. Client   Minit Mart
    Designers   Babcock, Schmid, Louis,
                    & Partners

3. Client   Minit Mart
    Designers   Babcock, Schmid, Louis,
                    & Partners

4. Client   Metropolitan Foundation
    Designer   Todd Edmonds

5. Client   Rhonda Abrams
    Designer   Jennifer Long

6. Client   Desautel Hege Communications
    Designers   Darin Klundt & Henry Ortega

7. Client   Executive Lending Group
    Designers   Brian Gage & Darin Klundt

(opposite)
Design Firm Wallace Church Ass., Inc.

    Client   Maxfli Golf Balls
    Designers   Stan Church, John Waski,
                    & Derek Samue

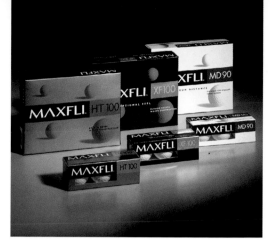

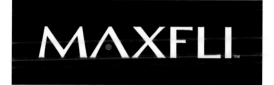

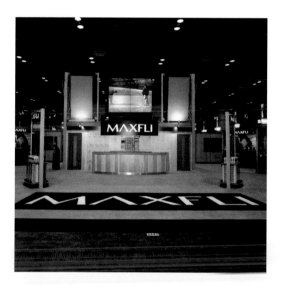

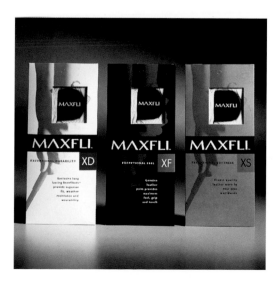

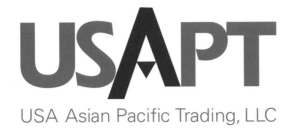

USA Asian Pacific Trading, LLC

1.

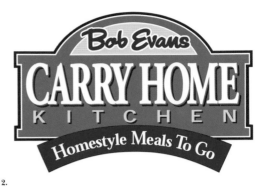

2.

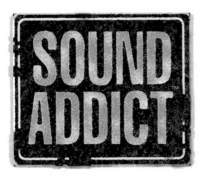

3.

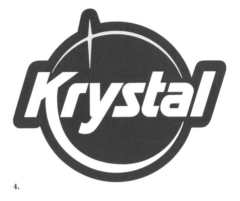

4.

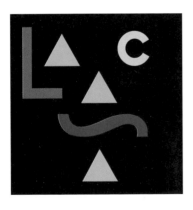

5.

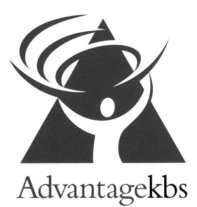

Advantagekbs

6.

CYBERPATH

7.

8.

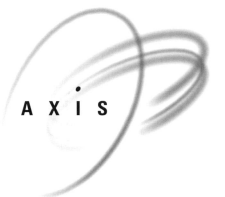

9.

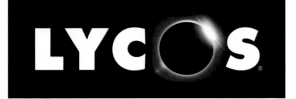

10.

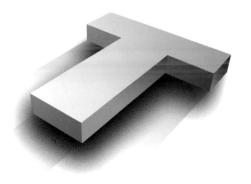

11.

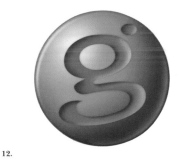

12.

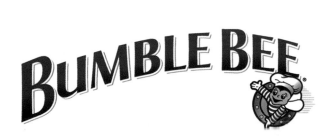

13.

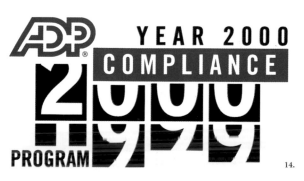

14.

OpenCon Systems, Inc.
WORLDWIDE COMMUNICATIONS SOLUTIONS

15.

1 - 4
**Design Firm Babcock, Schmid, Louis
           & Partners**
5
Design Firm Imageignition
6 - 8, 14, 15
Design Firm David Morris Creative Inc.
9 - 13
Design Firm Wallace Church Ass., Inc.

1. Client   U.S.A. Asian Pacific Trading
    Designers Babcock, Schmid, Louis
              & Partners

2. Client   Bob Evans
    Designers Babcock, Schmid, Louis
              & Partners

3. Client   Audio Technica
    Designers Babcock, Schmid, Louis
              & Partners

4. Client   Krystal
    Designers Babcock, Schmid, Louis
              & Partners

5. Client   La Casa Films
    Designer   Adrian Bellesguard

6. Client   Advantage Kbs
    Designer   Glenn Gontha

7. Client   OCS - Open Con Systems
    Designer   Denise Spirito

8. Client   Corporate Computing Expo
    Designer   Glenn Gontha

9. Client   The Axis Group, IIC
    Designers Stan Church, Wendy Church,
              & Lucian Toma

10. Client   Lycos
    Designers Stan Church & Craig Swanson

11. Client   Tri-State Graphics
    Designers Stan Church, Wendy Church,
              & Lucian Toma

12. Client   Green Media Cultivation
    Designers Nin Glaister & Paula Bunny

13. Client   Bumble Bee Tuna
    Designers Stan Church & Diana King

14. Client   ADP
    Designer   Matt Gilbert

15. Client   OCS - Open Con Systems
    Designer   Matt Gilbert

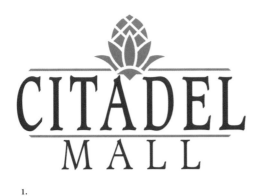

1.

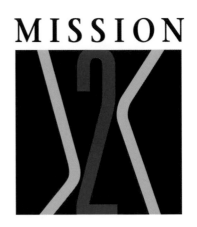

2.

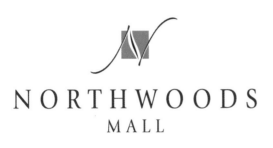

3.

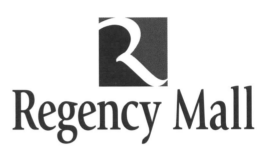

4.

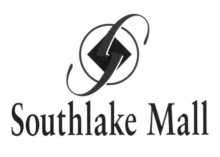

5.

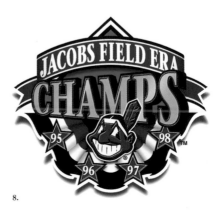

6.

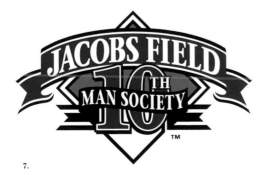

7.

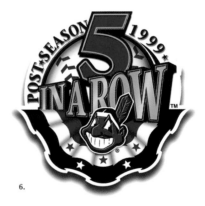

8.

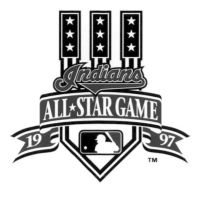

9.

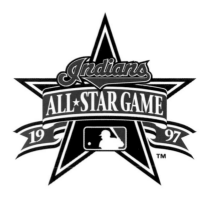

10.

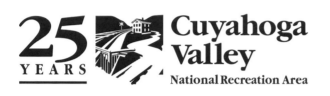

11.

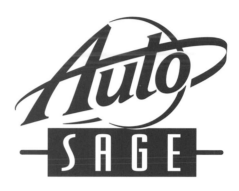

12.

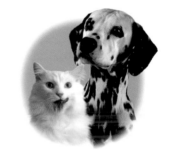

14.

BEACON PLACE

13.

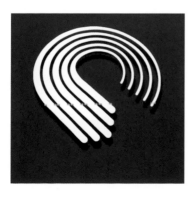

15.

(all)

Design Firm Herip Associates

1. Client   The Richard E. Jacobs Group
   Designers   Walter M. Herip, John R.
               Menter, & Rick Holb

2. Client   The Richard E. Jacobs Group
   Designers   John R. Menter &
               Walter M. Herip

3. Client   The Richard E. Jacobs Group
   Designers   John R. Menter, Rick Holb,
               & Walter M. Herip

4, 5
   Client   The Richard E. Jacobs Group
   Designers   John R. Menter &
               Walter M. Herip

6 - 8
   Client   Cleveland Indians
   Designers   John R. Menter &
               Walter M. Herip

9, 10
   Client   Major League Baseball
   Designers   Walter M. Herip &
               John R. Menter

11. Client   CVNRA
    Designers Walter M. Herip

12. Client   Ernst & Young, LLP
    Designers Walter M. Herip &
               John R. Menter

13. Client   Dalad Group
    Designers John R. Menter &
               Walter M. Herip

14. Client   Bioproducts, Inc.
    Designers Walter M. Herip, John R.
               Menter, & Rick Holb

15. Client   Stark Enterprises
    Designers Walter M. Herip, John R.
               Menter, & Rick Holb

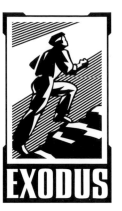

1.

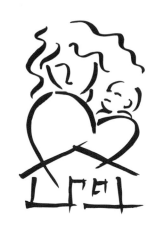

2.

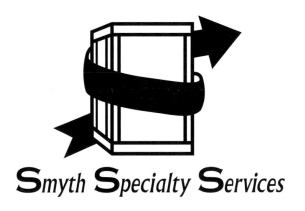

3.

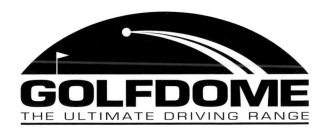

4.

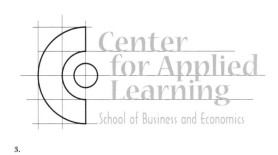

5.

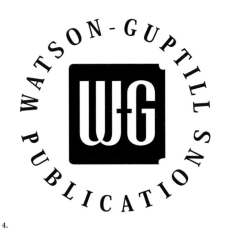

6.

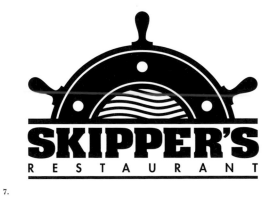

7.

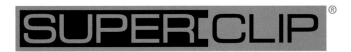

8.

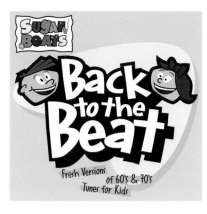

9.

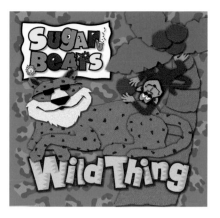

10.

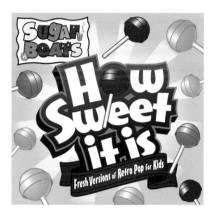

11.

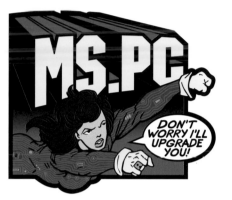

12.

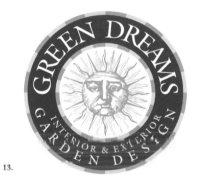

13.

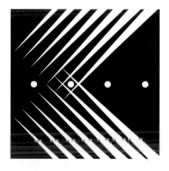

14.

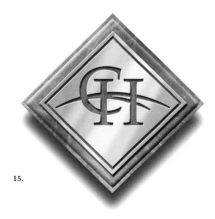

15.

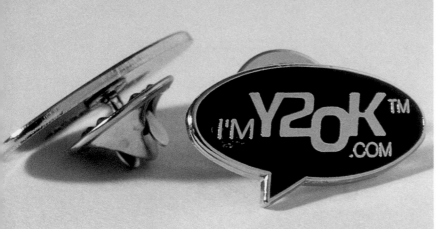

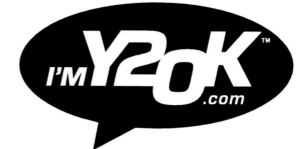

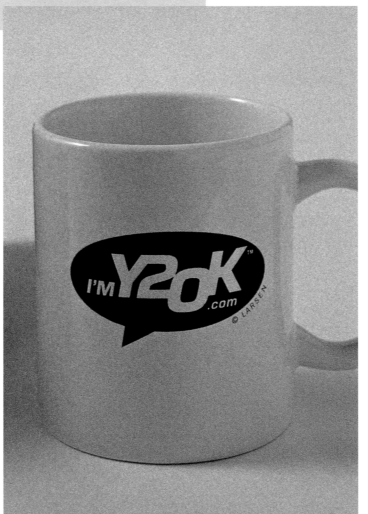

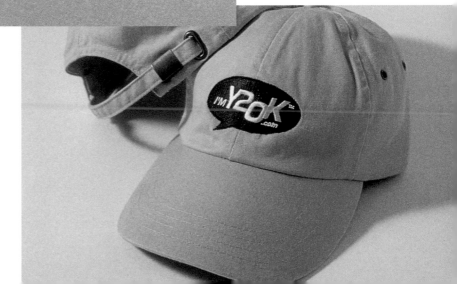

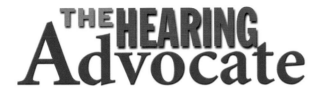

1.

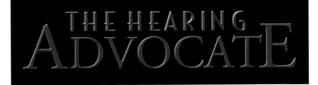

2.

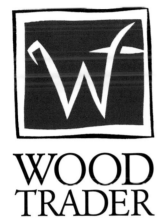

WOOD
TRADER

3.

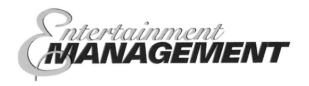

4.

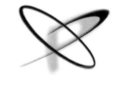

5.

out ☾
HOUSE
STUDIO
graphics, art & design

6.

SUCCESS
at FELICIAN
ACCELERATED DEGREE PROGRAMS

7.

1, 2, 4 - 7
Design Firm Outhouse Studio
3
Design Firm Nesnadny + Schwartz

1, 2
   Client   Ingroup Networking
   Designers Alex Lindquist & Jolanta Hyjek

3. Client   WoodTrader
     Designers Timothy Lachina, Gregory
                Oznowich, & Brian Lavy

4. Client   Entertainment Management
     Designers Alex Lindquist & Jolanta Hyjek

5. Client   Pulse Plastic Products, Inc.
     Designers Alex Lindquist & Jolanta Hyjek

6. Client   Outhouse Studio
     Designer   Alex Lindquist

7. Client   Ingroup Networking
     Designer   Alex Lindquist

(opposite)
Design Firm Larsen Design + Interactive

     Client   Larsen's I'm Y2OK Campaign
     Designers Tim Larsen, Sascha Boecker,
                & Elise Williams

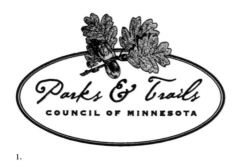

1.

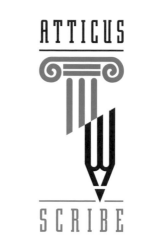

2.

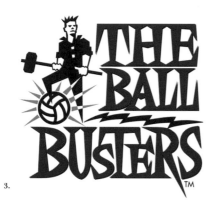

3.

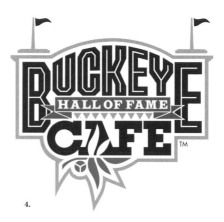

4.

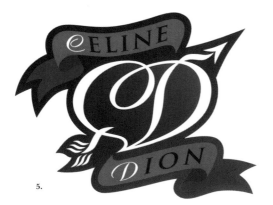

5.

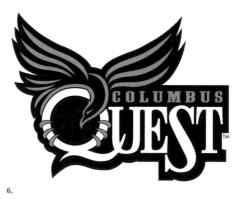

6.

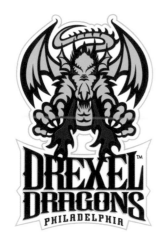

7.

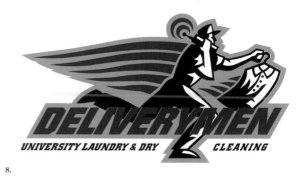

8.

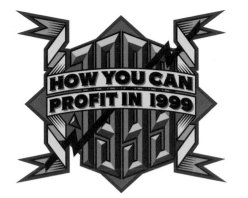

9.

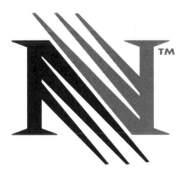

10.

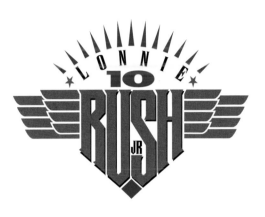

11.

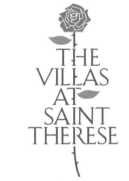

12.

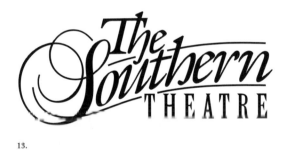

13.

THE
VILLAS
AT
SAINT
THERESE

14.

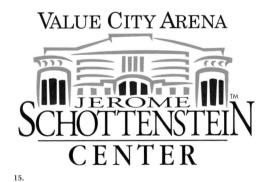

15.

1
Design Firm Larsen Design + Interactive
2 - 15
Design Firm Rickabaugh Graphics

1. Client   Minnesota Parks &
             Trails Council
   Designer   Todd Mannes

2. Client   Atticus Scribe
   Designer   Eric Rickabaugh

3. Client   The Ball Busters
   Designer   Eric Rickabaugh

4. Client   Buckeye Hall of Fame Cafe
   Designer   Eric Rickabaugh

5. Client   Celine Dion
   Designer   Eric Rickabaugh

6. Client   The Columbus Quest
   Designer   Eric Rickabaugh

7. Client   Drexel University
   Designers Eric Rickabaugh & Rod Smith

8. Client   University Laundry &
             Dry Cleaning
   Designers Eric Rickabaugh & Dave Cap

9. Client   Your Money Magazine
   Designer   Eric Rickabaugh

10. Client   Your Money Magazine
    Designers Eric Rickabaugh & Dave Cap

11. Client   Ohio State Motorsports
    Designers Eric Rickabaugh &
             Anthony Mosca

12. Client   Nationwide Insurance
    Designer Eric Rickabaugh

13. Client   The Southern Theatre
    Designer Eric Rickabaugh

14. Client   The Catholic Diocese
    Designer Eric Rickabaugh

15. Client   The Ohio State University
    Designer Eric Rickabaugh

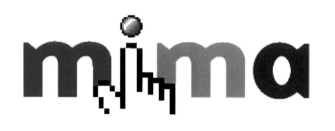

1.

2.

nexen™

3.

THE MINNEAPOLIS INSTITUTE OF ARTS

4.

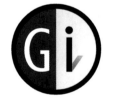

GartnerInstitute

5.

6.

GREAT PLAINS

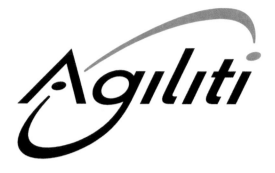

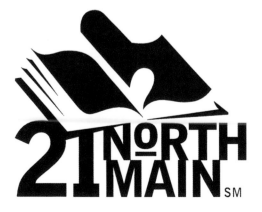

7.

1 - 7

Design Firm	Larsen Design + Interactive

1. Client   Minnesota Interactive Marketing Association
   Designers   Richelle J. Huff, Emily Eaton, & Peter Langlais

2. Client   Agiliti
   Designers   Paul Wharton & Brad Serum

3. Client   Nexen
   Designers   Jo Davison & Bill Pflipsen

4. Client   The Minneapolis Institute of Arts
   Designers   Todd Nesser, Peter de Sibour, Todd Mannes, Pepa Reimann, & Mark Wagner

5. Client   Gartner Institute
   Designers   Paul Wharton & Todd Mannes

6. Client   Great Plains Software
   Designers   Richelle J. Huff, Mike Haug, Bill Pflipsen, Sascha Boeker, Chad Amon, & Michael Hersrud

7. Client   21 North Main
   Designers   Jo Davison, Mark Saunders, & Todd Nesser

(opposite)

Design Firm	Larsen Design + Interactive

   Client   Target
   Designers   Paul Wharton, Peter de Sibour, & Chris Zastoupil

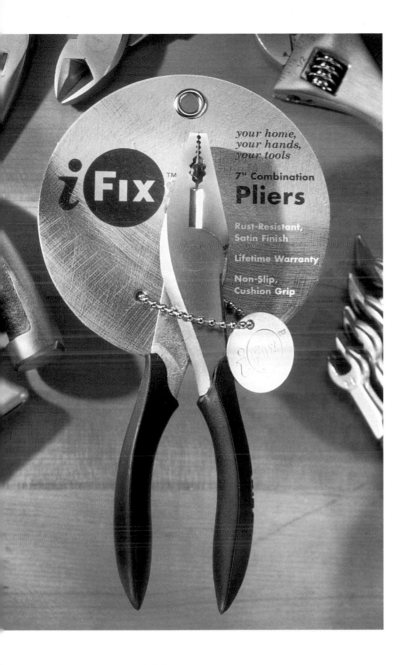

your home,
your hands,
your tools

7" Combination
Pliers

Rust-Resistant,
Satin Finish

Lifetime Warranty

Non-Slip,
Cushion Grip

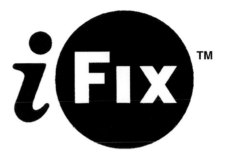

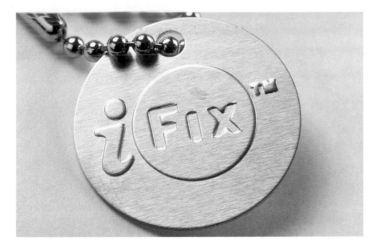

your home,
your hands,
your tools

8" Adjustable
Wrench

SAE and Metric

Lifetime Warranty

Non-Slip, Cush

315

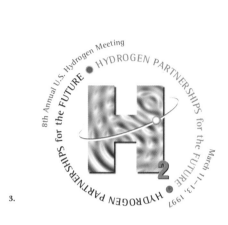

1.

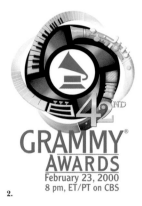

2.

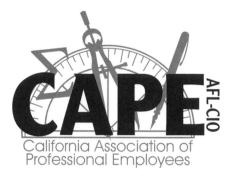

3.

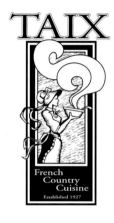

4.

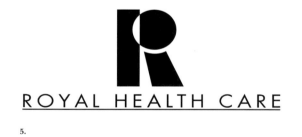

5.

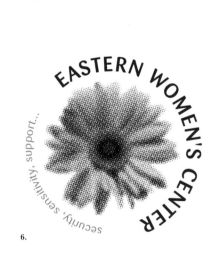

6.

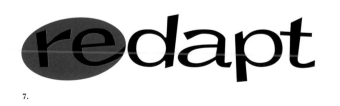

7.

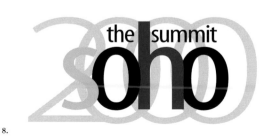

8.

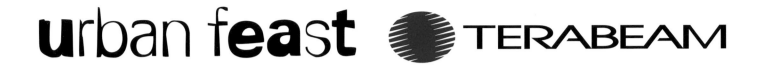

9.

10.

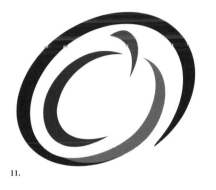

11.

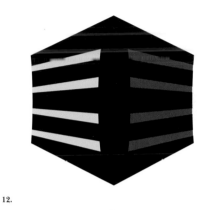

12.

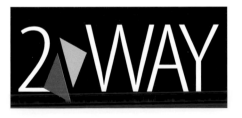

13.

BURTON & DOYLE Ltd.

14.

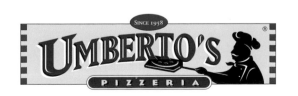

15.

1 - 6
Design Firm Mark Deitch & Associates, Inc.
7, 8, 10 - 13
Design Firm Tim Celeski Studios
9
Design Firm Nesnadny + Schwartz
14 - 15
Design Firm Adkins/Balchunas

1. Client   CAPE
   Designer   Sara Patterson

2. Client   NARAS
   Designer   Raoul Pascual

3. Client   National Hydrogen Association
   Designer   Lisa Kokenis

4. Client   Taix Restaurant
   Designers Radul Pascual & Joe Ibarra

5. Client   Royal Health Care
   Designer   Lisa Kokenis

6. Client   Eastern Women's Center
   Designer   Lisa Kokenis

7. Client   Redapt Systems & Peripherals
   Designer   Tim Celeski

8. Client   Small Office/Home Office
   Designer   Tim Celeski

9. Client   Urban Feast
   Designers Joyce Nesnadny, Cindy Lowrey,
              & Michelle Moehler

10. Client   Terabeam Corporation
    Designer Tim Celeski

11. Client   Producebiz. com
    Designer Tim Celeski

12. Client   Innovation
    Designer Tim Celeski

13. Client   2Way Corporation
    Designer Tim Celeski

14. Client   Sbarro
    Designers Jerry Balchunas &
              Susan DeAngelis

15. Client   Sbarro
    Designers Jerry Balchunas & Steve Rebello

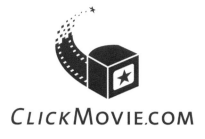

1.

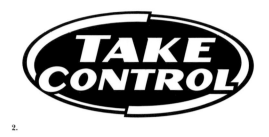

2.

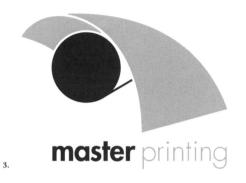

3.

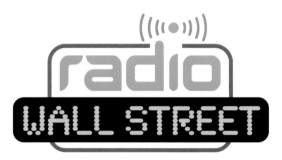

4.

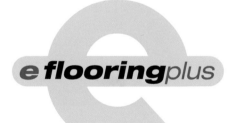

5.

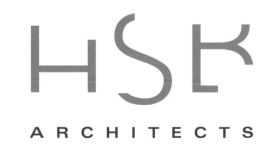

6.

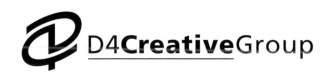

7.

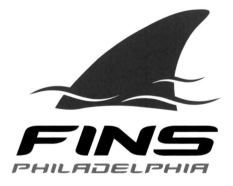

8.

WYSE·LANDAU

9.

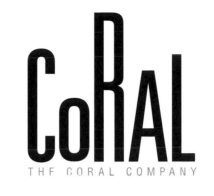

10.

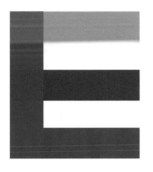

11.

12.

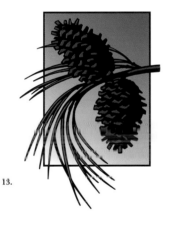

13.

SMITH+Co

14.

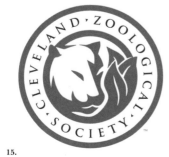

15.

1, 2
Design Firm Derek Yee Design
3, 8 - 11, 15
Design Firm Nesnadny + Schwartz
4 - 7
Design Firm D4 Creative Group
12 - 14
Design Firm Michael Courtney Design

1. Client   Click Movie.com
   Designer   Derek Yee

2. Client   Oracle
   Designer   Derek Yee

3. Client   Master Printing, Inc.
   Designers   Cindy Lowrey & Stacie Ross

4. Client   Radio Wall Street
   Designer   Wicky W. Lee

5. Client   E Flooring Plus
   Designer   Wicky W. Lee

6. Client   Fins Philadelphia
   Designer   Wicky W. Lee

7. Client   D4 Creative Group
   Designer   Wicky W. Lee

8. Client   Hengst Streff Bajko Architects
   Designers   Timothy Lachina, Michelle
                Mohler & Gregory Oznowich

9. Client   Wyse Landau Public Relations
   Designers   Joyce Nesnadny &
                Michelle Mohler

10. Client   Coral Company
    Designers   Cindy Lowerey & Stacie Ross

11. Client   Crossey International
    Designer   Joyce Nesnadny

12. Client   Fleischmann Office Interiors
    Designers   Michael Courtney, Dan Hoang,
                Heidi Favour, & Brian O'Neill

13. Client   Evergreen Printing
    Designer   Michael Courtney

14. Client   Smith & Co.
    Designers   Michael Courtney &
                Brian O'Neill

15. Client   Cleveland Zoological Society
    Designers   Timothy Lachina &
                Gregory Oznowich

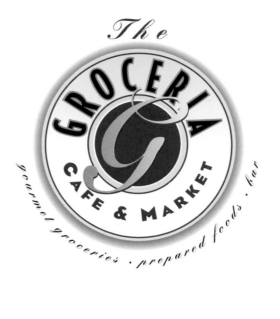

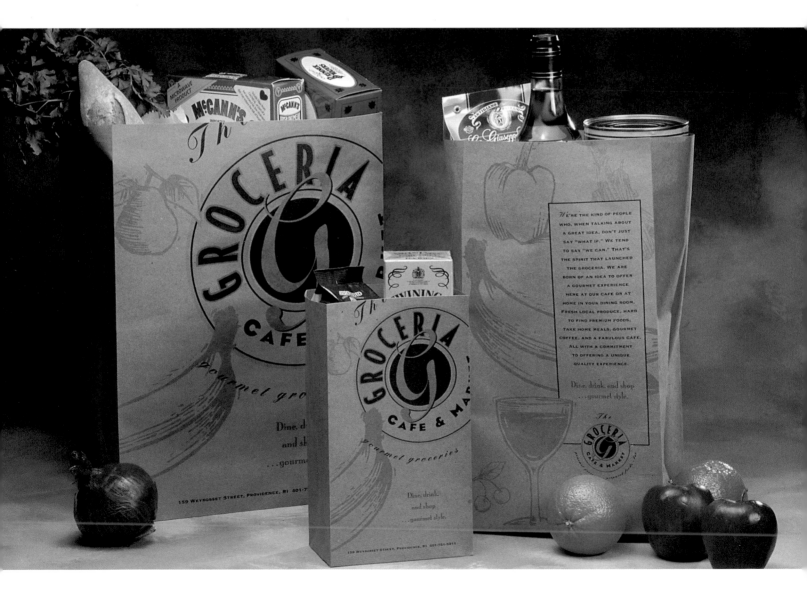

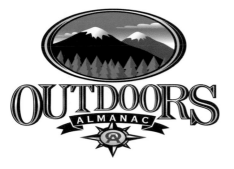

1.

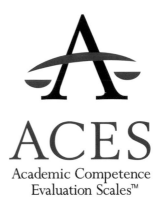

ACES
Academic Competence
Evaluation Scales™

2.

Symmorphix

3.

Derek Yee Design

4.

a!
apress

5.

MY NEWS

6.

PROJECT PANAMA

7.

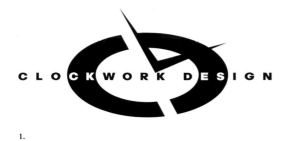

1.

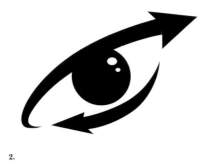

2.

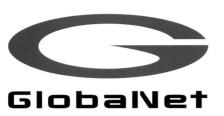

3.

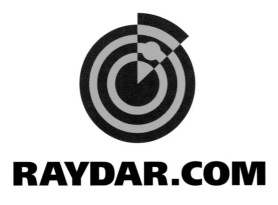

4.

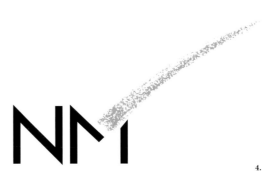

6.

5.

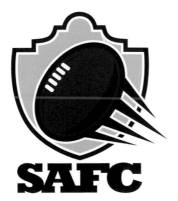

7.

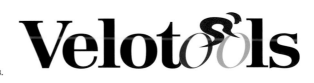

8.

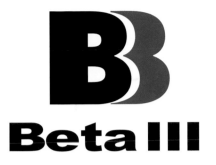

Beta III

9.

10.

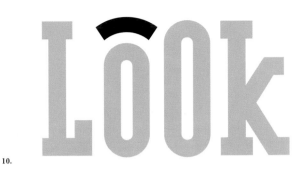

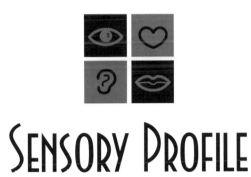

SENSORY PROFILE

11.

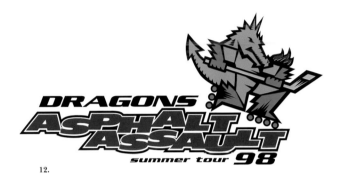

12.

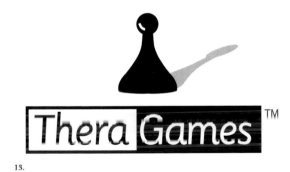

13.

TSD

14.

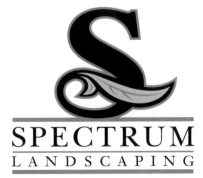

SPECTRUM
LANDSCAPING

15.

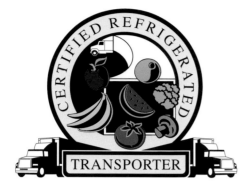

1.

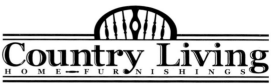

Country Living

Solid Wood. Solid Quality. Ready-to-Finish Furniture!

2.

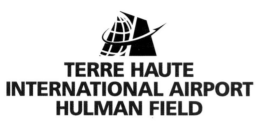

TERRE HAUTE
INTERNATIONAL AIRPORT
HULMAN FIELD

3.

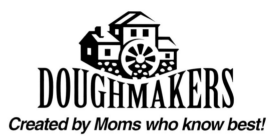

Created by Moms who know best!

4.

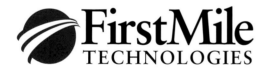

FirstMile
TECHNOLOGIES

5.

LEAGRECHANDLER
& MILLARD LLP

ATTORNEYS AT LAW

Solutions for Business Success℠

6.

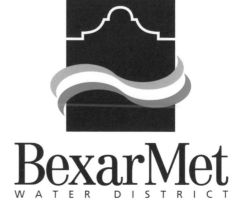

BexarMet
WATER DISTRICT

7.

1
Design Firm   **Dennis S. Juett &**
              Associates Inc.
2 - 6
Design Firm   **Miller & White Adv., Inc.**
7
Design Firm   **Clockwork Design**

1.   Client   Allen Lund Company
    Designer   Dennis S. Juett

2.   Client   Country Living
    Designers   Bill White & Tim Keller

3.   Client   Terre Haute
              International Airport
    Designers   Brian Miller & Bruce Morgan

4.   Client   Doughmakers
    Designers   Brian Miller, Bruce Morgan,
              & Tim Keller

5.   Client   Estridge
    Designer   Brian Miller & Bruce Morgan

6.   Client   Leagre Chandler & Millard
    Designers   Bill White & Bruce Morgan

7.   Client   Bexar Metropolotan
              Water District
    Designers   Steve Gaines & Terri Gaines

(opposite)
Design Firm   **Hitachi Data Systems**

    Client   Hitachi Data Systems
    Designer   Kim Ocumen

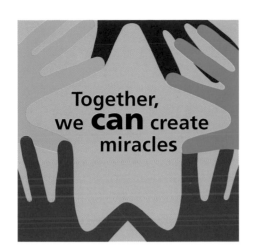

Together,
we **can** create
miracles

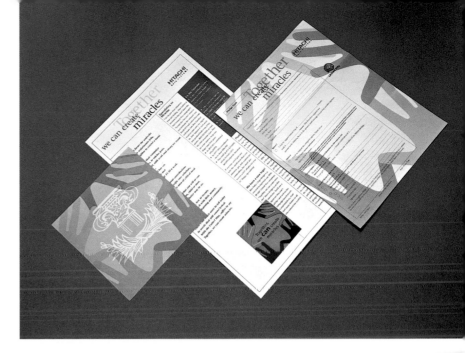

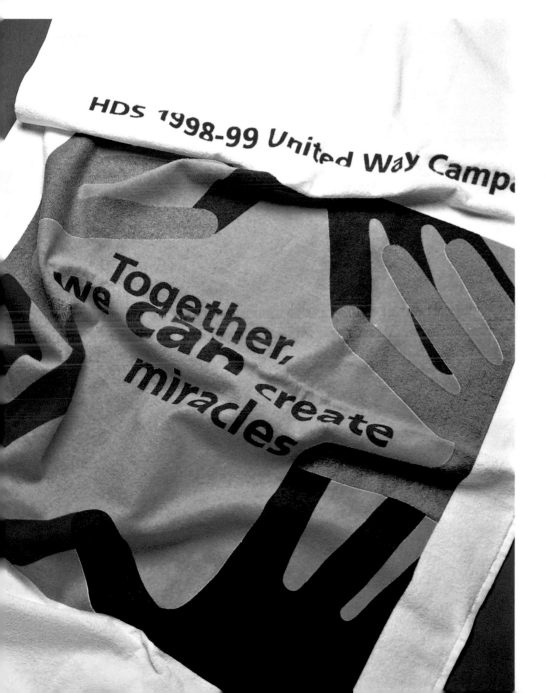

HDS 1998-99 United Way Campa

Together,
we can
create
miracles

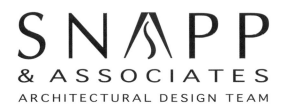

1.

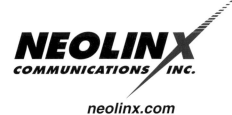

neolinx.com

2.

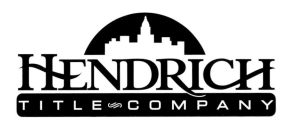

3.

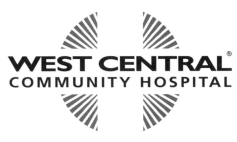

A Partner In The
Union Hospital Health Group

4.

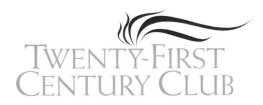

5.

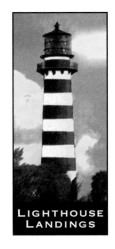

Lighthouse
Landings

6.

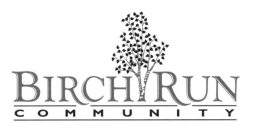

7.

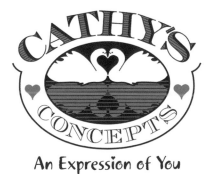

An Expression of You

8.

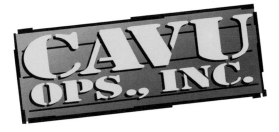

9.

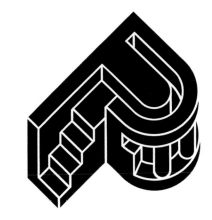

10.

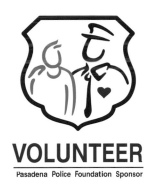

VOLUNTEER

Pasadena Police Foundation Sponsor

11.

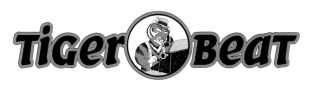

12.

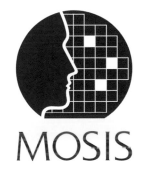

MOSIS

13.

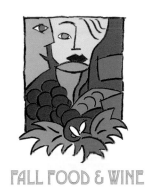

FALL FOOD & WINE

14.

THE ATHENAEUM FUND

15.

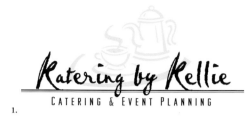

1.

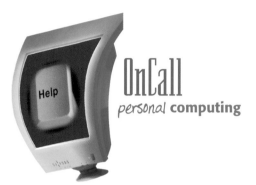

2.

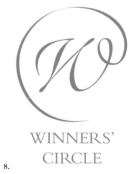

3.

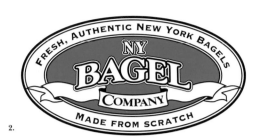

4.

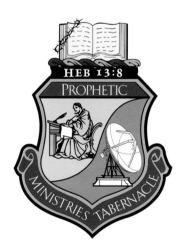

5.

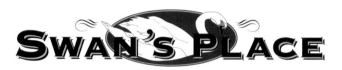

6.

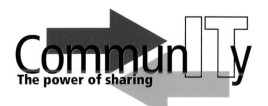

7.

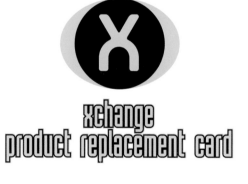

8.

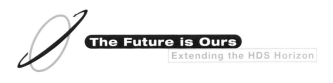

9.

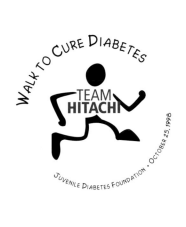

10.

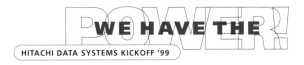

11.

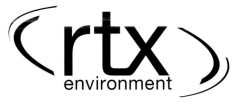

12.

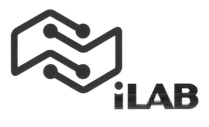

13.

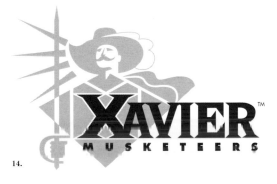

14.

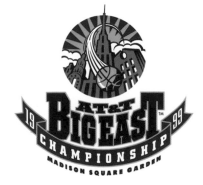

15.

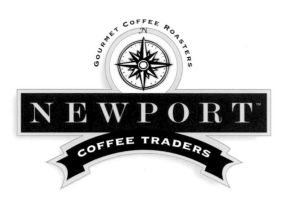

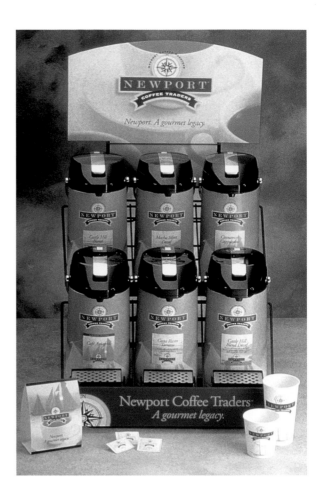

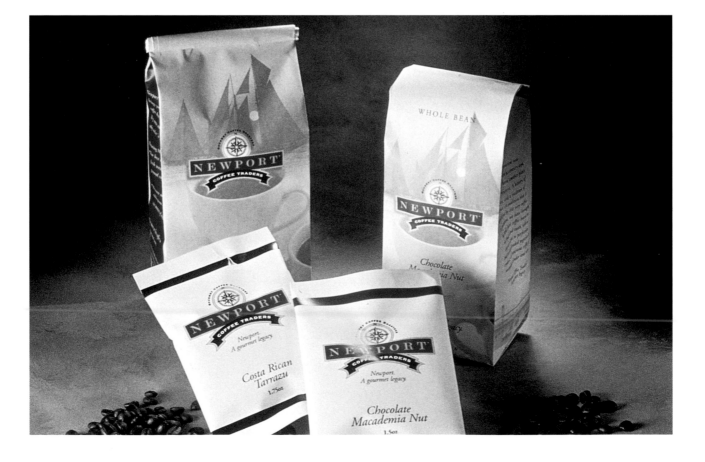

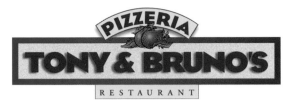

1.

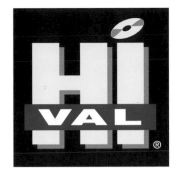

2.

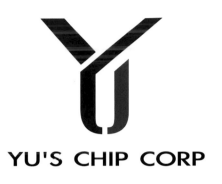

YU'S CHIP CORP

3.

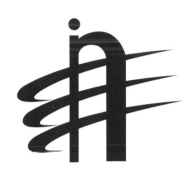

4.

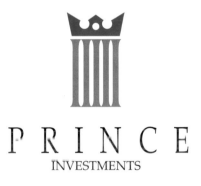

PRINCE
INVESTMENTS

5.

6.

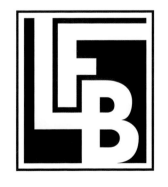

7.

1
Design Firm Adkins/Balchunas
2 - 5
Design Firm Vivatt Design Group
6, 7
Design Firm Mark Deitch &
               Associates, Inc.

1. Client   Sbarro
   Designers   Jerry Balchunas &
               Michelle Phaneuf

2. Client   HI-VAL
   Designer   Dan Wen

3. Client   Yu's Chip Corp.
   Designer   Dan Wen

4. Client   Inwin Development, Inc.
   Designer   Dan Wen

5. Client   Prince Investments
   Designer   Dan Wen

6. Client   UCLA Medical School
   Designers   Lisa Kokenis & Joe Ibarra

7. Client   Landsman, Frank & Bloch
   Designer   Raoul Pascual

(opposite)
Design Firm Adkins/Balchunas

Client   Autocrat, Inc.
Designers   Jerry Balchunas, Michelle
             Phaneuf, & Susan DeAngelis

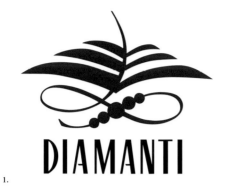

1.

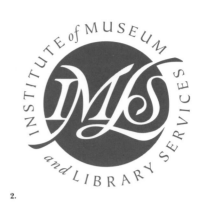

2.

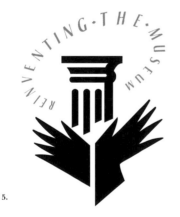

3.

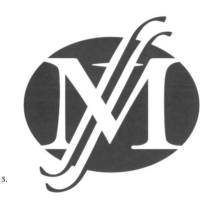

4.

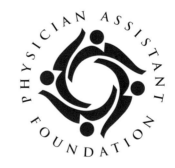

5.

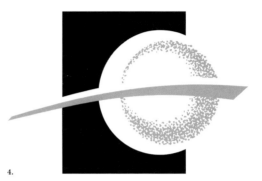

6.

AGA

7.

Aggrenox™

8.

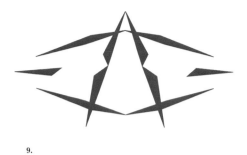

9.

10.

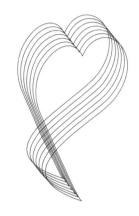

11.

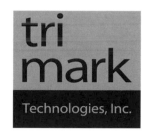

12.

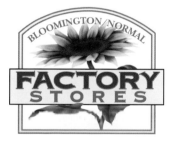

13.

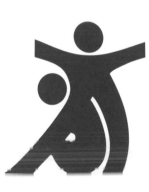

11.

actos™

15.

1 - 7		
Design Firm	Dever Designs	
8 - 15		
Design Firm	CMC Design Associates	

1. Client — Diamanti
   Designer — Jeffrey L. Dever

2. Client — Institute of Museum & Library Services
   Designer — Jeffrey L. Dever

3. Client — Martin's Furniture
   Designers — Emily Martin Kendall & Jeffrey L. Dever

4. Client — Carnegie Endowment for International Peace
   Designers — Jeffrey L. Dever & Emily Martin Kendall

5. Client — American Association of Museums
   Designer — Jeffrey L. Dever

6. Client — American Association of Physician Assistants
   Designer — Jeffrey L. Dever

7. Client — American Gas Association
   Designer — Jeffrey L. Dever

8. Client — Abelson-Taylor, Inc.
   Designer — Chris Cacci

9. Client — Spectrum Research & Development
   Designer — Chris Cacci

10. Client — Center for Fertility & Reproduction
    Designer — Chris Cacci

11. Client — Heart Source
    Designer — Chris Cacci

12. Client — Trimark Technologies
    Designer — Chris Cacci

13. Client — B & M Management
    Designer — Chris Cacci

14. Client — Center for Speech & Language Disorders
    Designer — Chris Cacci

15. Client — Abelson-Taylor, Inc./Lilly
    Designer — Chris Cacci

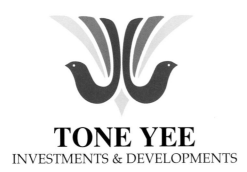

VIVATT
design group

1.

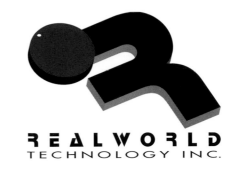

REALWORLD
TECHNOLOGY INC.

2.

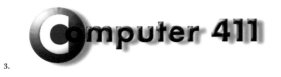

3.

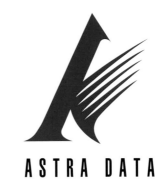

ASTRA DATA

4.

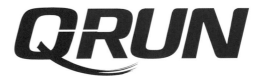

TONE YEE
INVESTMENTS & DEVELOPMENTS

5.

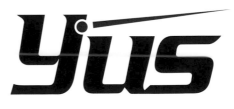

6.

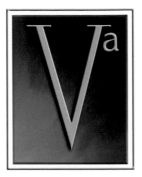

7.

1 - 7
Design Firm Vivatt Design Group
8, 9
Design Firm Hornall Anderson
         Design Works

1.	Client	Vivatt Design Group	6. Client	QRUN
	Designers	Dan Wen & Steven Wei	Designer	Dan Wen
2.	Client	Realworld Technology, Inc.	7. Client	Yus Group
	Designer	Eric Woo	Designer	Dan Wen
3.	Client	Computer 411	8. Client	Food Services of America
	Designer	Eric Woo	Designers	Jack Anderson, Cliff Chung,
4.	Client	Astra Data		Heidi Favour, Debra McCloskey,
	Designer	Dan Wen		& Julie Lock
5.	Client	Tone Yee	9. Client	Tigerlily
		Investment & Developments	Designers	Jack Anderson, Lisa Cerveny,
	Designer	Dan Wen		Sonja Max, & Mary Hermes

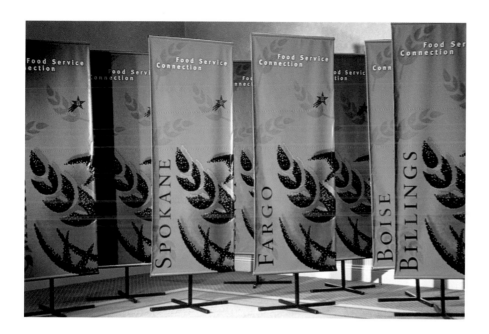

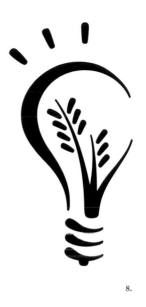

8.

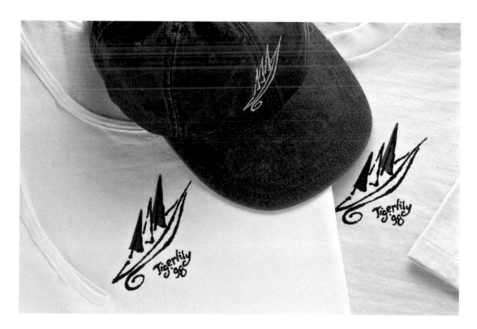

9.

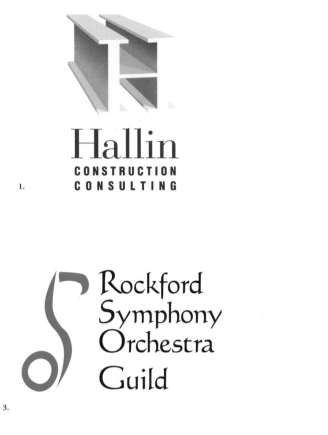

Hallin
CONSTRUCTION
CONSULTING

1.

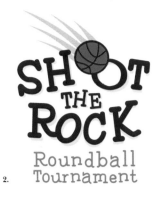

SHOOT THE ROCK
Roundball
Tournament

2.

Rockford
Symphony
Orchestra
Guild

3.

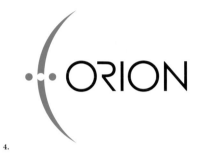

ORION

4.

CWS

5.

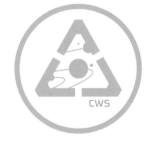

ACCLAIM TECHNOLOGY

6.

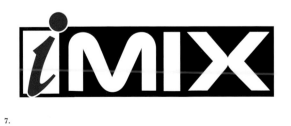

iMIX

7.

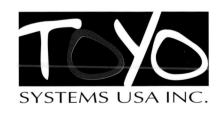

TOYO
SYSTEMS USA INC.

8.

336

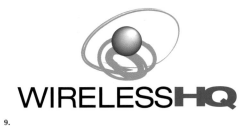

9.

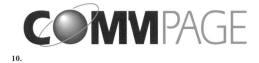

10.

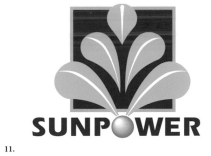

11.

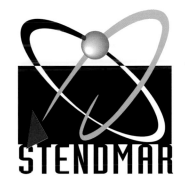

12.

Elliott

13.

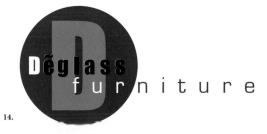

14.

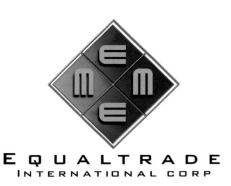

15.

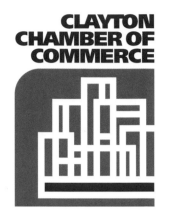

1.

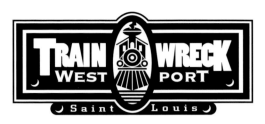

2.

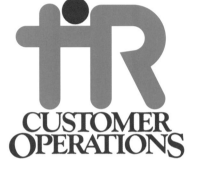

3.

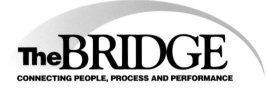

4.

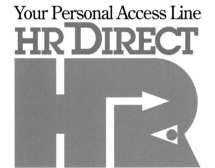

5.

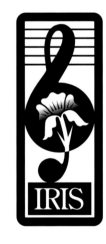

6.

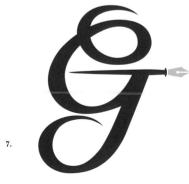

7.

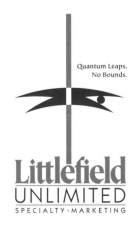

8.

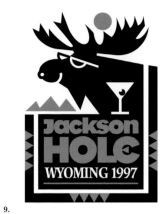

9.

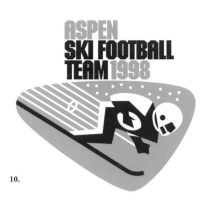

10.

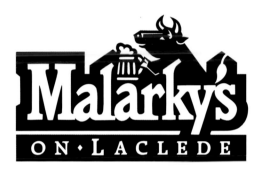

11.

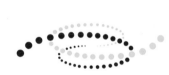

12.

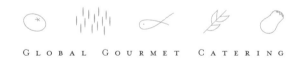

GLOBAL GOURMET CATERING

13.

capstan

14.

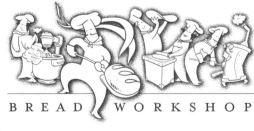

BREAD WORKSHOP

15.

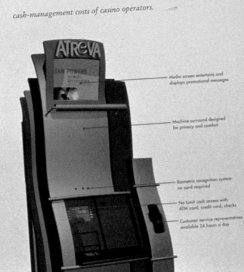

innoVisions™

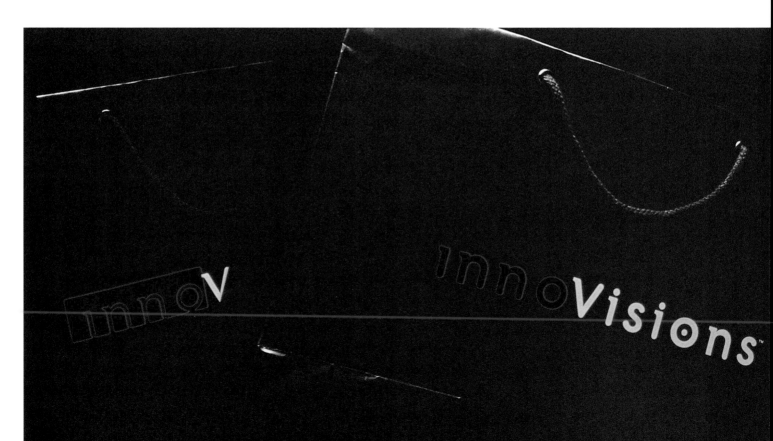

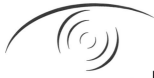

Hellmann Photography

1.

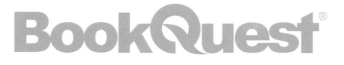

2.

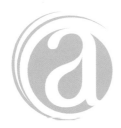 school of information studies

3.

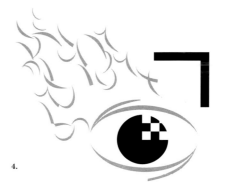

4.

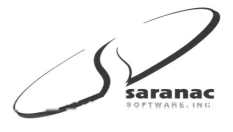

ALTERNATIVE HEALING CENTER

5.

saranac
SOFTWARE, INC.

6.

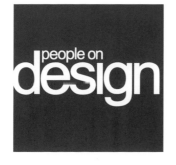

7.

pixelprecision

1.

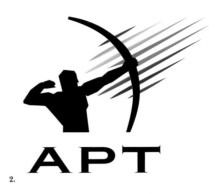

APT

2.

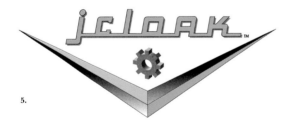

Force5™

software

3.

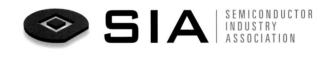

PanelLink®

D I G I T A L

4.

jcloak™

5.

SIA

SEMICONDUCTOR
INDUSTRY
ASSOCIATION

6.

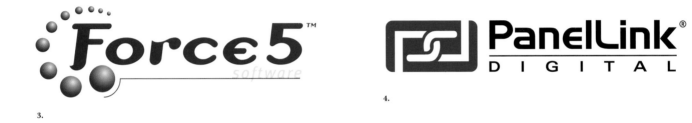

Chamber of Commerce
MOUNTAIN VIEW

7.

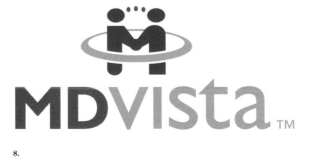

MDVista™

8.

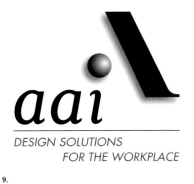

aai

DESIGN SOLUTIONS
FOR THE WORKPLACE

9.

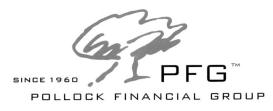

SINCE 1960 PFG™
POLLOCK FINANCIAL GROUP

10.

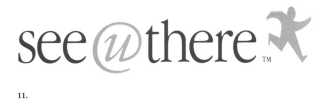

11.

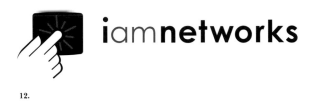

iam**networks**

12.

e**balance**™

13.

power**client**™

14.

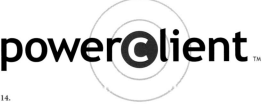

en Vision identity, inc.

15.

	(all)	
	Design Firm	**en Vision Identity, Inc.**
1.	Client	Pixel Precision
	Designer	Karl Kromer
2.	Client	APT
	Designer	Vadim Goretsky
3.	Client	Force 5 software
	Designer	Shepherd Brown
4.	Client	PanelLink Digital
	Designer	Erin Mathis
5.	Client	Force 5 software
	Designer	Shepherd Brown
6.	Client	Semiconductor Industry Association
	Designer	Karl Kromer
7.	Client	Mountain View Chamber of Commerce
	Designers	Nicole Bloss & Iva Dasovic
8.	Client	MD Vista
	Designer	Nicole Bloss

9.	Client	aai
	Designer	Karl Kromer & Shepherd Brown
10.	Client	Pollock Financial Group
	Designer	Vadim Goretsky
11.	Client	See U There
	Designer	Karl Kromer
12.	Client	i am networks
	Designer	Karl Kromer
13.	Client	eBalance, inc.
	Designer	Nicole Bloss
14.	Client	PowerClient
	Designer	Nicole Bloss
15.	Client	en Vision identity, inc.
	Designer	Nicole Bloss

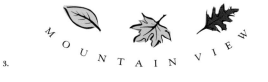

1.

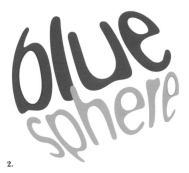

2.

DIVERSITY FORUM

M O U N T A I N   V I E W

3.

Silicon Image

4.

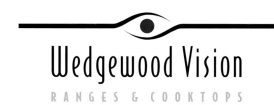

Wedgewood Vision

R A N G E S   &   C O O K T O P S

5.

Atwood Compliance Systems

6.

Splendor & MAJESTY

7.

1, 2
Design Firm Ocean Avenue Design
3, 4
Design Firm en Vision identity, inc.
5 - 7
Design Firm Conflux Design

1. Client   Howlett Surfboards
    Designer   Lynn E. Phillips

2. Client   Blue Sphere
    Designer   Lynn E. Phillips

3. Client   Diversity Forum
                 Mountain View
    Designer   Shepherd Brown

4. Client   Silicon Image
    Designers   Nicole Bloss &
                 Shepherd Brown

5. Client   Atwood Mobile Products
    Designer   Greg Fedorev

6. Client   Atwood Mobile Products
    Designer   Greg Fedorev

7. Client   Starlight Theatre
    Designer   Greg Fedorev

(opposite)
Design Firm Squires & Company

Client   Fast Park
Designer   Veronica Vaughn

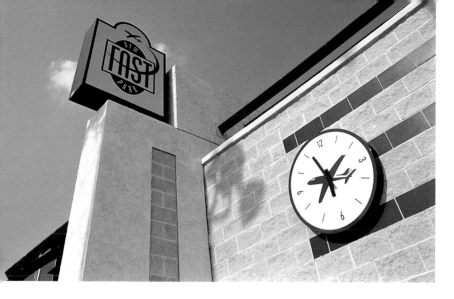

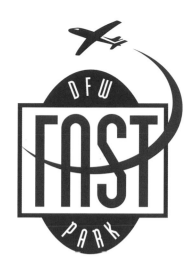

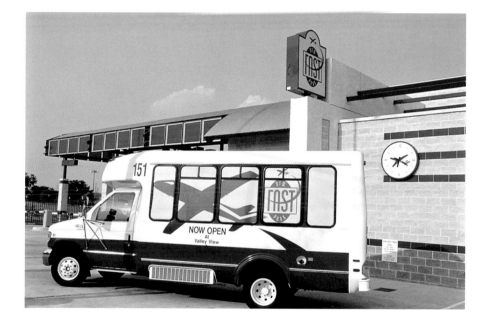

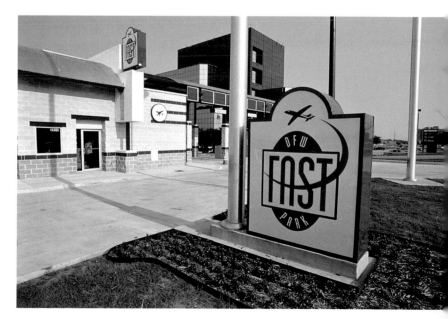

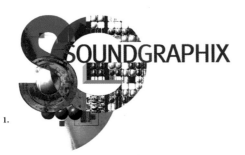

1.

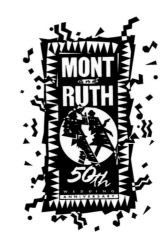

2.

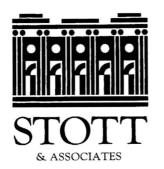

3.

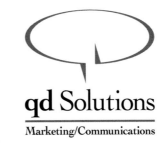

4.

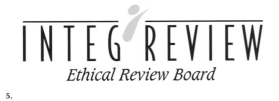

Ethical Review Board

5.

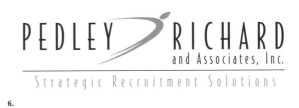

6.

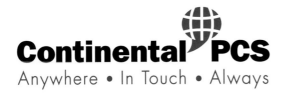

7.

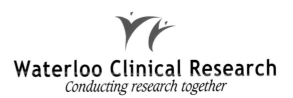

8.

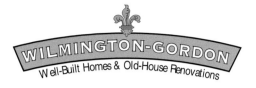

9.

CycleSolutions

10.

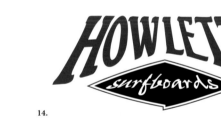

11.

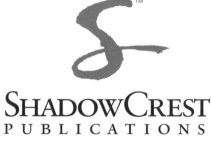

12.

HOWLETT
surfboards

14.

13.

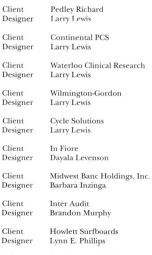

SHADOWCREST
P U B L I C A T I O N S

15.

1		
	Design Firm	**Interactive media**
2, 3		
	Design Firm	**Mickelson Design**
4 - 10		
	Design Firm	**Lewis Design**
11		
	Design Firm	**Aslan Graphics**
12		
	Design Firm	**Wild Onion Design, Inc.**
13		
	Design Firm	**Squire & Company**
14, 15		
	Design Firm	**Ocean Avenue Design**

1.	Client	SOUNDGRAPHIX
	Designer	Catsua Watanabe
2.	Client	Mont & Ruth
	Designer	Alan Mickelson
3.	Client	Stott & Associates
	Designer	Alan Mickelson
4.	Client	qd Solutions
	Designer	Larry Lewis
5.	Client	IntegReview
	Designer	Larry Lewis

6.	Client	Pedley Richard
	Designer	Larry Lewis
7.	Client	Continental PCS
	Designer	Larry Lewis
8.	Client	Waterloo Clinical Research
	Designer	Larry Lewis
9.	Client	Wilmington-Gordon
	Designer	Larry Lewis
10.	Client	Cycle Solutions
	Designer	Larry Lewis
11.	Client	In Fiore
	Designer	Dayala Levenson
12.	Client	Midwest Banc Holdings, Inc.
	Designer	Barbara Inzinga
13.	Client	Inter Audit
	Designer	Brandon Murphy
14.	Client	Howlett Surfboards
	Designer	Lynn E. Phillips
15.	Client	ShadowCrest Publications
	Designer	Lynn E. Phillips

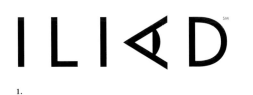

1.

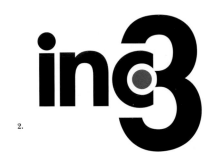

2.

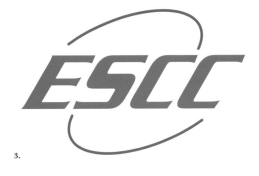

3.

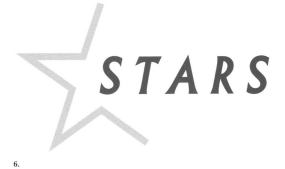

M.A. Weatherbie & Co., Inc.

4.

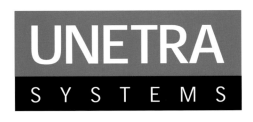

5.

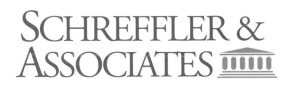

6.

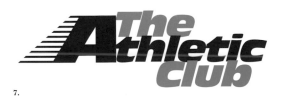

7.

SCHREFFLER &
ASSOCIATES

8.

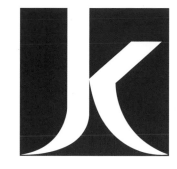

9.

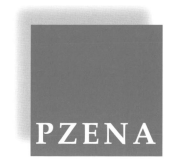

10.

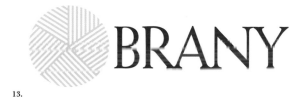

11.

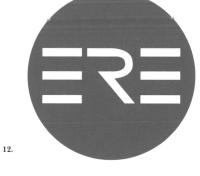

12.

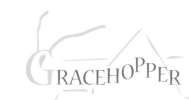

14.

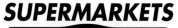
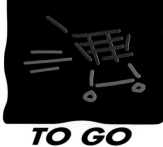

15.

13.

1
Design Firm Sibley Peteet Design
2 - 15
Design Firm inc3

1. Client   Chase Bank
    Designer   Tom Hough

2. Client   inc3
    Designers   Harvey Appelbaum &
               Nick Guarracino

3. Client   ESCC
    Designers   Harvey Appelbaum &
               Nick Guarracino

4. Client   M. A. Weatherbie & Co.
    Designers   Harvey Appelbaum &
               Nick Guarracino

5. Client   Unetra Systems
    Designers   Harvey Appelbaum &
               Nick Guarracino

6. Client   North Shore
    Designers   Harvey Appelbaum &
               Nick Guarracino

7. Client   The Atheltic Club
    Designers   Harvey Appelbaum &
               Valerie Viola

8. Client   Schreffler & Associates
    Designers   Harvey Appelbaum &
               Nick Guarracino

9. Client   J - K Orthotics & Prosthetics
    Designers   Harvey Appelbaum &
               Nick Guarracino

10. Client   Pzena Investment Management
     Designers   Harvey Appelbaum &
                Nick Guarracino

11. Client   Care Management Group
     Designers   Harvey Appelbaum &
                Nick Guarracino

12. Client   ERE
     Designers   Harvey Appelbaum &
                Nick Guarracino

13. Client   Biomedical Research Assoc.
               of NY
     Designers   Harvey Appelbaum &
                Nick Guarracino

14. Client   Gracehopper
     Designers   Harvey Appelbaum &
                Nick Guarracino

15. Client   Supermarkets To Go
     Designers   Harvey Appelbaum &
                Nick Guarracino

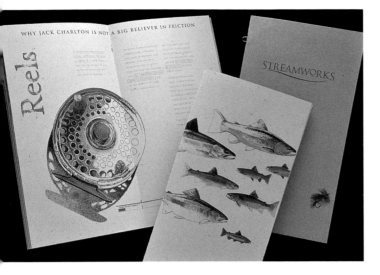

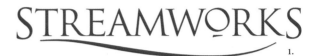
1.

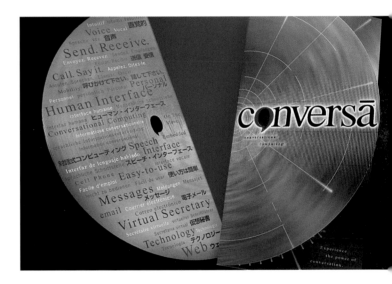

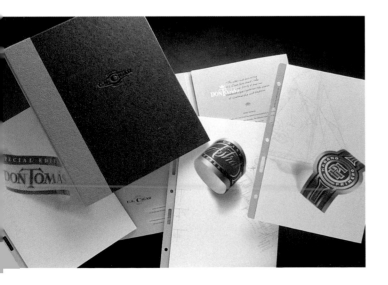

2.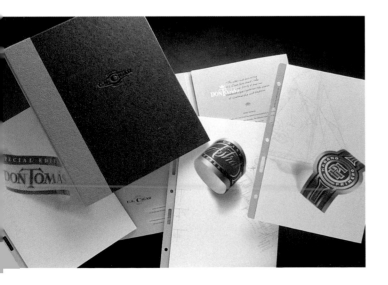

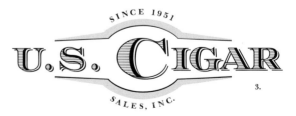
3.

350

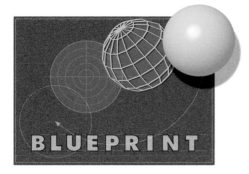

4.

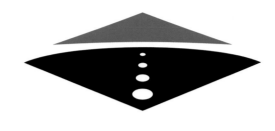

5.

PRIMACY

6.

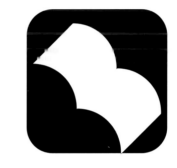

7.

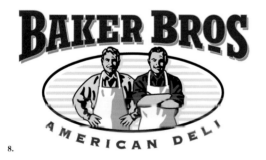

8.

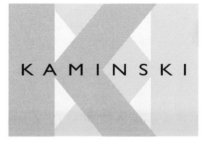

KAMINSKI

9.

10.

1 - 3
Design Firm   **Hornall Anderson Design Works**

4 - 10
Design Firm   **Sibley Peteet Design**

1. Client   Streamworks
   Designers   Jack Anderson, Belinda Bowline, Andrew Smith, & Ed Lee

2. Client   Conversa
   Designers   Jack Anderson, Kathy Saito, & Alan Copeland

3. Client   U.S. Cigar
   Designers   Jack Anderson, Larry Anderson, Mary Hermes, Mike Calkins, & Michael Brugman

4. Client   THE SABRE GROUP
   Designer   Brent McMahan

5. Client   Trans Solutions
   Designer   Joy Price

6. Client   Skin Ceuticals
   Designer   Joy Price

7. Client   Bentonville Public Library
   Designer   David Beck

8. Client   Baker Bros
   Designer   Tom Hough

9. Client   Karen Kaminski
   Designer   Roger Ferris

10. Client   John Hutton
   Designer   Brent McMahan

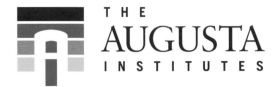

The Cornerstone of Motorola's Future

1.

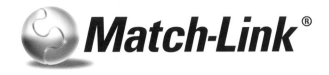

2.

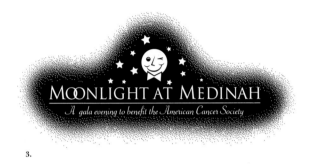

3.

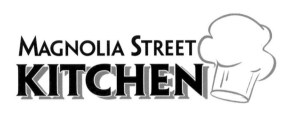

4.

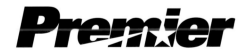

5.

6.

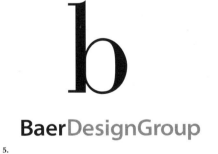

7.

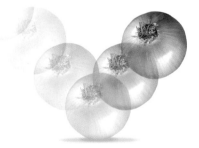

8.

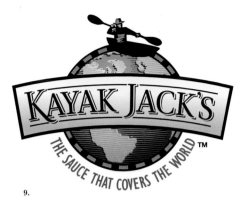

9.

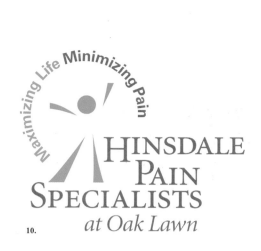

HINSDALE PAIN SPECIALISTS *at Oak Lawn*

10.

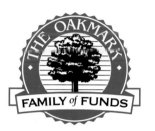

THE OAKMARK FAMILY *of* FUNDS

11.

HARLOW & ASSOCIATES P.C.
Certified Public Accountants • Tax Consultants

12.

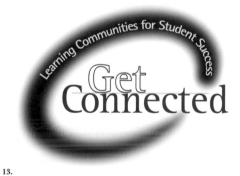

13.

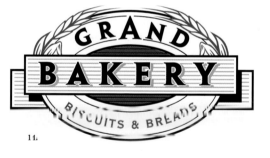

11.

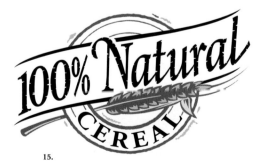

15.

1 - 5, 9 - 15
Design Firm Baer Design Group
6 - 8
Design Firm Wild Onion Design, Inc.

1. Client — Motorola University
   Designers — Todd D. Baer, Dominy Burkhart, & Julie Rigby

2. Client — Cendant
   Designer — Todd D. Baer

3. Client — American Cancer Society
   Designer — Todd D. Baer

4. Client — Haagen Grocers
   Designer — Todd D. Baer

5. Client — Baer Design Group
   Designers — Geoff Stone, Dominy Burkhart, & Todd D. Baer

6. Client — Wild Onion Design Inc.
   Designer — Barbara Inzinga

7. Client — Premier Auto Finance, Inc.
   Designer — Barbara Inzinga

8. Client — Professional Organization for Association Executives
   Designer — Barbara Inzinga

9. Client — Kayak Jack
   Designer — Todd D. Baer

10. Client — Hinsdale Pain Specialists
    Designer — Toy Nakajima

11. Client — Harris Associates LLP
    Designer — Todd D. Baer

12. Client — Harlow & Associates
    Designer — Todd D. Baer

13. Client — Harper College
    Designer — Dominy Burkhart

14. Client — Haagen Grocers
    Designer — Todd D. Baer

15. Client — Food Club
    Designer — Todd D. Baer

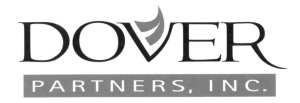

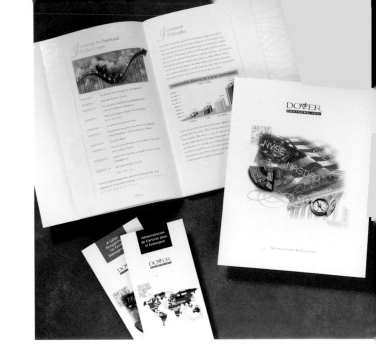

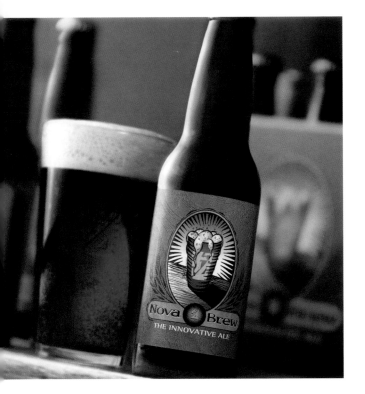

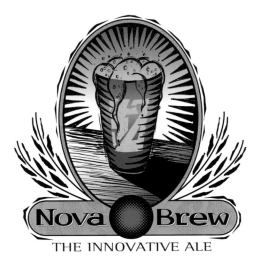

THE INNOVATIVE ALE

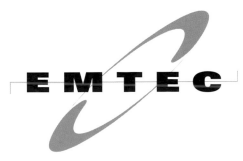

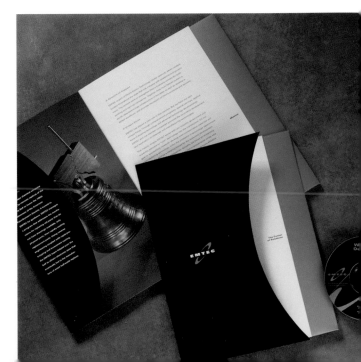

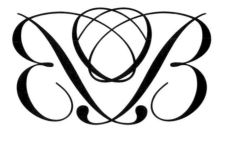

1.

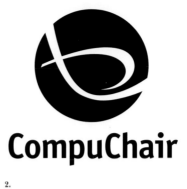

CompuChair

2.

M O U N T A I N
trading co.

3.

baskets
BY DESIGN

4.

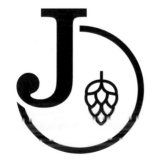

5.

6.

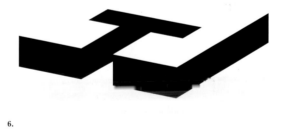

7.

1 - 3
Design Firm Nova Creative Group, Inc.
4 - 10
Design Firm Graphica
                Communication Solutions

1. Client   Dover Partners, Inc.
    Designer   Kris Hosbein

2. Client   Nova Creative Group, Inc.
    Designer   Tim O'Hare

3. Client   EMTEC
    Designer   Jack Denlinger

4. Client   Best In Bows
    Designer   Craig Terrones

5. Client   CompuChair
    Designers   Craig Terrones &
                  Robin Walker

6. Client   Mountain Trading Co.
    Designer   Craig Terrones

7. Client   Baskets by Design
    Designers   Robin Walker &
                  Craig Terrones

8. Client   Jaenicke, Inc.
    Designer   Craig Terrones

9. Client   Tarragon
    Designer   Craig Terrones

10. Client   Solid Vision, Inc.
    Designer   Christa Fleming

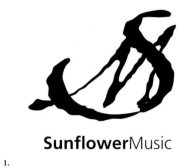

SunflowerMusic

1.

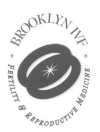

BROOKLYN IVF

FERTILITY & REPRODUCTIVE MEDICINE

2.

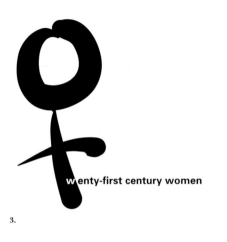

wenty-first century women

3.

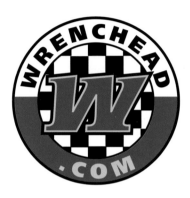

WRENCHEAD
W
.COM

4.

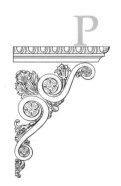

brightidea.com

5.

print promotions, inc

6.

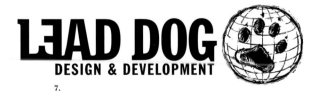

LEAD DOG
DESIGN & DEVELOPMENT

7.

P

8.

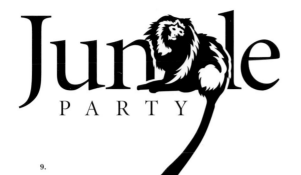

9.

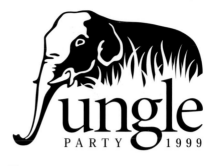

10.

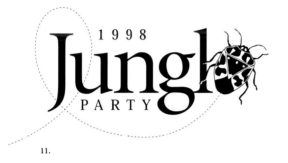

11.

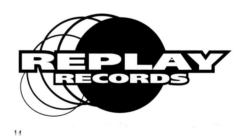

12.

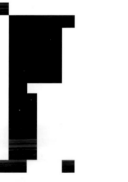

13.

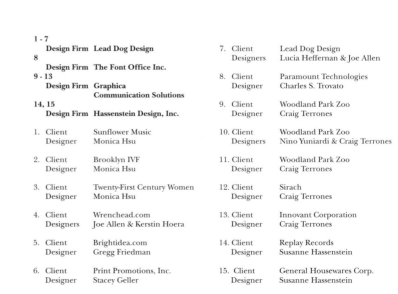

14

440A FINE™

Chicago Cutlery

15.

1 - 7			7.	Client	Lead Dog Design
	Design Firm	Lead Dog Design		Designers	Lucia Heffernan & Joe Allen
8					
	Design Firm	The Font Office Inc.	8.	Client	Paramount Technologies
9 - 13				Designer	Charles S. Trovato
	Design Firm	Graphica Communication Solutions	9.	Client	Woodland Park Zoo
14, 15				Designer	Craig Terrones
	Design Firm	Hassenstein Design, Inc.	10.	Client	Woodland Park Zoo
1.	Client	Sunflower Music		Designers	Nino Yuniardi & Craig Terrones
	Designer	Monica Hsu	11.	Client	Woodland Park Zoo
2.	Client	Brooklyn IVF		Designer	Craig Terrones
	Designer	Monica Hsu	12.	Client	Sirach
3.	Client	Twenty-First Century Women		Designer	Craig Terrones
	Designer	Monica Hsu	13.	Client	Innovant Corporation
4.	Client	Wrenchead.com		Designer	Craig Terrones
	Designers	Joe Allen & Kerstin Hoera	14.	Client	Replay Records
5.	Client	Brightidea.com		Designer	Susanne Hassenstein
	Designer	Gregg Friedman	15.	Client	General Housewares Corp.
6.	Client	Print Promotions, Inc.		Designer	Susanne Hassenstein
	Designer	Stacey Geller			

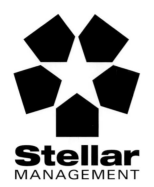

Stellar
MANAGEMENT

1.

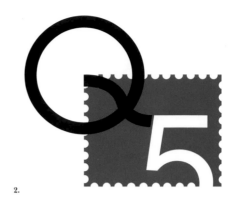

2.

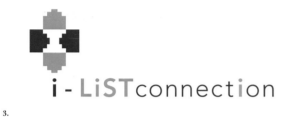

i-LiSTconnection

3.

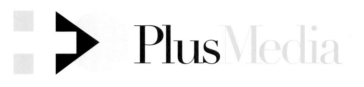

PlusMedia

4.

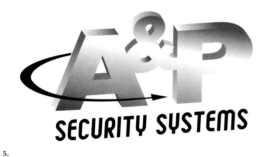

SECURITY SYSTEMS

5.

TRI
ARCH

6.

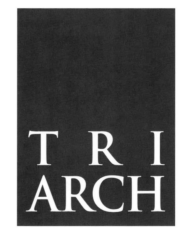

musicLens™

7.

1 - 4
Design Firm The Font Office Inc.
5 - 7
Design Firm Hassenstein Design, Inc.

1. Client   Stellar Management
   Designer   Charles S. Trovato

2. Client   Q-5 List Marketing
   Designer   Charles S. Trovato

3. Client   I-List Connection
   Designer   Charles S. Trovato

4. Client   PlusMedia
   Designer   Charles S. Trovato

5. Client   A & P Security Systems
   Designer   Susanne Hassenstein

6. Client   TriArch
   Designer   Susanne Hassenstein

7. Client   DDD Design
   Designer   Susanne Hassenstein

(opposite)
Design Firm   Hornall Anderson
   Design Works

Client   Foster Pepper Shefelman
Designers   John Hornall, Julie Keenan,
   Katha Dalton, & Nicole Bloss

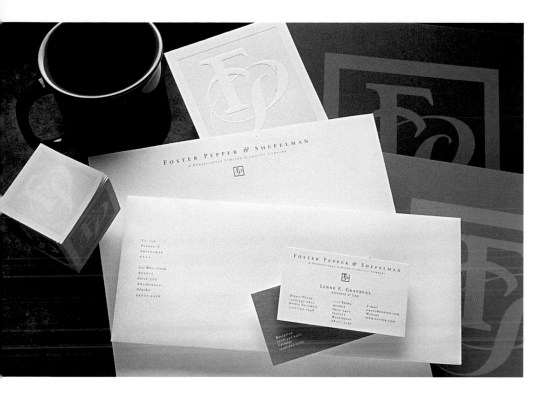

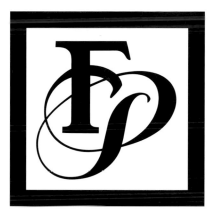

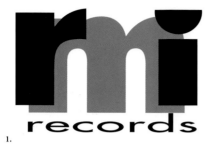

records

1.

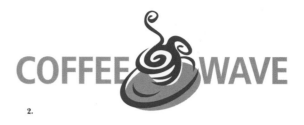

COFFEE WAVE

2.

Insight
Insurance Services, Inc.

3.

SUMMIT COMMUNICATION SERVICES, INC.

4.

SIXTH INTERNATIONAL

TEACHING FOR
INTELLIGENCE
CONFERENCE
2000

5.

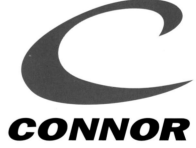

CONNOR

6.

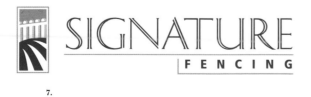

SIGNATURE
FENCING

7.

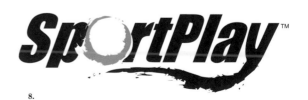

SportPlay™

8.

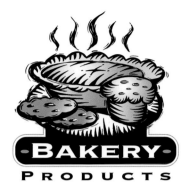

9.

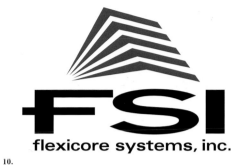

10.

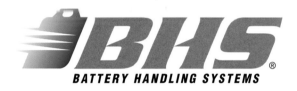

11.

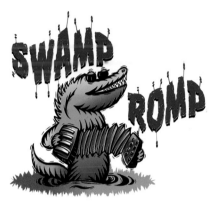

12.

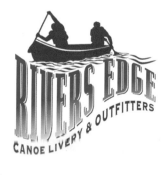

13.

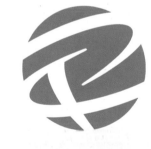

14.

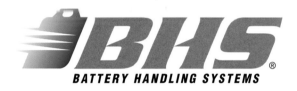

15.

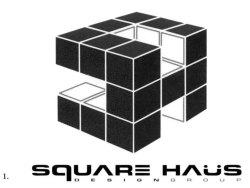

1.

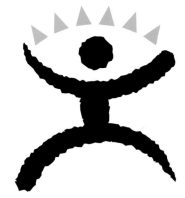

2.

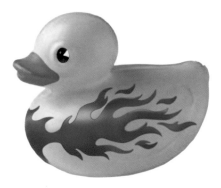

3.

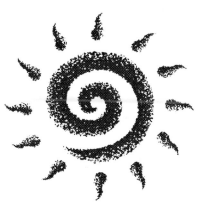

4.

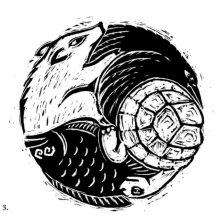

5.

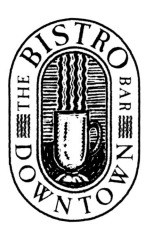

6.

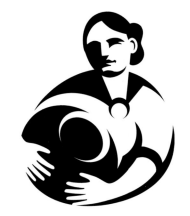

7.

8.

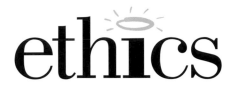

9.

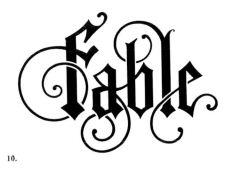

10.

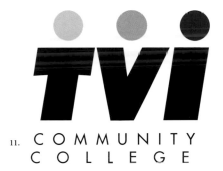

11. COMMUNITY COLLEGE

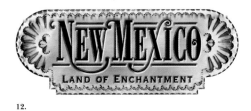

12.

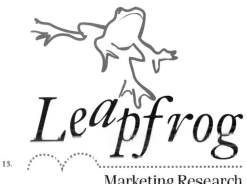

13.

Marketing Research

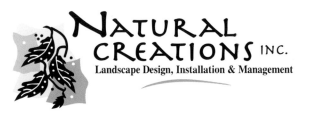

14.

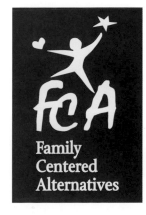

15.

1					
	Design Firm	Square Haus Design Group	8.	Client	Suncare
2 - 12				Designer	Mark Chamberlain
	Design Firm	Rick Johnson & Co., Inc.			
13 - 15			9.	Client	Samaritan Institute
	Design Firm	Design Directions		Designer	Mark Chamberlain
1.	Client	Square Haus Design Group	10.	Client	Fable
	Designer	Dion M. Isselhardt		Designer	Mark Chamberlain
2.	Client	Deming Duck Race	11.	Client	TUI
	Designer	Mark Chamberlain		Designer	Mark Chamberlain
3.	Client	Rio Grande Nature Center	12.	Client	New Mexico
	Designer	Mark Chamberlain			Department of Tourism
				Designer	Mark Chamberlain
4.	Client	New Mexico Optics		Tin Work	Fred Lopez
		Industry Association			
	Designer	Mark Chamberlain	13.	Client	Leapdrog Marketing
				Designer	Melissa Muldoon
5.	Client	Albuquerque Convention &			
		Visitors Bureau	14.	Client	Natural Creations
	Designer	Mark Chamberlain		Designer	Melissa Muldoon
6.	Client	Double Tree Hotel	15.	Client	Family Centered
	Designer	Mark Chamberlain			Alternatives Counseling
				Designers	Melissa Muldoon
7.	Client	Susan B. Fomen Foundation			
		of Central New Mexico			
	Designer	Mark Chamberlain			

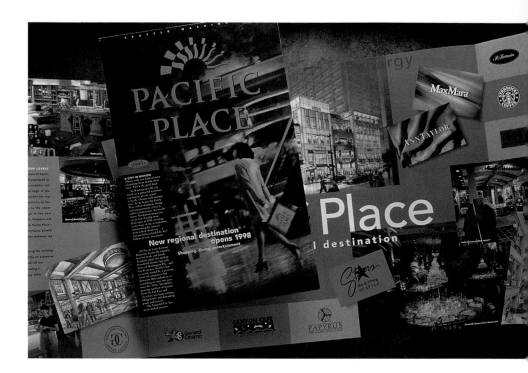

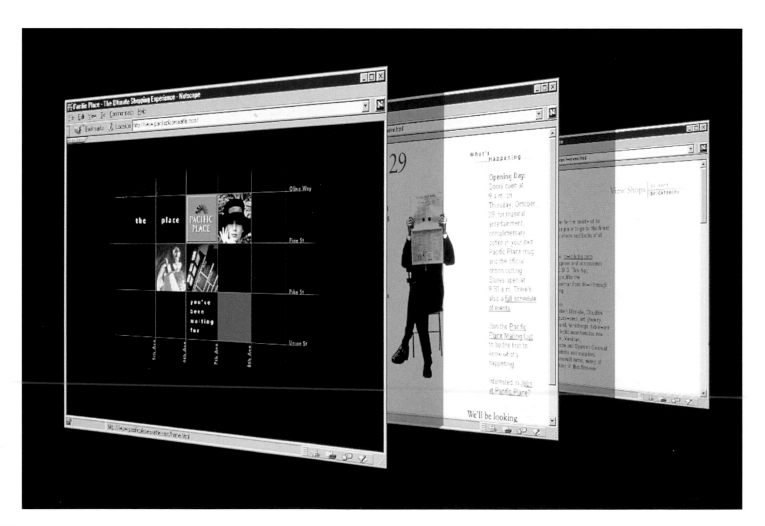

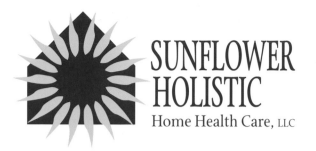

1.

HOPE
CHRISTIAN CHURCH

2.

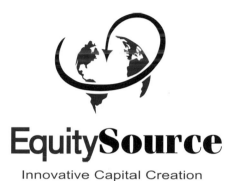

EquitySource

Innovative Capital Creation

3.

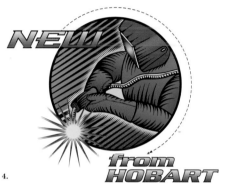

4.

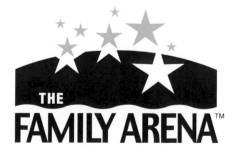

5.

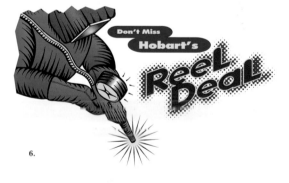

6.

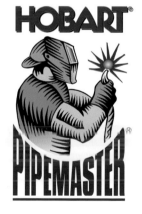

7.

(opposite)
Design Firm Hornall Anderson
Design Works

Client   Pacific Place
Designers   Jack Anderson, Heidi Favour,
             & David Bates

1 - 3
Design Firm Design Directions
4 - 7
Design Firm Nova Creative Group Inc.

1. Client   Sunflower Holistic
   Designer   Melissa Muldoon

2. Client   Hope Church
   Designer   Melissa Muldoon

3. Client   Equity Source
   Designer   Melissa Muldoon

4. Client   Hobart Welding Products
   Designer   Tim O'Hare

5. Client   Hobart Welding Products
   Designer   Tim O'Hare

6. Client   Hobart Welding Products
   Designer   Tim O'Hare

7. Client   Family Arena
             Management Enterprise
   Designer   Dwayne Swormstedt

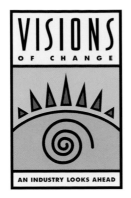

1.

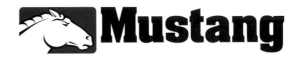

2.

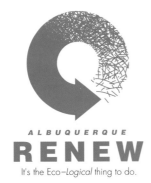

3.

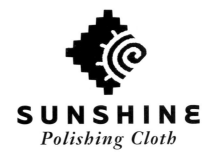

4.

5.

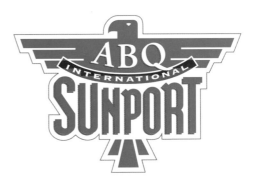

6.

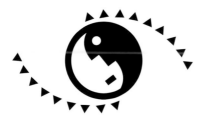

7.

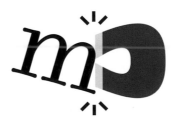

8.

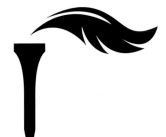

9.

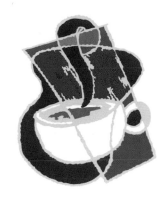

10.

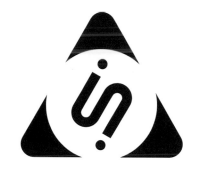

11.

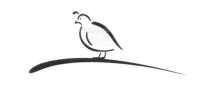

QUAIL RANCH

A natural way of life

12.

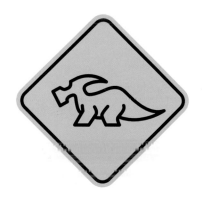

14.

13.

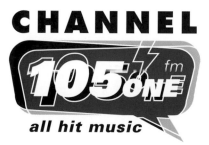

15.

(all)

Design Firm   Rick Johnson & Co.

1.	Client	Public Service Co. of New Mexico
	Designer	Lisa Graff
2.	Client	Giant Industries
	Designer	Molly Davis
	Illustrator	Brad Goodell
3.	Client	City of Albuquerque
	Designer	Tim McGrath
	Copywriter	Tim Pegors
4.	Client	Rio Grande
	Designer	Tim McGrath
5.	Client	New Mexico Economic Development
	Designer	Tim McGrath
6.	Client	Albuquerque International Sunport
	Designer	Lisa Graff
7.	Client	On-Site Solutions
	Designer	Tim McGrath

8.	Client	Media Dynamics
	Designer	Tim McGrath
9.	Client	Santa Ana Golf Club
	Designer	Tim McGrath
10.	Client	Gold Street Caffe
	Designer	Rick Gutierrez
11.	Client	Interactive Solutions, Inc.
	Designer	John Reams
12.	Client	Quail Ranch
	Designers	Tim McGrath & Lisa Graff
	Copywriter	Katie Duberry
13.	Client	Albuquerque Women's Resource Center
	Designer	Tim McGrath
14.	Client	New Mexico Museum of Natural History
	Designer	Tim McGrath
15.	Client	Simmons Radio Group
	Designer	Tim McGrath

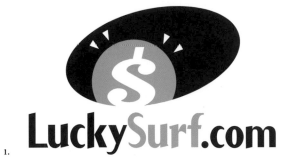

LuckySurf.com
1.

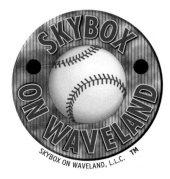

2.

flair

3.

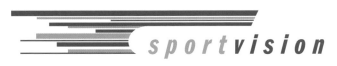

4.

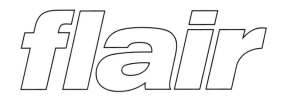

5.

NEXT PHASE

6.

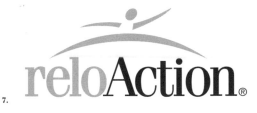

7.

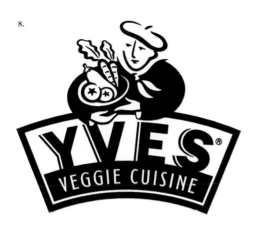

8.

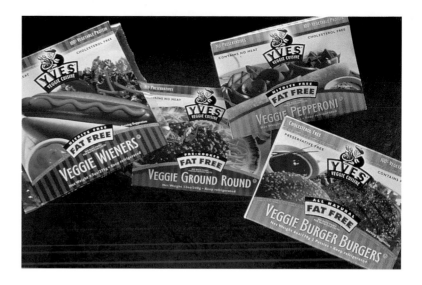

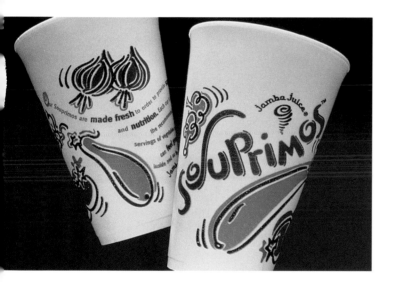

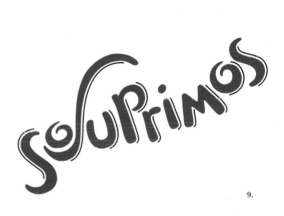

9.

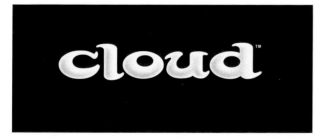

10.

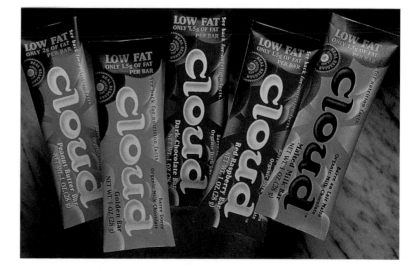

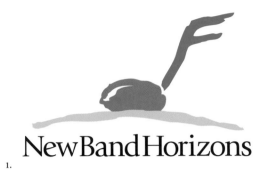

NewBandHorizons

1.

2.

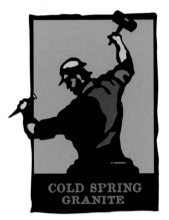

COLD SPRING
GRANITE

3.

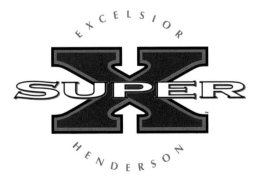

Continental Harmony

NEW MUSIC FOR THE MILLENNIUM

4.

 AMERICAN COMPOSERS FORUM

5.

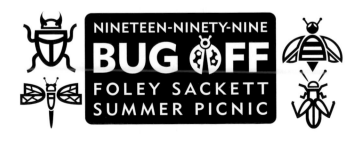

6.

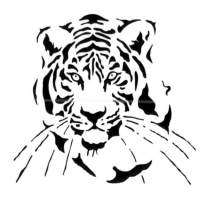

7.

8.

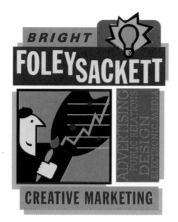

9.

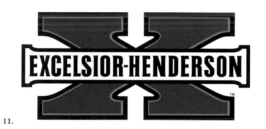

11.

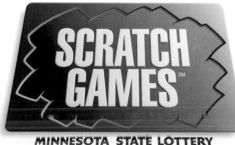

13.

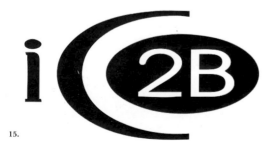

15.

W. A. Lang Co.

90TH ANNIVERSARY

10.

ROAD BUILDERS CREW CLUB

12.

Field's Classic

MARSHALL FIELD'S TOURNAMENT OF LPGA CHAMPIONS

14.

1 - 14
Design Firm Foley Sackett, Inc.

15
**Design Firm Hornall Anderson
Design Works**

1. Client	American Composers Forum	
Designer	Tim Moran	
2. Client	Asia Grille	
Designers	Michelle Willinganz & Joan Meath	
3. Client	Cold Spring Granite	
Designer	Chris Cortilet	
4. Client	American Composers Forum	
Designer	Tim Moran	
5. Client	American Composers Forum	
Designer	Michelle Willinganz	
6. Client	Excelsior - Henderson Motorcycles	
Designers	Michelle Willinganz & Chris Cortilet	
7. Client	Leeann Chin, Inc.	
Designer	Chris Cortilet	

8. Client	Foley Sackett, Inc.
Designer	Michelle Willinganz
9. Client	Foley Sackett, Inc.
Designer	Michelle Willinganz
10. Client	W. A. Lang Co.
Designer	Michelle Willinganz
11. Client	Excelsior-Henderson Motorcycles
Designer	Michelle Willinganz
12. Client	Caterpillar
Designer	Wayne Thompson
13. Client	Minnesota State Lottery
Designer	Joan Meath
14. Client	Marshall Fields
Designer	Michelle Willinganz
15. Client	IC2B
Designers	Jack Anderson, Mary Chin Hutchison, & Andrew Smith

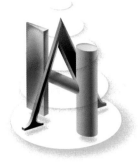

1.

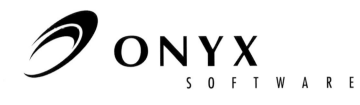

2.

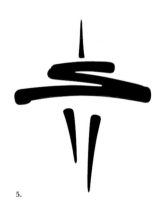

3.

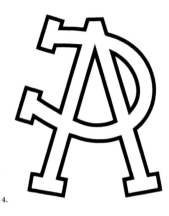

4.

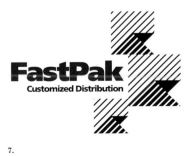

5.

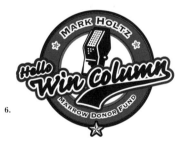

6.

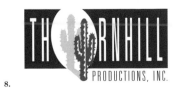

7.

8.

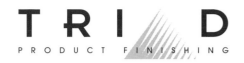

9.

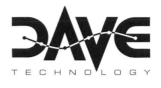

10.

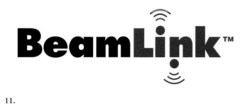

11.

Braunbach
Granite

12.

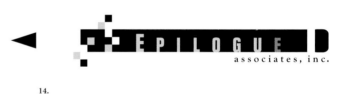

14.

13.

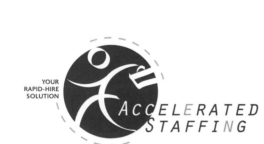

15.

1 - 5
Design Firm Hornall Anderson
Design Works
6 - 13
Design Firm Hallmark Levy Smith
14, 15
Design Firm White Communications, Inc.

1.	Client	Hornall Anderson Design Works
	Designers	Jack Anderson & David Bates
2.	Client	Onyx Corporation
	Designers	John Hornall, Debra McCloskey, Holly Finlayson, & Jana Wilson Esser
3.	Client	Ground Zero
	Designers	Jack Anderson, Kathy Saito, Julie Lock, Ed Lee, Heidi Favour, & Virginia Le
4.	Client	Anderson Pellet
	Designers	Jack Anderson & David Bates
5.	Client	Space Needle
	Designers	Jack Anderson, Mary Hermes, Gretchen Cook, Julie Lock, Amy Fawcett, & Andrew Smith

6.	Client	Mark Holtz
	Designer	Chuck Hodges
7.	Client	FastPak
	Designer	Cesar Hallmark
8.	Client	Thornhill Productions, Inc.
	Designer	Rick Levy
9.	Client	Triad
	Designer	Rick Levy
10.	Client	Dave Technology
	Designer	Rick Levy
11.	Client	BeamLink
	Designers	Rick Levy
12.	Client	Braunbach
	Designer	Sean Gregory
13.	Client	Black Pearl
	Designer	Chuck Hodges
14.	Client	Epilogue Associates, Inc.
	Designer	Karen B. White
15.	Client	Executives Network, Inc.
	Designer	Karen B. White

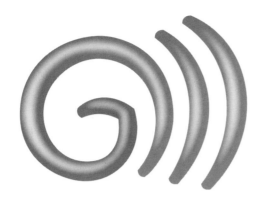

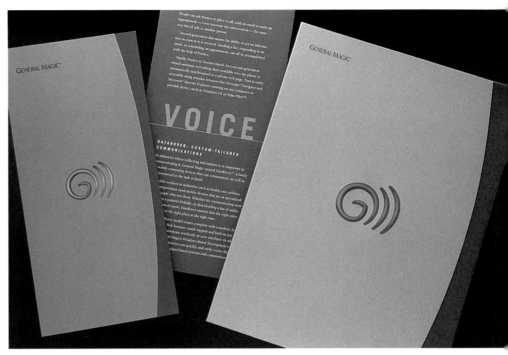

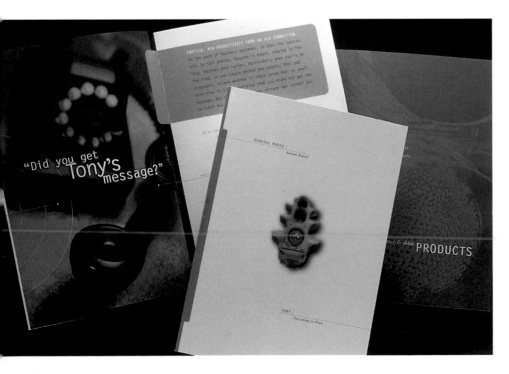

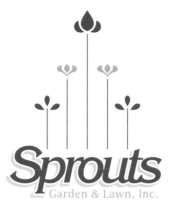

1.

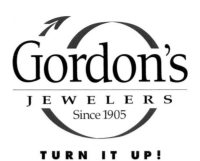

2.

TURN IT UP!

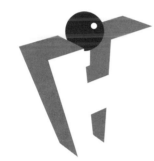

3.

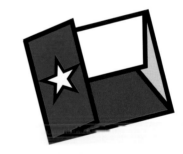

4.

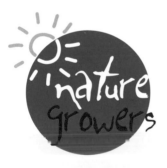

5.

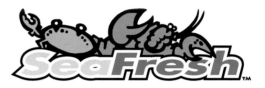

6.

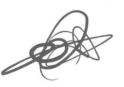

Hallmark Levy Smith
Marketing & Creative, Inc.

7.

(opposite)		(all)	
Design Firm	**Hornall Anderson Design Works**	**Design Firm**	**Hallmark Levy Smith**
Client	General Magic	1. Client	Sprouts Garden & Lawn, Inc.
Designers	Jack Anderson, Jana Nishi,	Designer	Cesar Hallmark
	Mary Chin Hutchison, Larry		
	Anderson, Michael Brugman,	2. Client	Gordon's Jewelry
	& Denise Weir	Designer	Chuck Hodges
		3. Client	Huge Image
		Designer	Cesar Hallmark
		4. Client	Sea Fresh
		Designer	J.R. Mounger
		5. Client	Nature Growers
		Designer	Cesar Hallmark
		6. Client	Paris Packaging
		Designers	Sean Gregory & Rick Levy
		7. Client	Hallmark Levy Smith
		Designers	Cesar Hallmark

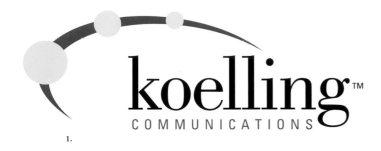

1.

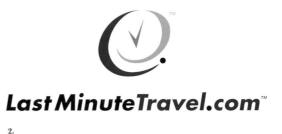

LastMinuteTravel.com™

2.

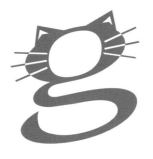

Gray Cat

GRAPHIC DESIGN

3.

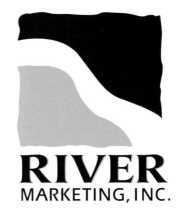

RIVER

MARKETING, INC.

4.

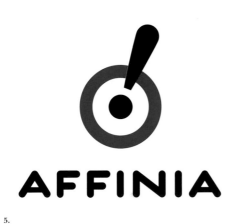

AFFINIA

5.

6.

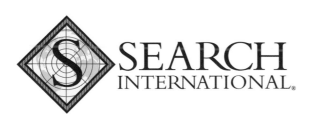

SEARCH

INTERNATIONAL®

7.

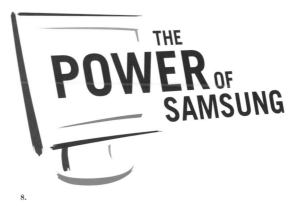

8.

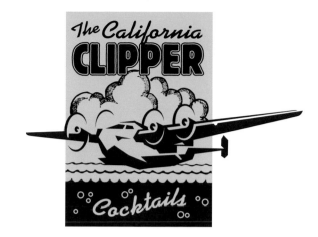

9.

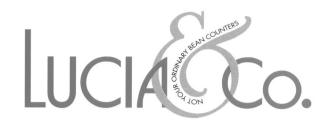

10.

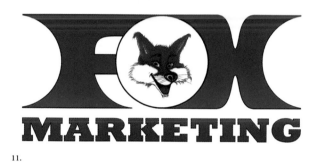

11.

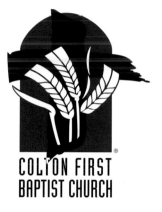

COLTON FIRST
BAPTIST CHURCH

12.

DAVID HOPKINS

PAINT & DRYWALL
INCORPORATED

13.

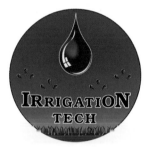

14.

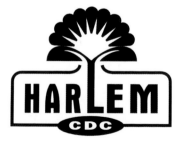

Harlem Community
Development Corporation

15.

1, 2, 5, 8
Design Firm Muccino Design Group
3, 9
Design Firm Gray Cat Graphic Design
4, 7
Design Firm River Marketing, Inc.
6
Design Firm The Graphic Expression, Inc.
10, 12, 13
Design Firm P.K. Design
11, 14
Design Firm Fox Marketing
15
Design Firm Granola Graphics

1. Client   Koelling Communications
    Designers   Alfredo Muccino & Julia Held

2. Client   Last Minute Travel.com
    Designers   Alfredo Muccino &
                  Joshua Swanbeck

3. Client   Gray Cat Graphic Design
    Designer   Lisa Empleo

4. Client   River Marketing, Inc.
    Designer   Jennifer Sailer

5. Client   Affinia
    Designers   Alfredo Muccino, Michael
                  Lee, & Colm Sweetman

6. Client   ePatients.com

7. Client   Search International
    Designer   Jennifer Sailer

8. Client   Samsung Electronics
    Designer   Alfredo Muccino &
                  Joshua Swanbeck

9. Client   The California Clipper
    Designer   Lisa Empleo

10. Client   Lucia & Co.
    Designer   Phyllis Kates

11. Client   Fox Marketing

12. Client   CFB Church
    Designer   Phyllis Kates

13. Client   Hopkins Paint & Drywall
    Designer   Phyllis Kates

14. Client   Irrigation Tech.

15. Client   Harlem Community
                  Development Corp.
    Designer   Paul Howard

377

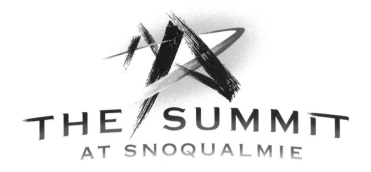

1.

2.

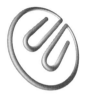

workengine™

3.

gettuit.com

4.

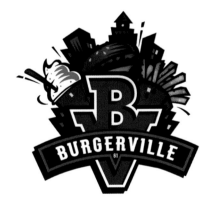

5.

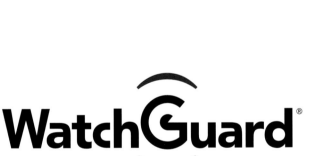

TECHNOLOGIES, INC.

6.

magicTalk™

7.

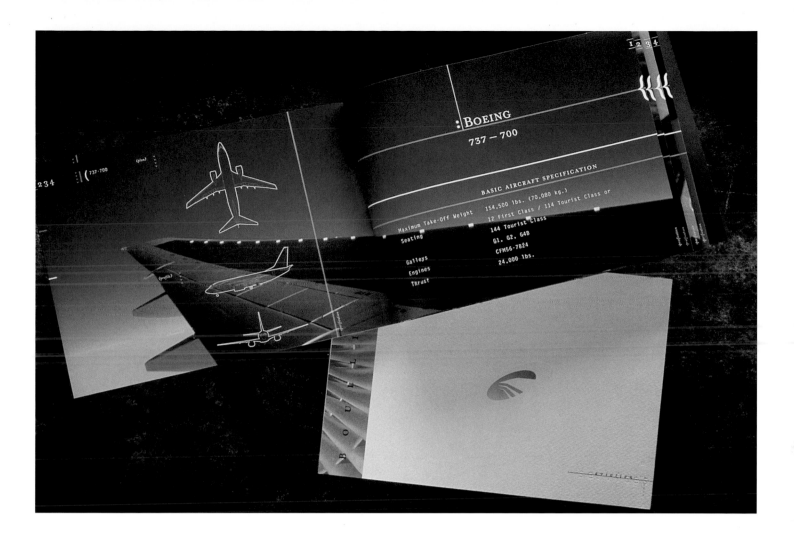

BOULLIOUN

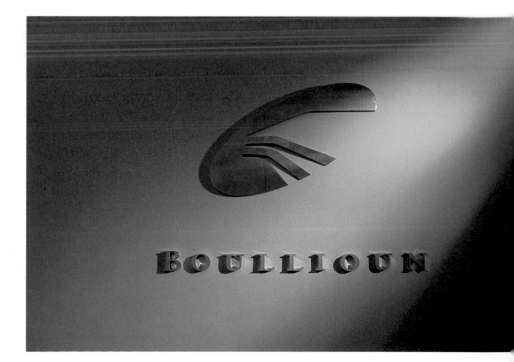

Index

383